BUILDING
UNDERSTANDING
TOGETHER

A Constructivist Approach to Early Childhood Education

D1072725

BUILDING UNDERSTANDING TOGETHER

....

A Constructivist Approach to Early Childhood Education

Sandra Waite-Stupiansky, Ph.D.
Edinboro University of Pennsylvania

Delmar Publishers
an International Thomson Publishing company I ⓣ P®

Albany • Bonn • Boston • Cincinnati • Detroit •London •Madrid
Melbourne • Mexico City • New York • Pacific Grove • Paris • San Francisco
Singapore • Tokyo •Toronto • Washington

NOTICE TO THE READER

Cover Design: Brucie Rosch

Delmar Staff
Publisher: William Brottmiller
Senior Editor: Jay Whitney
Associate Editor: Erin O'Connor Traylor
Senior Editorial Assistant: Glenna Stanfield

Production Coordinator: James Zayicek
Art and Design Coordinator: Timothy J. Conners

COPYRIGHT ©1997
By Delmar Publishers
A division of International Thomson Publishing Inc.

The ITP logo is a trademark under license
Printed in the United States of America

For more information, contact:
Delmar Publishers
3 Columbia Circle, Box 15015
Albany, New York 12212-5015

Thomas Nelson Australia
102 Dodds Street
South Melbourne, 3205
Victoria, Australia

International Thomson Editores
Campos Eliseos 385, Piso 7
Col Polanco
11560 Mexico D F Mexico

International Thomson Publishing Asia
221 Henderson Road
05-10 Henderson Building
Singapore 0315

International Thomson Publishing Europe
Berkshire House 168-173
High Holborn
London, WC1V7AA
England

Nelson Canada
1120 Birchmount Road
Scarborough, Ontario
Canada M1K 5G4

International Thomson Publishing GmbH
Königswinterer Strasse 418
53227 Bonn
Germany

International Thomson Publishing - Japan
Hirakawacho Kyowa Building, 3F
2-2-1 Hirakawacho
Chiyoda-ku, Tokyo 102
Japan

1 2 3 4 5 6 7 8 9 10 XXX 02 01 00 99 98 97

Library of Congress Cataloging-in-Publication Data
Waite-Stupiansky, Sandra.
      Building understanding together : a constructivist approach to
early childhood education / Sandra Waite-Stupiansky.
      p.   cm.
      Includes bibliographical references and index.
      ISBN 0-8273-6835-6
      1. Early childhood education—United States.   2. Constructivism
(Education)—United States.   3. Early childhood education—United
States—Curricula.   4. Piaget, Jean, 1896–1980.   I. Title.
LB1139.25.W35   1997
372.21—dc20   96-41892
                                                              CIP

Contents

*This book is dedicated to the hundreds
of children whose words and actions helped me
construct all of the ideas herein.*

Foreword

First of all, what a great refresher this book is for the instructor. How powerfully it gathers important concepts together and invites the reader to add to the productive examples given. How aptly this book pulls apart areas for scrutiny; and then synthesizes them together at the end of the book—integration at a high level. The personal touches in the vignettes by this master teacher/learner/author add a ring of authenticity both the beginner and the experienced reader will value. The perspectives on each area (e.g., play) are well chosen and get right to the heart of the matter.

The last bi-annual meeting of the National Association of Early Childhood Teacher Educators (NAECTE) focused on the theme of constructivism. This way of thinking/theorizing about education is of long-time, but also "cutting-edge" interest to our profession. This book serves our changing needs exceptionally well, especially as we move closer and closer to the implementation of constructivist programs, both in the classroom and in teacher education. I am certain that the reader will find this book's constructivist framework well-organized and engaging, and will want to tell others about it.

Sara W. Lundsteen
Regents Professor, Program in Early
Childhood, University of North Texas
Former President of the National
Association of Early Childhood Teacher Educators

*Who dares to teach
must never cease to learn.*

John Cotton Dana

Preface

As if it were yesterday, I remember leading my first class of kinder-gartners in a discussion about what they wanted to be when they grew up. One little girl looked at me and asked, "What do *you* want to be when you grow up?" I sighed and said, "I was thinking of becoming a teacher. Perhaps even a kindergarten teacher." The little girl realized the humor implied in her question and my answer. Yet, twenty years later I realize that her question was on target. I was a kindergarten teacher by occupation back then. Only in the last several years do I feel that I have "grown up" to be the teacher I wanted to be.

Teaching young children is one of the most complex professions imaginable. During my first several years of teaching I was over-whelmed with what I did not know about children, how they learn, and how I should teach them. Returning to graduate school convinced me that the more I learned, the more I needed to learn. Somewhere along the way I discovered Piaget's theory of constructivism. His the-ory convinced me to shift my emphasis from teaching and to start to examine how children learn. This book is about what I have learned about teaching after my lens was focused on children's learning.

I wrote this book for people new to constructivist approaches and for people who would like a "refresher" course on the main concepts underlying constructivism and its applications. Although constructivist concepts apply to learners of all ages, this book focuses on children between the ages of three and eight. There are many interpretations of constructivism, many of which will be discussed on the pages that fol-low. I do not pretend to present the only interpretation of Piaget's ideas. What follows is a presentation of his theory and suggested implications that I have found in my own classrooms. Each chapter contains vignettes or examples of how the theory looks in practice. Most of these vignettes stem from my real-life experiences with the children I have worked with over the years. Quite honestly, I think that they have done as much teaching as I have; hence the title of the book, *Building Understanding Together: A Constructivist Approach to Early Childhood Education*. Each new teacher must construct an understanding of the complexities of teaching and learning that makes sense to him or her. This book contains many of my own constructions; I invite you to consider them and decide if they make sense to you.

The application of the concepts presented in this book would create radical reforms in the way we teach young children. Once one accepts the basic premises of constructivism, changes in teaching follow naturally. I know that my teaching has changed. These changes will become clear to the reader in the pages to follow.

How are constructivist approaches different from traditional methods of teaching? Constructivist teachers teach toward the *Big Ideas*, or the framing concepts of a subject (Schifter & Fosnot, 1993). All subject disciplines have basic concepts within which other concepts fit. Understanding these *Big Ideas* gives the learner the scaffolding, or framework, necessary to fill in the details and applications. This book presents many of the underlying, *Big Ideas* of constructivism for the reader to think about and shows how to apply them in preschool, kindergarten, and primary settings.

The ideas in this book are grounded in the work and theory of Jean Piaget (1896–1980). Piaget was a Swiss developmental psychologist who began his career as a biologist. His first publication, at the age of 10, was on albino sparrows. At age 15, he published reports on freshwater mollusks. After pursuing a doctorate in the natural sciences, Piaget turned his attention to psychology.

In 1920, he was invited to collect data on children's responses to a reasoning test at a laboratory school in Paris. Instead of simply tabulating the children's correct answers, he became interested in the patterns of their incorrect responses. By listening to the children's reasons for their incorrect answers, Piaget's studies in children's thinking began (Labinowicz, 1980). Over the next 60 years, Jean Piaget tirelessly observed and interviewed children to gain insight into their thinking and reasoning at different developmental levels. He wrote over 35 books and many articles describing his findings.

Although he did not consider himself an educator, Jean Piaget's insights into children's thinking have helped educators reform teaching practices to reflect the children's active role in the construction of their own knowledge.

For students new to Piaget's ideas, the terms and definitions may seem abstract and difficult to grasp upon first reading. Yet, developing an understanding of the basic assumptions of constructivism will help in understanding all of the chapters that follow. Vignettes describing constructivist classes in action will illustrate the principles described and give the reader a window into the teacher's actions and thinking.

Each of the chapters that follow Chapter 1 will highlight common areas of the curriculum in preschool, kindergarten, and primary classrooms. Each chapter will use a constructivist lens to focus on the underlying *Big Ideas* for each subject or area. Furthermore, guiding principles of constructivist approaches will encapsulate the application of constructivist theory to practical applications of the theory. Dividing the curriculum into subject areas is not a constructivist notion. In fact, constructivism views knowledge as overlapping and integrated. Although not a constructivist, Sir Halford John MacKinder put it aptly: "Knowledge is one. Its division into subjects is a concession to human weakness."

Dividing the chapters by subject areas was a concession made in order to illustrate how constructivist teaching relates to traditional approaches. For now, we relate to a framework that focuses on math, literacy, social studies, and so on, as different subjects. However, as the reader will find, there are many areas of overlap and processes in common to many of these subject areas. And children learn many subjects and concepts simultaneously. For them, knowledge is one.

In order to describe the way that the subject areas fit together, a puzzle metaphor is helpful. When looking at a puzzle, the whole cannot be complete with pieces missing. A curriculum that leaves out any of the disciplines cannot create a whole picture that makes sense to the child. Similarly, an isolated piece of the puzzle cannot stand alone. The whole puzzle must have all of its pieces to make sense. Similarly, a constructivist curriculum must be seen as a whole held together by a strong theoretical framework based on how children learn. The theoretical framework presented in this book is not new; it is based upon the 75 years of research begun by Jean Piaget and continued by many after him.

After the chapters focusing on different subject areas, the last chapter of the book will "put the curriculum back together" the way that children learn naturally. These chapters focus on the learning environment, integration of the curriculum, and meeting the needs of all children.

I invite the reader to seek to understand the basic tenets and applications of constructivism, question ideas that do not fit existing notions of teaching and learning, and discuss ideas and practices put forth in the book with others. Interviewing and observing children will lead to even deeper levels of understanding. Readers who become actively involved in the learning process and really think about what constructivist theory means will construct their own understanding of this approach to teaching and learning. This book offers an invitation and a source of disequilibrium to start the reader on the exciting path toward deeper understanding of constructivist views applied to teaching and learning. I hope that the reader will discover, as I did, that once started on the constructivist path, it is hard to ever go back.

Acknowledgments

As with all authors, I write about ideas that are the outcome of my personal and professional experiences. Acknowledging all of the important people whose ideas have influenced mine is impossible, but I will try to name a few. Foremost, I thank the children whose learning I have studied, pondered, and tried to influence. They have been and always will be my best informants on how children learn. In particular, I thank the children from my 1995–1996 kindergarten/first-grade class at the Miller Research Learning Center of Edinboro University of Pennsylvania. Their faces are in the photos of this book and tell a story that words alone cannot. I thank them for allowing me to capture their learning in photos. Two children whose faces do not appear in these pages but are ever-present in my thoughts are Nathan and Kristin Stupiansky. Being their parent has been the most constructive experience of all.

I am indebted to the teachers who stimulated, challenged, and supported my own learning: Alec Dale, David Anderson, Glenn Thompson, and Bill Delamarter of Allegheny College; Bill Corsaro, Jo Prentice, Norm Overly, David Gallahue, and Egon Guba of Indiana University; and Cathy Twomey Fosnot of City College of the City University of New York. I am also indebted to Kathy Merski of the Erie Art Museum, who guided me through all of the stages of photography for this book and also contributed several of the photos.

I am grateful to the many colleagues and friends who made suggestions on how to present the ideas of constructivism in meaningful, accurate ways, in particular Harriet Alger, Rosemary Omniewski, Patricia Diebold, and Dale Hunter of Edinboro University of Pennsylvania; Nancy Sayre of Clarion University of Pennsylvania; Ed Klugman of Wheelock College; Sara Lundsteen of the University of North Texas; Ginny DiRaimo, Judith Olmstead, Pam Dailey-Lang, Lynn Cohen, and Leslie McFadden. I thank the students at Edinboro University of Pennsylvania who suffered through the many drafts of this book and urged me to bring it to fruition. Thanks are also owed to

Erin O'Connor Traylor and Jay Whitney of Delmar Publishers for giving me the opportunity to share my ideas with a wider audience.

There are two people without whom this book would never have happened: Ilene Rosen, whose wise and careful editing helped clarify my thinking and writing from the beginning to the end of this project, and Nick Stupiansky, whose support as colleague, coauthor, friend, and spouse never wavered.

I would like to extend a special thank you to the following reviewers for their comments and recommendations:

Juila Beyeler
University of Akron/Wayne
Orrville, OH

Jane Leatherman
Gulford Tech. Community College
Summerfield, NC

Melonye Curtis
Amarillo College
Amarillo, TX

Dr. Cynthia Paris
Rider College
Lawrenceville, NJ

Dr. Arlene Hambrick
Bluefield College
Welch, WV

Elizabeth Stanley
Marion, CT

To all of these people, thank you for contributing to my thinking in more ways than you will ever know.

SWS

CHAPTER ONE

....

Understanding Constructivism: The Big Ideas

*Constructivism**, the term that Jean Piaget (1973) coined to describe his theory of how people learn, refers to the process of change or knowledge construction that occurs in one's thinking as learning occurs. Piaget redirected the way we think about knowledge. He theorized that knowledge is a process, a way of thinking. Traditionally, knowledge has been treated as a collection of facts and information. Piaget demonstrated that knowing something involves much more than being able to recite memorized information. Knowing involves organizing information and forming a conceptual foundation within which new knowledge can fit. Knowledge is never static; it changes and transforms with each new discovery. Furthermore, the learner has an active part in the knowing process.

Piaget contributed three main ideas that revolutionized the ways we think about learning and teaching. These three ideas are **operational thinking**, the **process of knowledge construction**, and the **active role of the learner**. Let's look at how Piaget explained each of these.

CHILDREN AS OPERATIONAL THINKERS

Perhaps the most widely known aspect of Piaget's theory is the notion of stages of operational thinking. In order to understand how a child reasons, one must understand the concept of operational thinking. An operation is the fundamental component of logical reasoning. Operations are logical, reversible relationships that exist in a person's mind. Operations are formed through actions and interactions with real objects and people (Piaget & Inhelder, 1969). Children begin to mentally perform these actions as they become more sophisticated

* For a full explanation of the theoretical and historical roots of Piaget's constructivism theory, see DeVries and Kohlberg, 1987; Fosnot, 1996; or Kamii, 1985b.

thinkers. For example, addition and its reverse, subtraction, are operations. An addition problem such as $2 + 3 = 5$ can be logically reversed to $5 - 3 = 2$. Children construct this addition/subtraction operation through multiple experiences adding and subtracting real objects. For many years of their development, children are dependent on objects to perform the operations of addition and subtraction.

Piaget described several of the stages through which children progress according to the type of operational thinking they use: **preoperational, concrete operational,** and **formal operational.** Preoperational thinkers, commonly between the ages of two and seven, reason in a rather serendipitous manner. They jump around in their logical explanations in a way that most adults—or operational thinkers—have trouble following. For example, when asked, "Why do bubbles float?" a four-year-old responded with, "Because they pop when I touch them." Later, this same four-year-old was asked, "Would the bubbles still float if they didn't pop when you touched them?" The child, finding no discrepancy in the logical connection, said "Yes." This preoperational thinker is not connecting one idea to another in a logical, reversible manner, and it does not seem to bother her.

Concrete operational thinkers, on the other hand, who are generally between the ages of six and eleven, move from performing operations within the context of real, concrete materials toward being able to move beyond a dependence on the objects. For example, a six-year-old working with two red counters and three green counters can add them together and say that now there are five counters. Furthermore, this child can see that if one takes away the two red counters, three green ones remain. If asked how many will remain if only green counters are taken away, most six-year-olds will perform the action on the counters to arrive at the answer. They still rely on their firsthand experiences with the counters to solve the problem. On the other hand, eleven-year-olds who have had multiple experiences with adding and subtracting real objects, can perform the operations mentally. They can separate the operation from the actual objects and apply the operations in a more abstract way. For example, an eleven-year-old can usually see the relationship between addition and subtraction as reversible and interconnected. When children reach formal operational thinking, they can apply addition and subtraction to many different kinds of numbers, such as decimals, fractions, and large numbers. Furthermore, they can apply their knowledge of addition to the operation of multiplication and see that multiplication is repeated addition. All of these operations are possible for older children if they first understand the operations as relationships performed on objects. They construct this understanding by working with real objects within many contexts. Thus, between the ages of six and eleven years, concrete operational thinking develops with experiences and maturation.

There is an important factor to remember when working with concrete operational thinkers. Just because the children can perform the operations with concrete objects does not mean they are ready to do the same operations at the symbolic level. Many six-year-olds are baffled by the symbolic notations (e.g., 2 + 3 = 5), even though they can perform the operation with counters. The children are still concrete operational thinkers because they attach their thinking to the actual materials. Older concrete operational thinkers who have learned the operations of addition and subtraction by repeated experience with real objects will be able to perform the actions mentally and symbolically, without actually using the objects.

As children move toward more sophisticated thinking, they can rely more on mental and symbolic operations in their reasoning. Children who are able to understand the abstract relationship of addition and subtraction without having to connect their thinking to actual objects are moving into formal operational thinking, which usually starts at about twelve years of age. However, the movement is gradual and full of regressions.

Operations occur in all logical thinking. Socially, a child who can perform mental operations can think through an if/then situation, such as "If I tell Mom that I like the cookies, then she will know that I ate them before dinner. If I do not tell her that I like the cookies, she will not know that I ate any before dinner" (See Figure 1.1). This example illustrates that children attempting their first acts of deceit, or telling their first lies, have become more sophisticated thinkers. They are actually using mental if/then operations in their reasoning.

Another example of an operation from a child's social experiences is two-way family relationships. The father-child relationship can be perceived from the father's point of view or the child's point of view. For example, "My father's child is me." Furthermore, the father is the child of the grandfather and the grandfather is the father of the father (See Figure 1.1). These multiple roles and relationships take time for the child to construct and reverse. They are internalizing logical, reversible, operations about their family relationships. Later they will be able to apply these operations to other families and more complex relationships.

Language is full of operations. Questions are inverses of statements. The order of words can be reversed to create new meanings. Consider the different possible meanings of the following: "I will go to the store," "Will I go to the store?" and "To the store I will go." Children construct an understanding of the reversible operations of language by using language expressively and hearing it in their own conversations. They experiment with the different forms and functions of language.

Figure 1.1 Examples of Operational Thinking

Operational thinking permeates logical reasoning. Children must construct the logic of operations over time, starting with observable, concrete experiences. As they become sophisticated operational thinkers, usually late in elementary school, children can perform mental operations at progressively more formal, abstract levels. Development of symbolic, operational thinking does not stop at the end of childhood. Adults continue to bring meaning to abstract symbols and continue to develop their logical reasoning skills as they construct new ideas and knowledge. When new concepts are introduced to adults, they too often need to start with a concrete example or a concept they already know, then progress into more abstract, symbolic levels of understanding.

Egocentrism

Another concept essential to understanding Piagetian theory is egocentrism. Piaget defines **egocentrism** as centering or focusing only on one's own perspective or perception (Piaget, 1967). Thus the root word,

Figure 1.2 Movement from Centering to Decentering

centrism is in the word *egocentrism*. As children develop their reasoning and thinking skills, they become less centered on their own points of view and become able to "decenter" or take others' points of view (See Figure 1.2). The ability to understand the perspectives of others or consider multiple views on the same topic is another characteristic of formal operational thinking. Decentering allows one's social relationships, problem-solving abilities, and logical reasoning to become more sophisticated because a person who can decenter can look at a situation from a variety of perspectives.

Symbolic Representation

A child's ability to use symbolic thinking is important in constructivist theory. According to Piaget, children in their first several years are closely tied to their immediate experiences. They do not think about an idea much longer than the moment it occurs. When they begin to use mental images and language, children have a means of representing or keeping a thought for longer than the moment. A six-month-old who is playing with a set of keys that drop out of sight will probably not look for the keys (See Figure 1.3a). Piagetian theory says this is because the keys are "reabsorbed" by the environment (Piaget & Inhelder, 1969, p. 12). Yet, that same child at ten months will look for the keys when they fall out of sight. Piaget explained this by saying that now the child has "object permanence"—he is able to hold the image of the keys in his head (Piaget & Inhelder, 1969). A little later, when the child is approximately 18 months old, he moves to another level of symbolic representation when he picks up the car keys and pretends to drive a car. The child uses the keys and his improvisation to symbolize driving a car. When the child is three or four years old, he may pretend to drive a car without using the keys, but with mimed actions and the making of carlike sounds (See Figure 1.3b). This mimed form of pretending is a higher form of symbolic representation because the child symbolizes some of the objects of the play (e.g., the car) without the actual objects. The child is no longer dependent on the concrete objects for his pretending. At even higher levels of representation, children can understand abstract symbolism such as metaphors. For example, an eleven-year-old child will probably understand the metaphor "key to my heart" as referring to the abstract feeling of love that can be unlocked by a special person or action. Other forms of abstract symbolism tap into the child's imagination, such as the symbolic meaning in art forms and literature. As children become more sophisticated in their use of symbolic representation, they can bring meaning to the more abstract and less obvious symbols they encounter in dance, literature, music, and the visual arts.

Children's understanding of symbolic representation develops in predictable ways. According to constructivism, there is a continuum for representing or symbolizing objects and ideas that ranges from the concrete to the abstract. On the concrete level, the objects represent themselves. At the next level, a replica can symbolize the object. Replicas have many characteristics of the actual objects, such as a model airplane or a plastic horse. Learning the spoken word for the object is the next step and allows the child to talk or think about the objects outside of their presence. Another type of abstraction is a photo or diagram. This graphic representation no longer feels or moves like the real object, but a child who has had firsthand experience with the object can bring to it the already developed understanding of its meaning. A high level of abstraction would be the symbols or letters used to spell the word for the object. Nothing in these symbols sounds like, moves like, or feels like the real

Figure 1.3a Beginning Symbolic Thinking

thing. Being able to understand words or symbols demands that a child has already constructed meaning from multiple experiences with the actual objects. Thus, the abstract levels of understanding are based upon the child's concrete, firsthand experiences.

objects themselves	replicas/ models	spoken words	pictures	written words	concepts/ metaphors
CONCRETE					ABSTRACT

At the highest level, which would not be expected until a child enters formal operational thinking around the age of eleven, would be the ability to apply the concrete object to a nonliteral meaning. Examples of this would be understanding phrases such as, "Don't bite the hand that feeds you" or "All nature is my bride" (to quote Thoreau). Understanding the application of the concrete object to its metaphoric meaning involves a high level of abstract operational reasoning.

Figure 1.3b Later Symbolic Thinking

Children need to progress through levels of representation at a rate that fits their levels of understanding. If highly abstract symbols are presented too quickly, such as flash cards with words printed on them, children may achieve only surface-level memorization without deeper understanding.

VIGNETTE 1.1

Teaching to the Students' Level of Symbolic Representation

Jim Taylor, a teacher of four- and five-year-olds, has been preparing to teach a series of lessons on apples. Last year he used pictures of various types of apples and taught the children the correct name for the apples (McIntosh, Red Delicious, Golden Delicious, Granny Smith, Paula Red).

Then, he instructed the children to color in outlines of the apples, matching the colors to the apple names, which were printed at the bottom of the page. Even though Mr. Taylor thought they had learned the apple names well, when they took a trip to an apple orchard, the children could not remember much about the apples or their names.

This year, Mr. Taylor has decided to follow a more constructivist approach to the apple unit. He knows now that the children need to construct their knowledge about apples. Further, he knows that the written words for the apple types are probably too abstract for the children to understand at this point in their development.

Mr. Taylor has set up a series of learning experiences for the children to draw apples, taste the various types of apples, and make many foods from apples, such as apple sauce, apple pie, and apple cider. Throughout the activities, the children use the vocabulary related to apples, compare and contrast the tastes, textures, and appearances of the apples, and construct all kinds of knowledge about the apples from firsthand experiences.

At the end of the unit, Mr. Taylor is amazed at how much the children remember about apples. They discuss the attributes of Paula Reds and McIntoshes as they argue with one another about which kind is best. Months later, they point out apple trees as they ride in the bus to a field trip. Mr. Taylor's class understands much more about apples this year; and they will bring this knowledge with them when they are ready to write—in the symbolic form of letters—the words for what they have learned.

Conservation

An important element in logical reasoning, according to Piaget, is the process of **conservation**. Conserving involves the ability to understand that things that look different can still be the same in some way. Consider the famous Piagetian example of the two balls of clay that are the same size when they are in ball form but, according to a non-conserver, are different sizes when one is rolled into a snake. Before a child develops the ability to conserve, she depends on her **perception,** not her **conception** (DeVries & Kohlberg, 1987). The clay in the snakelike shape looks like more, so it must be more. Similarly, non-conserving children perceive water poured into a differently shaped glass as being more if the water level appears to be higher.

Conservation is closely tied to the logical notion of equivalence. Two things can be the same in some ways, but different in others. For example, to the operational thinker who has developed the ability to conserve, 3 + 4 is the same as 6 + 1, yet they look quite different. Or Tanya's mom is a mother to Tanya in the same way that Joey's mom is a mother to Joey; yet they are different people. On a more abstract level, a theme or moral in two different pieces of literature can be the same, even though the protagonists, setting, and plot are totally different. Conservation involves the ability to perceive sameness and equality beneath obvious, superficial appearances.

Conservation and operational thinking are interdependent. One type of thinking cannot develop without the other. Perhaps that is why the famous Piagetian tasks involving conservation using clay and water are often used to gain insight into a child's level of operational reasoning.

Teaching Toward Conservation

Ms. Lesley Dale is a kindergarten teacher. She provides a midmorning snack every day for the 20 five- and six-year-old children in her class. One day, she puts baskets of small crackers at each snack table. She tells the children that they can have as many crackers as can fit in a 3-ounce paper cup. Several minutes into snack time, she hears Max and Hannah disagreeing about how many crackers each has. Max has poured his crackers onto a napkin. Hannah is eating her crackers out of the paper cup. When Ms. Dale inquires about the reason for the disagreement, Hannah tells her that Max took more crackers than he was supposed to.

Ms. Dale asks the children at the table if they can suggest a way to find out if this is the case. Robert suggests that Max put the remaining crackers back into his cup to see if there are more than the cup would hold. Max agrees to do this. When he replaces his crackers, they fill approximately three-quarters of the volume of the cup. Hannah still is not satisfied. She insists that when he pours the crackers back onto the napkin that he will have more. Knowing that Hannah is focusing on the physical appearance of the pile of crackers, Ms. Dale has another idea. She suggests that Hannah pour her crackers onto a napkin to see if they look like approximately the same amount as Max's. Hannah agrees to try this strategy. After pouring out her crackers and making a pile bigger than Max's pile, she exclaims, "Now I have more than Max!" Satisfied with the distribution of crackers, she goes on eating her snack.

Ms. Dale knows that Max is able to see that he has the same amount of crackers, whether they are in the cup or poured onto the napkin. Piaget calls this the ability to conserve. Hannah is not using conservation in her reasoning yet. Ms. Dale knows that with repeated experiences, such as the present argument with Max, and developmental maturity, Hannah will move toward using conservation in her thinking. Ms. Dale knows that she cannot teach conservation directly, yet social disagreements will help provide the context for Hannah's learning.

CHILDREN AS CONSTRUCTORS OF KNOWLEDGE

One of Piaget's most enlightening ideas was his system for classifying knowledge into different types, based on how a learner comes to know each type. Although the differentiation between the types is often blurred, the classification system helps us connect *what* we want children to learn with *how* to teach different types of knowledge.

Types of Knowledge

As interpreted by one of Piaget's students, Constance Kamii, the three types of knowledge are **physical knowledge**, **logical-mathematical knowledge**, and **social-conventional knowledge** (Kamii, 1985b).

Physical knowledge, according to Piaget, involves the physical properties of objects, such as the hard and shiny physical attributes of glass or the cold and slippery nature of ice. Physical knowledge is *discovered* as the child interacts with the actual objects. The source of the knowledge is the object itself. The information about the object is taken in directly through the learner's five senses of sight, touch, hearing, taste, or smell. Thus, teaching physical knowledge must include opportunities for discovery and hands-on experimentation with actual objects that use one or more of the senses. These firsthand opportunities for discovery are *how* children learn about physical attributes and physical knowledge.

Logical-mathematical knowledge involves relationships between and among objects, ideas, and people. Children *construct* logical-mathematical knowledge as they begin to understand these relationships. For example, three-year-old Paul randomly selects different-sized blocks to construct his block tower. On the other hand, five-year-old Kimia carefully selects blocks in progressively smaller sizes to create a pyramid-like tower. Both children use the same blocks, yet Kimia has constructed a scheme, or mental strategy, to order the blocks in a logical manner. This serial order does not come from the blocks themselves, but from her mental scheme of the relationships among them. Thus, the source for her logical-mathematical knowledge is her mental operations or thinking.

Teaching logical-mathematical knowledge includes providing opportunities for solving realistic problems, manipulating objects in thought-provoking ways, questioning others and oneself, and articulating one's own logical reasoning without the fear of failure. Teachers who pose questions that create disequilibrium in the children's minds and allow children time and opportunity to grapple with their own solutions are teaching logical-mathematical thinking. Children do not memorize or internalize logical-mathematical knowledge from an adult model. They construct logical-mathematical knowledge for themselves.

The third type of knowledge, **social-conventional knowledge**, emanates from the culture within which the child is raised. Social-conventional knowledge includes the conventions of the culture, such as vocabulary and rules of conduct. The word *yes* has the same meaning as the words *si* or *oui*, but in English-speaking cultures, children learn to say *yes*. Similarly, in some cultures, it is considered impolite to wear a hat indoors; whereas in other cultures it is impolite not to cover one's head in certain buildings, such as places of worship. In fact, these two rather contradictory social conventions can occur in the same culture, and children need to memorize where it is appropriate to wear a hat and where it is not acceptable. These are examples of social-conventional knowledge. Children must learn social-conventional knowledge from others who already know the conventions. For the most part, they must memorize social conventions until they become habitual. Social-conventional knowledge cannot be discovered through interactions with physical objects, like physical knowledge. Nor can it be constructed through logic, like logical-mathematical knowledge. Social-conventional knowledge is learned through repetition, reminders, and imitation of others within the culture.

Rarely can the three types of knowledge be separated from each other. Just about every learning experience uses physical, logical-mathematical, and social-conventional knowledge (See Figure 1.4). For example, when learning about the properties of solar energy, children learn the vocabulary for the phenomena they experience—*hot, sun, radiate, heat waves*—terms that are determined by the language of their culture (social-conventional knowledge). These terms are necessary to communicate about their experiences. The physical knowledge of solar energy includes the properties of hot and cold and light and dark. These properties must be discovered and experienced directly by the child. Most children have experienced the light and warmth of the sun, so they can draw upon their prior knowledge as they connect new discoveries. Logical-mathematical knowledge is constructed as children come to understand the relationships between the location of the sun and the length of their shadows, for example, or how the sun feels warmer on their skin at different times of the day and different times of the year. Children begin to bring order to their experiences and use this order to understand and make predictions.

Figure 1.4 Types of Knowledge

VIGNETTE 1.3

Incorporating Three Types of Knowledge into Learning

Cindy Charland, a teacher of three- and four-year-old children, notices that her class is showing a keen interest in popcorn. Their interest was sparked when a child brought to school a cob of corn that she had grown in her garden. The children do not believe that the corn on the cob can turn into the popped corn they are used to eating. Ms. Charland asks if they would like to try popping the corn.

After reading about how to dry the corn and prepare it for popping, Ms. Charland is ready. She sets up an air-pop machine in the middle of a large, clean sheet spread on the floor. The children gather around the sheet, excitedly anticipating the popcorn treat. Ms. Charland passes around the unpopped kernels of popcorn. She uses the vocabulary *kernels, cob,* and *husk* (social-conventional knowledge). She shows them a cob of corn and allows them to rub off the kernels. The children notice how the unpopped kernels feel "hard, shiny, and sharp" and look "brownish-yellow, small, and teardrop shaped" (physical knowledge and social-conventional knowledge). As the popcorn pops, the children notice its smell and the change in appearance (physical knowledge).

Ms. Charland asks the children what made the popcorn pop. They come up with several explanations, for example, "They bounce around and hit into each other hard enough to pop open," and "The machine has little pins in it that pop the kernel like a balloon." Ms. Charland asks if anyone has ever popped popcorn another way. Several children offer responses, such as in the microwave oven or the fireplace. Ms. Charland asks if the microwave or fireplace has something in common with the popcorn popper. One child blurts out, "They both get hot!" (logical-mathematical knowledge).

"Ah ha," says Ms. Charland. "Do you think that the heat has something to do with the popcorn popping?" Several children say "Yes." The rest of the children are not so sure. Ms. Charland knows that the concept of heat causing a physical expansion and mini-explosion inside the popcorn kernel is too abstract for the children to understand. Yet she knows that some of them are beginning to see the cause-effect relationship between the heat and the corn popping (logical-mathematical knowledge). Some of the children still cling to their theories of bumping kernels or little pins, which make sense to them at this point. Ms. Charland makes a mental note to herself that a next experiment could be to shake the kernels vigorously without a heat source and see if they could make them pop. She also will show the children the inside of the popcorn popper when it cools off so that they could look for little pins.

In the meantime, the children and Ms. Charland enjoy their freshly popped popcorn scooped up by eager hands from the sheet surrounding the popper. Ms. Charland knows that she has helped the children gain a great deal of physical, logical-mathematical, and social-conventional knowledge related to popcorn.

All three types of knowledge are important, but they are learned in different ways. Constructivist teachers adjust their strategies to help children discover, construct, or memorize according to the knowledge or concepts they want children to learn; yet they remember that all three types must be integrated. Subsequent chapters will show more specific examples of how the types of knowledge influence the way we teach children.

A criticism of traditional models of teaching is that teachers approach most knowledge like it is social-conventional knowledge, which must be committed to memory through drill and practice (Kamii, 1985b). For example, number equations (such as 2 + 2 = 4) are often taught through flash cards, computer drill-and-practice programs, and timed tests. Constructivists would argue that a child's understanding of number equations is based upon the child's construction of logical-mathematical relationships, that is, the child's understanding of the operation of addition and its inverse, subtraction (Kamii, 1985b).

Additionally, previous experiences with sets of objects (e.g., counting hands, fingers, and feet) and other developmental cognitive constructs contribute to the child's level of understanding of such operations and, consequently, the symbolic notations for these operations. A child cannot understand a number sentence such as 2 + 2 until she has constructed the logical-mathematical reasoning the sentence represents. She may be able to memorize and recite 2 + 2 = 4, but she will not be able to transfer the knowledge to other similar problems, such as 2 + 3 = 5 or 4 − 2 = 2. Without logical-mathematical knowledge, the child's understanding is only at the surface level. If teachers understand that logical-mathematical knowledge cannot be approached as a memorization task, they will provide opportunities for children to use their budding logical reasoning skills with real objects to solve the same problems.

Accommodation and Assimilation

According to Piagetian theory (Piaget & Inhelder, 1969), people incorporate new knowledge into their thinking in two basic ways. If information is so new that it does not "fit" existing ways of thinking, the current thinking is reorganized and new conceptual frameworks are developed to replace earlier ones. This is called **accommodation**. On the other hand, if new ideas fit the learner's current ways of thinking, the new information is assimilated, or added, without major reorganization of existing frameworks. Thus, **assimilation** of new information strengthens existing knowledge.

To illustrate the difference between assimilation and accommodation, consider a three-year-old child who is familiar with dogs of many shapes and sizes. He has developed a conceptual framework for classifying dogs in his mind. Now when he sees a dog, he can fit it into his framework. Even if the dog has unique characteristics, it still barks, acts, and looks like a dog. He can assimilate new information about this dog into his preconceived definition of dogs. Perhaps this same child has never seen a horse, except in picture books and on television. The first time he sees a horse, he may think that it is a dog until he finds that the smell, sounds, and size do not fit his classification framework for dogs. He must develop a new framework within which to fit horses. He must accommodate his thinking to fit the new information (See Figure 1.5).

Teaching for accommodation differentiates constructivist approaches from traditional approaches. Traditional notions of learning as an accumulation of information are related to Piaget's process of assimilation. The departure from traditional views of learning occurs with accommodation, or changes in the way knowledge is organized. Traditionally, we

Figure 1.5 Assimilation and Accommodation

perceived learning as filling the mind with facts and knowledge. This view of teaching and learning has been called the "banking notion" of education (Freire, 1990). Children's minds are regarded as empty banks into which teachers deposit knowledge, like coins. Learners are passive recipients who start with empty banks. Teachers decide what coins of knowledge the children should internalize.

Learners are expected to assimilate the new information in the form the teacher has determined (Brooks & Brooks, 1993). Assessment is usually based on the students' right or wrong answers on a test. In the traditional view of learning, students are usually not expected or asked to engage in higher level thinking and critiquing of what they are learning. Instead, they are expected to give back information in the exact form it was given to them. This form of teaching and learning lends itself to rote memorization and a surface-level understanding of concepts (Kamii & Kamii, 1990).

On the contrary, according to constructivism, learning involves a deep level of understanding that either relates to what the learner already knows or forces the learner to change his or her way of thinking to accommodate new knowledge. Learning involves an active processing of new and existing knowledge as the learner strives to understand, to interpret, and to make sense out of each new experience.

In the words of Kamii (1985b):

> Children learn by *modifying* old ideas, according to constructivism, rather than simply by accumulating new bits of information. . . . In traditional instruction, children are assumed to learn by internalizing knowledge; therefore, teachers simply correct the errors and present right answers, believing that the learner will then absorb this wisdom (p. 49).

Teaching for Accommodation and Assimilation

Paula Dunbar, a first-grade teacher who uses a constructivist approach, uses children's literature to help the children learn that there is usually more than one point of view in any story. She decides to teach several lessons on point of view after some of the children have disagreed about an event that happened on the playground. Several children have accused others of provoking a fight with name-calling. When Ms. Dunbar asks the children to describe the event, diverse points of view emerge, depending on which child is telling the story. Some children say it started because of name-calling, while others insist that it was unprovoked. She encourages the children to listen to each other, yet their emotional involvement prevent them from being objective listeners.

To help the children understand that two parties can perceive the same events very differently, Ms. Dunbar reads the children a book that retells the famous story of the "Three Little Pigs," but from the wolf's point of view (Scieszka, 1989). The story, as told by the wolf, relates how he had a terrible cold, including a bad case of sneezes. According to the wolf, he did not intentionally blow down the straw and stick houses of the first two little pigs. Further, he only ate the pigs because they were dead and he did not want to waste good food. In this version of the story, the wolf claims that he was "framed."

Ms. Dunbar uses assimilation in her lesson by starting with a story familiar to the children. They know "The Three Little Pigs," thus they can *assimilate* the knowledge of the characters, plot, and theme of the story to what they already knew. There is a comfortable fit between the story and their existing knowledge. Ms. Dunbar also encourages *accommodation* on the part of the children. The wolf's point of view probably does not fit the children's current thinking about the story. They have to accommodate their thinking in order to understand the wolf's perspective. Thus, if this lesson is successful, the children will begin to change or accommodate their own thinking to understand that others may have points of view quite different from their own.

Ms. Dunbar realizes that one lesson will not result in deep levels of understanding and accommodation. Yet, by relating the new knowledge— the wolf's point of view—with an example from their own lives—the playground disagreement—the children will begin to make the accommodations in their thinking and move toward more sophisticated thinking. Ms. Dunbar thinks that this strategy is much more effective than simply telling the children that people have different points of view. The children need to learn through real-life experiences, helped by a familiar story with a new twist. Ms. Dunbar knows that she is teaching *toward* accommodation because the children must form the connections within their own thinking. Accommodation is not a process that can be taught directly.

The learner's ability to think and to reason become progressively more sophisticated as a result of experience, conceptual development, and physical maturation. None of these factors—experience, conceptual development, or maturation—can be isolated as either a cause or effect of the other, because they all affect each other. Because of the interactive nature of many factors in the development of thinking, Piaget has been called an "interactionist."

Equilibrium

Piaget, borrowing from the field of biology, used the notion of equilibrium—the striving by all organisms to maintain balance—to explain the forces that propel learning (Fosnot, 1996). If new information, experiences, or ideas do not fit into a person's existing thinking, a state of cognitive imbalance or disequilibrium results. The discomfort created by this disequilibrium provokes the learner to change previous ways of thinking in order to establish a balance between the new knowledge and old knowledge. Thus, the process of accommodation is sparked by cognitive disequilibrium. Constructivist teachers strive to create the right amount of disequilibrium for the children so that they will seek to accommodate their thinking and move toward more sophisticated reasoning.

CHILDREN AS ACTIVE LEARNERS

Children actively construct knowledge according to constructivist theory. Never passive, children try to make sense of and bring meaning to each new experience. They do this as they play, form social relationships, and develop their thinking.

Figure 1.6 Traditional Versus Constructivist Approaches

Importance of Play

In early childhood classrooms, play provides the perfect context for constructing knowledge (See Figure 1.6). There are many definitions of play that will be explored in more depth in Chapter 4. One of the defining features of play is that the players have control or autonomy over their decisions within their play. This includes the freedom to develop rules and procedures for the play. When two or more children play together, they must negotiate and agree on these rules in order for the play to continue. They manipulate materials according to their ideas, experiment, test hypotheses, pretend to take on different roles, and work out their fears. When children play, they try out their thinking in a safe setting. Above all, children are active cognitively and physically in their play.

Importance of Social Interactions

According to constructivism, social interactions are essential for learning. Through comparison of viewpoints and open dialogue, children begin to take into account others' perspectives. It is through social interactions that children begin to think objectively and autonomously. They come to realize that they cannot focus only on their own perspectives.

In social terms, shifts in thinking occur when the learner experiences disequilibrium between what he already knows or thinks and the actions and thinking of others. For example, a child who centers on his own desire to play with a particular toy may encounter a second child who also desires the same toy. After many tugging matches and similar social interactions, the child gradually begins to take into consideration that others have desires as strong as his own (See Figure 1.7).

Figure 1.7 Learning Through Social Conflicts

Social interactions provide a multitude of social problems to be solved. A child must decide how to get the swing on the playground from a child who has claimed it first, how to invite someone to read with her, or how to convince another child to do a project her way. The context provided by social interactions among peers is a natural learning environment in which logical reasoning can develop. The feedback is usually immediate, and the motivation to succeed is high.

Learning through social interactions and social conflicts is a gradual but essential process that requires many experiences to master, as well as the development of cognitive reasoning skills. Constructivist teachers know that over time and with many social experiences, children will begin to realize that others have perspectives, needs, and desires of their own and that these must be recognized and accounted for in their own behavior and thinking. A goal for the teacher is to help children see and hear the viewpoints of others and become social problem-solvers themselves.

Intellectual Autonomy

As stated earlier, according to constructivism, learning is more than the accumulation of facts and concepts. Learning is movement toward more advanced and sophisticated thinking. Sophisticated thinkers can take into account information from a variety of sources, as well as several points of view, and use developed reasoning to come to their own conclusions. This type of thinking is called **intellectual autonomy** (Kamii, 1985b). Intellectual autonomy is a goal of constructivist education, though one that children will not reach until adolescence or early adulthood. Children must proceed through a series of universal, less-sophisticated ways of thinking before reaching autonomous reasoning. They need to have countless experiences with the physical and social world and reach developmental maturity before becoming autonomous, abstract thinkers. The roots for autonomous thinking are formed during the concrete, first-hand experiences of the early childhood years.

Intellectual Heteronomy

If autonomous thinking is a goal for education, its converse, **intellectual heteronomy**, should be defined. Autonomy is the ability to think for oneself. *Heteronomy* means that others have power or control over one's thinking. Children who are more heteronomous in their thinking believe what others tell them without questioning. With regard to moral issues, heteronomy is characterized by people making decisions because of the rewards or punishments they will receive from others.

Conversely, autonomous thinkers make decisions based upon their own convictions and beliefs (Kamii & DeVries, 1993). For example, a child who works hard in school in order to earn high grades acts heteronomously. A child who works hard because of intrinsic interest in the subject is more autonomous. Of course there are times when the context affects the degree of the child's autonomous reasoning. Yet, traditionally, schools have promoted heteronomy over autonomy in students. Constructivist approaches try to build upon a child's interests and convictions and downplay external rewards that promote heteronomous dependence on others.

Motivation to learn, in a constructivist classroom, comes from the child's curiosity and natural need to know. Extrinsic rewards, fear of punishment, and traditional grading systems work against the child's intrinsic motivation to make sense out of the world. If children work toward pleasing the teacher instead of satisfying their natural search for understanding, they will not progress toward intellectual autonomy (See Figure 1.8).

Figure 1.8 Autonomous and Heteronomous Thinking

Autonomous thinkers are not necessarily defiant or disrespectful of those in authority roles. Much to the contrary, they are respectful of others' perspectives and responsibilities. By engaging in social interactions with peers and others who do not exert extreme power over them, children gain an understanding of others that is necessary for this type of mutual respect. These concepts will be explored further in Chapter 3.

TEACHERS AS CONSTRUCTIVIST EDUCATORS

As has been illustrated in this chapter, traditional notions of how a student learns have been questioned by Piaget and his successors in their theories and careful research focusing on how children approach and interpret new knowledge (Kamii, 1985b; Piaget, 1973). Constructivism views the learner as an active participant in the learning process. Learners bring with them a wealth of knowledge and individual characteristics that enter into each learning act. Preconceived notions, reasoning skills, maturation level, and earlier experiences affect the way learners perceive and interpret each new experience. Piaget conducted many experiments showing how children interpret and explain their reasoning at different ages or developmental levels. As children gain new experiences and develop physically and mentally, they go through a series of predictable shifts in their thinking. Thus, constructivist teachers of young children expect and allow children to reason differently than adults, older children, and each other. The child's reasoning—even when erroneous—helps teachers understand the child's operational thinking.

Since constructivist teachers view students as active participants in their own learning, planning for their learning begins with the learners and their pre-existing knowledge and ways of thinking about the world. The focus of the teaching/learning activities shifts from the teachers and refocuses on the learners.

....

VIGNETTE 1.5

Focusing on Students'
Prior Knowledge

Carlos Ramos, a second-grade teacher, prepares to teach a unit on light. This is the third year that he has taught this same unit. The second-grade science curriculum guidelines state that by the end of the unit, the children will be able to do the following:

- Identify and define translucent, opaque, and transparent properties of objects
- Predict the resulting colors when mixing two primary-colored filters

- Explain and demonstrate that shadows result from the blocking of a light source
- Explain that light rays bend when they pass through or strike some surfaces

The first year that Mr. Ramos taught this unit, he used the textbook as the source of information for the children. He directed them in reading the chapter on light silently, then he had children read aloud from the text, paragraph by paragraph, while the others read along silently. Mr. Ramos did not do any of the suggested experiments with light; instead he relied on the text's descriptions of the experiments to demonstrate the concepts. He did notice that the children entered the unit with all different levels of understanding about the properties of light. Some children had obviously experimented with shadows, color mixing, and magnifying glasses on their own. Yet, Mr. Ramos treated all of the children the same, not making any allowances for the children's varying levels of understanding. All of the children started at the same place in the book and proceeded together through the chapter. At the end of the unit, Mr. Ramos played several word games with the class that reviewed the facts about light. Then he gave a pencil-and-paper, multiple-choice test from the teacher's guide. The children did well on the test, so Mr. Ramos assumed that they understood the properties of light well enough to go on to the next unit. Yet Mr. Ramos was concerned that the children did not seem to be very interested in the unit.

The second year that Mr. Ramos taught the unit, he still used the textbook as the main source of information. However, he decided to make it more interesting by supplementing the written materials with several experiments that he demonstrated for the children. The children again scored well on the end-of-unit test; but, several months later, Mr. Ramos noticed that the children had forgotten most of what they had learned about light. The children were unable to transfer knowledge of the properties of light rays to help them understand the properties of sound waves in another unit, even though they had correctly answered the test questions about light rays.

Mr. Ramos decides this year to use more constructivist approaches to teaching the unit on light. He is becoming convinced that in order to plan effective, interesting learning experiences for the children, he must find out what they already know and think about the properties of light. Thus, he decides to start the planning process by assessing the children's thinking.

Mr. Ramos sets up several small experiments with the purpose of finding out what the children already think about light before the unit begins. In one of these experiments, Mr. Ramos fills a large glass jar with water. He then asks the children if they think that this glass of water could make his hand get bigger. All of the children agree that this was impossible. He slowly lowers his hand into the glass of water, which makes his hand appear larger when viewed from the side of the glass. The children respond with "oohs" and "ahs." He repeats this process several times, then asks a child in the class to do the same. Next, Mr. Ramos asks the children to describe what happened and write their ideas—or hypotheses—about why they think his hand appeared bigger. After the children write their ideas, he asks them to design an experiment to discover if they are right and write the steps to their experiment in their journals. He then uses their experiments to allow the children to explore the properties of light. After each experiment, the children, working in cooperative learning groups, record their findings. Each group reports back to the whole class about their findings. The children's inquiries guide the rest of the unit.

Thus, Mr. Ramos starts with the children's hypotheses and their suggested experiments to plan a series of learning experiences that will let the children challenge pre-existing notions about the properties of light. He knows that if the children pursue some of their own ideas, they will be more interested in the results and remember their discoveries. They will seek answers to their own questions. In Piagetian terms, through active experimentation, the children experience disequilibrium between what they already think and their new discoveries. When their experiments turn out in the way they predicted, they assimilate the experiences into their existing thinking. When the experiments surprise them, they accommodate their thinking to account for the new learnings. Mr. Ramos finds that the children's interest in light is much higher this year than in the past two years. Also, later in the year, the children remember the concepts they learned through their own discoveries, and they can apply these concepts to new areas of investigation. Mr. Ramos is surprised to discover that another outcome is that the children are thinking and acting like scientists. He realizes that the process of scientific inquiry may be as important for the children to learn as the properties of light.

The theory of constructivism, as first proposed by Piaget and later interpreted and expanded upon by others, revolutionizes the way we think about teaching and learning. Teaching strategies, according to constructivism, must match the child's developmental level to the types of knowledge being taught, promote autonomous thinking, actively involve the learner, and lead to the development of increasingly more sophisticated levels of understanding and reasoning.

Teaching using constructivist approaches does not mean lowering expectations for learning. If anything, expectations are raised for deeper levels of understanding on the part of the children. When a child learns about the position of the sun and the length of shadows by actively experimenting and devising her own hypotheses, she will remember and use that knowledge. She comes to know the relationship between her body, the sun, and her shadow in a way that it makes sense to her. In other words, when a child accommodates her thinking by bringing personal meaning to new experiences, she does not forget what she has learned. She learns at a deep level of understanding that will influence all later learning.

The ancient proverb summarizes the essence of constructivism most eloquently: "I hear, I forget. I see, I remember. I do, I understand." Constructivist teachers teach for understanding.

CHAPTER TWO

Children's Social Understanding

As defined by the National Council for the Social Studies, social studies is the integrated study of many disciplines, including economics, geography, history, political science, psychology, and sociology. By definition, social studies must be multidisciplinary and interdisciplinary. One of the major purposes of the social studies curriculum is to help students develop the knowledge, skills, and attitudes they will need to become responsible citizens (National Council for the Social Studies [NCSS], 1994). For children in the early childhood years (i.e., eight years old and younger), the roots of social studies form as they develop their understanding of people and groups of people. As children come to know the social world around them, constructivist teachers emphasize children's social interactions and emergent social relations as providing the context for learning. Children construct notions of their social world in much the same way as they construct notions of the physical world. As children experiment and interact with other people, they form the cognitive constructs that allow them to make predictions and understand the logic of their social environment.

A case in point would be a two-year-old child who knocks over a potted plant, all the while shaking her head and saying, "No, no, no." The parent responds by saying, "No, no," while scooping up the soil and plant. This sequence of actions has happened before. The child has constructed the relationship between her actions (knocking over the plant) and the parent's reaction (saying "No, no"). Yet the inhibitory meaning of the words, *no, no,* did not deter the child's action. Constructivists would argue that the child is forming a cause-and-effect logic about her social environment, just as she constructs cause-and-effect relationships about her physical explorations with the environment.

Understanding the social environment and social relations follows a progression from less- to more-sophisticated logical reasoning as a child has repeated and varied firsthand experiences with a variety of people and concomitantly develops the cognitive skills to account for these experiences. Children's earliest experiences are often within the family or with caregivers. Gradually, these social experiences take them into new social realms, introducing the children to their peers, people from different backgrounds and cultures, and new adults. Later as they become abstract thinkers, children come to understand physically distant events, such as historical events. Yet the roots to the children's understanding of remote and abstract social studies topics are always in their concrete, firsthand experiences (Wadsworth, 1978).

Constructivist approaches to teaching social studies are quite different from traditional approaches that emphasize the memorization of dates, names, and geographic locations. Rather than viewing socialization as the children's internalizing of adult knowledge and skills, constructivists believe that all information and experience is "interpreted, organized and acted upon from the child's point of view" (Corsaro, 1985, p. 53). Constructivist approaches build on the child's real-life experiences with families, peers, social institutions, and the similarities and differences within and among cultures. The goals of a constructivist social studies program include helping children develop different perspectives, become good decision-makers and problem-solvers, and develop respect for themselves and others as they prepare to become citizens in a democratic society. In the words of the National Council for the Social Studies (1994), to achieve these goals, students must learn "connected networks of knowledge, skills, beliefs, and attitudes that they will find useful both in and outside of school" (p. 163).

DISCIPLINES WITHIN THE SOCIAL SCIENCES

Before examining processes that underlie social studies, let us take a look at several of the specific fields of study within social studies. For the purposes of this book, the fields of history, geography, economics, political science, and community studies will be included.

History

Putting events within a historical context requires the development of many complex cognitive skills, such as being able to transport one's thinking over time and distance. It also involves collecting and analyzing historical data to piece together what life was like in other eras. For children to develop these skills, which are requisite to thinking like historians, they need to be able to go through a number of more basic cognitive processes, such as being able to put events into temporal order, to use measurements of time such as years, and to take on another person's perspective.

An egocentric child who perceives events from a singular, personal perspective, will be able to interpret historical events in increasingly more complex ways as she grows. But, history must connect to the child's current knowledge if the child is to bring meaning to it. For example, understanding the First Thanksgiving, that famous meal that was shared between the Pilgrims and Native Americans in the 1600s, demands that children cross time, cultures, and geographic locations. This ability develops gradually and is not completed in the early childhood period. The child's understanding begins with what they already know, such as sharing a meal with new friends, learning to eat new foods, and learning about new ways of dressing and speaking. The location in time (three hundred years ago) and space (Plymouth Rock, Massachusetts) are far removed from the children's experiences. To understand these concepts, children must first bring meaning and order to the concepts of yesterday, today, and tomorrow. Then, through real-life experiences and vicarious experiences, such as stories shared through literature and films, children come to recognize the gradations and range of yesterdays and tomorrows. They begin to understand that "yesterday" could be 24 hours ago or 24 centuries ago. Even so, understanding the definition of *pilgrims* as religious sojourners who could come from many religions, historical periods, and geographic locations is an even more abstract concept that takes many years for children to develop.

Constructivist teachers recognize that interpretation of history is gradual and dependent upon the child's cognitive development and firsthand experiences. They use this understanding to make history meaningful. Interpretation of historical events is culturally-bound and subjective. Children who learn to compare and contrast interpretations, who are exposed to original sources, such as diary entries and autobiographies, and who are encouraged to maintain a tentative attitude about their own interpretation of history learn to think like historians (Fromberg, 1995). Traditionally, history was taught as if it were a body of static knowledge, consisting of dates, accomplishments of famous people, and wars. This approach is not meaningful for young children. History is rich with stories of people's struggles, changes, and discoveries. If taught through the views of the people of different eras, children will come to understand these views. Not only do these approaches help children comprehend history, they offer a richer view of history. Children learn to collect data, to compare and contrast interpretations, and to conduct the work of historians, all the while constructing an understanding of history that makes sense to them.

Teaching Toward an Understanding of History

Ms. Pam Hewit, a second-grade teacher, wanted to help the 22 seven- and eight-year-old children in her class understand the meaning of Columbus Day in a deeper way than memorizing, "In 1492, he sailed the ocean blue," or the phrase, "He discovered America." To prepare for this unit, Ms. Hewit became a historical researcher herself. She went to the library and found books recalling Columbus's voyage, as told in his own diary. She read about the way he altered his estimates of the distance they covered so that his crew would not be alarmed. She watched movies that depicted the events leading to the voyage, the actual voyage, and the months that followed. Ms. Hewit wanted to learn so she could create as many firsthand experiences as possible, so the children could construct their own understanding of this historical event.

Using cardboard boxes, construction paper, and paint, she and the children set up a side of the classroom to look like a replica of one of Columbus's ships. Several children made the "captain's quarters," equipping and furnishing the space with cardboard replicas of what Columbus may have used in 1492, such as a primitive telescope, sundial, and captain's log. The class developed a list of other things the ship would have carried. They gathered ropes, sacks of potatoes, wood, salt, dried meat, and other materials they found at home. If they could not find some of the items, they made them out of paper, cardboard, and clay. They made a compass out of a bowl and cardboard, sails out of sheets, and masts out of cardboard tubes. The children also prepared and ate a meal like that which the sailors on Columbus's ship may have eaten. Ms. Hewit introduced the Columbus unit at the beginning of the school year so she could read to the children each week from Columbus's log, using his own words to describe what transpired on that particular date, leading up to the famous landing on October 12.

Ms. Hewit wanted the children to understand that there were people living on the land that Columbus discovered, the people that Columbus called "Indians" because he thought that he had landed in India. So, on the other side of the classroom, she and the children set up a Native American village like the ones that Columbus found. As one group worked on the ship replica, another worked on the Native American village, researching the foods, artifacts, types of homes, and clothing the residents would have used. On the 12th of October, the class re-enacted the first encounter between Columbus's crew and the native people. Ms. Hewit read to the children the words Columbus recorded that captured his surprise when he met the people whose clothes were few. The children composed a fictitious diary entry of one Native American's impressions of Columbus with his peculiar-looking attire and unrecognizable language. The children invited their parents to attend the finale to share the encounter experiences with them.

Ms. Hewit struggled with what to do about presenting the historical accounts of the ensuing struggles between the Native Americans and the first European settlements, which included death and destruction for both cultures. She did not want to give the children the false impression that the two cultures lived peacefully, yet she did not want to overwhelm them with some of the tragic and violent events that followed. She decided to ask the children what they thought would happen and the feelings they would experience if they had been there over 500 years ago. The children volunteered many of the strong feelings of distrust, misunderstanding, confusion, and intrigue that members of the two cultures must have felt. Ms. Hewit asked the children if they thought that living side by side was going to be easy and peaceful. The children's responses ranged from "yes" to "of course not." Ms. Hewit told the children that there were rough times ahead as the two cultures lived together on the same land. There were fights and some people died. Yet, many people became friends and some even married.

Ms. Hewit was satisfied at the end of the unit that the children had learned about history in a firsthand, meaningful way. They had engaged in the processes of history, including researching, re-enacting, and building representations of historical structures and artifacts. She knew that the children did not understand the historical events and their implications in the same way that adults could; but she knew that many of the children had laid the foundation for a deeper understanding of not only Columbus's story, but of other historical events they would encounter in the future.

Geography

If geography is thought of as encompassing ways of understanding and representing physical space in symbolic, visual-spatial forms such as maps, globes, reliefs, and other forms, constructivist theory is clear about approaches that lead to children's understanding of these forms. Children move from concrete, close approximations of represented objects to more abstract representations of the same objects. For example, a dollhouse is a close approximation of a real house, yet it differs in scale. A two-dimensional floor plan of the dollhouse is more abstract because it lacks many characteristics of the house. Bringing meaning to a floor plan of the dollhouse demands perspective (looking down at the roofless house from a bird's-eye view) and imagination (showing walls as lines and doors as arcs). Taking this example one step further, showing the house as a dot on a road map according to its location is even further removed from the actual house.

Children move toward understanding these geographic forms of representing space as they form meaningful representations themselves. As five-year-old children construct block buildings in the block corner, they form rectangular rooms with walls. They discover that when they look at their construction from several angles they see it differently. When they try to draw their construction, they have to think about how to represent it in two-dimensional form. If they take a photo of the building, they see it from the camera angle. Through experiences such as building with large blocks, constructing with link-together, small, plastic blocks, and forming objects with clay and other three-dimensional media, children construct knowledge of how other three-dimensional models work. As they explore two-dimensional ways of representing objects (e.g., photos and drawings), they develop an understanding of how the same concrete object can be presented in different forms.

Experiences with negotiating one's body through space, through movement activities where children need to go under, around, and over objects and each other, help them develop spatial skills. Moving toy cars on roads and bridges in the block area or on map mats brings action to the child's representations. Finding and developing patterns in the floor tiles, children's clothing, and picket fences across the street also help children find visual-spatial order, which will later transform into map-reading skills.

Expanding on these earlier experiences and leading the children toward more abstract representations of their world is appropriate for early elementary students. Graphing their lunch data, making maps of the classroom, playground, neighborhood, and other familiar places, and examining aerial photographs allow slightly older children to develop the knowledge base and processes necessary for reading and interpreting abstract depictions of geographic space such as maps.

VIGNETTE 2.2

Teaching Map Skills

Mr. Jim Cavanaugh, a kindergarten teacher, knew that one of the curricular objectives for his school district was to lay the foundations for map-reading skills in the kindergarten year. In the past, he had brought in simple maps of the community, located the children's homes on the map, and duplicated the maps for the children to color and take home. He was not satisfied that the children comprehended the meaning of the maps; rather, they seemed to approach it more like a paper and crayon-coloring task.

This year, Mr. Cavanaugh decided to experiment with a more constructivist approach and set up a series of experiences that would take the children from very concrete map-reading skills to more representational levels. Mr. Cavanaugh's school was a three-story structure with windows overlooking the playground area. The playground had the typical equipment found on many elementary school playgrounds: a sliding board, large swing set, sandbox, rotating merry-go-round, crossbars, and many wide-open spaces for running, chasing, and ball games.

The first experience that Mr. Cavanaugh planned for the children was a scavenger hunt. He took photographs of the playground equipment from various positions on the playground. He stood at the top of the sliding board ladder and took a picture of the slide. He sat on one swing and took a picture of the other swings. All in all he took 12 pictures from all different vantage points.

When the photos came back from developing, he had the children work in teams of two and try to figure out exactly where he was standing when he took the photo. The children took the photos with them as they excitedly tried different angles and locations. When they found the right location, they stayed there so that Mr. Cavanaugh could verify their finding. Some children performed this task with ease. Others had difficulty and used a trial-and-error approach. All of the teams were successful, so they traded photos and repeated the task. This "game" became so popular that Mr. Cavanaugh brought the photos out with them every day for two weeks, until the children's interest started to wane.

The next experience that Mr. Cavanaugh planned for the children was to build a replica of the playground in their room. He sectioned off a large area of the floor and put a plastic tablecloth on the floor. He provided clay and other materials for the children to use as they made the three-dimensional replica. Before starting, one of the children asked him if he would take a photograph of the playground from the third-floor window. Together, Mr. Cavanaugh and the children went upstairs and took the photograph. When the photograph came back from developing, the children realized that the playground equipment looked different in the two-dimensional photo. Yet they had enough experience with the playground to recognize the sliding board, swing set, and so on.

The map-building project took two weeks, with groups of children working on it during free-choice times. The children drew the sidewalks onto the tablecloth. Some children made bushes and trees, and the others made the equipment. When the map was done, some of the children asked if they could use little people figures and toy cars to "play" on the map. Mr. Cavanaugh said, "Of course."

At the end of the three weeks, Mr. Cavanaugh was satisfied that the children had a much deeper understanding of how maps are constructed and what they represent than in any of the previous years when he used already-made maps.

Economics

If economics is viewed as the study of the distribution of material resources, including the interdependent relationships of persons with each other and persons with their environments, children can engage in meaningful learning experiences that help them understand these relationships (Fromberg, 1995). As children visit persons "on the job" in a variety of work settings, they learn that accomplishing a task demands the contributions of many persons doing a variety of functions. As they work together on meaningful projects that are engineered for them to work together toward a final product, such as making cookies for a bake sale or putting together food baskets for the food bank, children become part of the interdependent workings of the economic and social system.

VIGNETTE 2.3

Teaching Economics to First Graders

Ms. Jody Olmstead and Ms. Aletha Rice were both first-grade teachers. As part of the first-grade unit on "The More We Work Together," which included objectives such as "The children will be able to identify the importance and function of workers within a variety of jobs," and "The children will use coins (pennies, nickels, dimes, and quarters) and one-dollar bills in meaningful contexts," Ms. Olmstead and Ms. Rice decided to combine their classes and work on a big project. They brought the idea to the children, asking them, "Can you think of something that we could make and sell?" After brainstorming many different options, the class narrowed it down to some sort of food. A multitude of ideas were generated, from cupcakes and cookies to popcorn balls and sandwiches. Together they decided that they could make hoagie sandwiches. The parents and teachers would be interested in buying them to eat for lunch or dinner. They were healthy and easy to make.

Next, the children and teachers had to decide what ingredients they needed for the hoagies. They generated a list of possible ingredients. Several children volunteered to go with their parents to the grocery store and find out how much each would cost. Three different children (and parents) would go to three different grocery stores so that they could compare the prices.

Several days later, the prices were in. Ms. Olmstead and Ms. Rice, with the help of the children, made large charts with the names of the items and the names of the store, cross-referenced with the prices. After all of the prices were put onto the chart, the teachers asked, "Where should we buy our ingredients?" The children recognized that overall one of the stores had lower prices than the others. They decided to go to that store for their shopping.

Next, they had to decide how much they needed of each ingredient. Together they decided that they could sell 100 hoagie sandwiches without much trouble. So, working in groups of four children, they estimated quantities of buns, slices of cheese and meat, lettuce, tomatoes, spread, and plastic wrap they would need to buy. Once again, Ms. Olmstead and Ms. Rice made a large chart to record all of the estimates. They discussed each estimate and arrived at a group consensus for the amount they should buy. Sometimes, they had to buy more than needed because the packages of ingredients were in groups of 8, 12, or 24. This became a math problem that the children took home as homework. Next, the children had to figure out how much it was going to cost to make 100 hoagies and the price of each hoagie. The class voted that they would like to make a small profit and use the profit to donate to the local food bank. The final verdict was that the hoagies would cost $1.50 each to make; but they would sell them for $2.00, making a $.50 profit. For homework, they had to figure out how much they would have to donate to the food bank.

To correlate with the unit on working together, Ms. Olmstead and Ms. Rice explained that everyone needed to have a job. There would be "bun cutters," "meat spreaders," and "hoagie wrappers," to name a few. Children filled out job applications, depending on which job they wanted. A selection committee (two students and the two teachers) made the final job placements. During this process, Ms. Olmstead asked the group if there might be another way that they could make the hoagies, other than the factory-type assembly line. One child suggested that they could make them like they do at home, each person would make one from start to finish, by moving along the table of ingredients. Then they could even put a little label on the hoagie, "Made by _____." Some of the children liked this idea, but others wanted to do an assembly line. Ms. Rice suggested that they try both ways and vote at the end which one worked best.

The children spent the next couple days taking orders and collecting the money. They kept a big chart to record how many hoagies had been ordered and how much money had been collected. When 100 had been sold, the class walked to the grocery store they had selected and bought all of the ingredients. The next day was "Hoagie-Making Day." All of the children washed their hands, took their jobs, and the assembling began. After 50 hoagies were made, the children switched to the one-person-making-each-hoagie model. After an hour and a half, 100 hoagies were ready to distribute to their buyers. They were bagged and labeled by the children.

The next day, the children and teachers went to the food bank to take the $50.00 they had earned. They decided that they liked the "one-person-one-hoagie" way of assembling the hoagies because of the sense of pride they took in the finished product, especially since their names were attached. Ms. Rice and Ms. Olmstead agreed that the objectives for the unit had been met. Next year, perhaps they could make a different "manufactured" product.

Children learn about the use of money as a means of acquiring goods as they "buy and sell" items in their dramatic play and through bake sales and trips to the grocery store. They learn about the larger notions of exchanging one good for another as they barter in the block center for a block that another child is using, as they trade bikes on the playground, and as they take turns using a favorite shovel at the sand table.

Children learn through stories and children's literature about the ways different families overcome economic hardships. They learn how people in different cultures make and use products similarly and differently than their own culture. Much of children's literature illustrates the power of cooperation, with even the smallest contributor making a difference when combined with the efforts of the group.

As in learning other subjects, economic concepts and experiences close to the child's real-life experiences allow the child to form meaningful connections between what he or she already knows and the new knowledge. Constructivist teachers draw upon and provide as many firsthand experiences as possible. Whenever this is not possible, vicarious experiences, such as those provided through good children's literature, help children experience reality through the characters in the stories.

Political Science

Political science involves the use of power, rules and laws, and governmental institutions (Fromberg, 1995). Piaget contended that children construct an understanding of rules and laws by engaging in situations with peers wherein they negotiate and come to agreement about the rules governing their own behavior. As primary-age children participate in a game of kick-ball on the playground, they need to agree on the rules, even if they are loosely applied, for the game to continue. As they argue about how children are tagged "out" and what happens after a foul ball, they come to agreement about the rules in operation. This social negotiation leads to an understanding of the importance and reasons for the rules of the legal and justice systems. A full understanding of the political and legal system does not come until much later than the early childhood years; but the early constructions that lead to this later understanding form in the early years.

Children learn about the responsibilities and power that accompany leadership positions as they experience both sides of the power scale. As the adults and authority figures around them use their power over them, children can experience a variety of situations. The children can be empowered and encouraged to make their own decisions and choices or they may be coerced to follow others' edicts. They will experience both extremes and many gradations in between. Constructivist teachers strive to allow children opportunities for autonomous decision making, which is predicated on childrens being encouraged to make decisions and consider the consequences. Educators can provide opportunities for democratic decision making by leading the children in class dicussions and voting on issues; providing student leadership opportunities, such as taking on responsible roles like the "people counter" or "locker checker"; and encouraging children to take action on issues that concern them (e.g., writing their requests for the lunch menu). Decision making and taking action that affects others can give children a sense of the responsibility that having power implies. As children see the effects of their efforts and experience the sense of satisfaction that comes from making a difference, they gain a sense of self-efficacy or confidence that they can have an impact on their world.

Community Studies

Young children come to understand the world around them starting with the world closest to them—their own social and family circles. If a child's social world can be imagined as a series of concentric circles with the child in the center and the child's family as the first circle, a child's social development moves from being centered upon himself to focusing on persons outside his immediate social circle, starting with peer groups, classmates, and eventually communities and cultural groups. During the first several years of life, the child begins to differentiate between himself and others and comes to recognize that he is one of many persons (Piaget, 1969).

Constructivist approaches build upon this natural thinking and introduce studies of communities starting with the innermost circles and moving to larger and more inclusive communities. Units of study may start with a focus on one's self and family in preschool, move to study of the classroom as a community in kindergarten, and study of the local community in first grade. Concepts such as the relationships of cities, states, countries, and continents become increasingly inclusive and demand a cognitive understanding that communities can be embedded in still larger communities, an understanding that develops during the elementary school years. Once children come to understand their own worlds, they can come to understand others'. They can assimilate information that is familiar, such as the way children play baseball in their own community and others'. They accommodate their thinking to include new ways of doing things: "We go places in a car, but children who live in cities ride on subways."

Community studies incorporate history, geography, economics, political science, and sociology. Children learn the roots of their community as they study its history through interviewing persons, visiting historical sites, learning the folktales and stories of the community, and other firsthand experiences. They learn about the interrelationships of geography and community life as they discover how the physical, geographic location of the community (e.g., on the shore of a large lake) affects its commerce and development. Moreover, they learn how the commerce and development of the community influences its physical environment (e.g., the runoff into the lake, the disposal of waste, the effect upon the fish and other water life). Understanding these reversible, interdependent relationships requires operational thinking, a skill that concrete operational thinkers can begin to perform if it connects to their real-life experiences.

VIGNETTE 2.4

Teaching About Community

Ms. Lori Martin is a preschool teacher in a local child care center. She has a class of three- and four-year-old children. They are beginning a unit on community helpers, which usually involves going to the police station, fire station, grocery store, and hospital. Since Ms. Martin had most of the four-year-olds last year, she decides that this year they could go on some different types of field trips. Fortunately, the child care center is right in the center of a small town, with many options within walking distance. She decides to ask the children what place they would like to visit in town so that they can see what the workers do there. The list that the children brainstorm is quite interesting, including the bank (where the robbers go), the car wash, the local fast-food restaurant, and the shoe store. Ms. Martin says that she will contact these places and see if they could go for a visit. Just about every person she calls says that a visit from the children would be welcome.

Ms. Martin knows that it would overwhelm the children to visit all of the places in a short time span, so she plans one visit per week for the next several weeks. She also sets up the dramatic play area of the classroom with materials the children will see workers use when they visit the different businesses; for example, money, adding machines, and a safe for the bank; cash register, ordering pads, plastic food, and utensils for the fast-food restaurant; tricycles, buffing cloths, and spray bottles for the car wash; and stools, feet sizers (borrowed from the shoe store), and shoes of many sizes for the shoe store. Upon returning from the visits each week, the children will be able to re-enact their experiences in the dramatic play center—and they sure do!

At the end of the unit, Ms. Martin is pleased with how the children remembered and acted out many of the actions they saw the workers doing. She is also pleased that the children chose the places to visit this year, places she probably would not have thought of herself. She can tell how important the children feel because their ideas made a difference. She decides that she will go through the same process next year. Maybe they will end up at the fire station, but maybe not! That will all depend on the children and their interests.

The child's education should not be limited to only her closest levels of community, even though these are the areas she will know best. Introduction to other cultures, placed within the context of what the child already knows, allows the child opportunities to build connections between her world and those of others. Cultural studies that emphasize commonalities among cultures, such as family bonds, kinds of shelter and transportation, games, and means of nourishing our bodies, encourage the child to connect what she already knows about her ways of doing things in her community and similar ways children do things in other cultures. Children's literature, folklore, songs, video presentations, and firsthand experiences such as trips and guest speakers bring these experiences within the child's level of understanding.

As children engage in sociodramatic play with a variety of props and community artifacts, such as a shoe store, grocery story, doctor's office, factory, and so on, they experiment with the roles and relationships within the community. They will pretend to be the store clerk, doctor, factory worker, as well as the mother, father, or baby, as they engage in the types of activities associated with these roles (Fromberg, 1995). This type of play is a way for the children to represent their ideas about their communities and is essential for their developing an understanding of how persons within communities relate to each other.

Thus, history, geography, economics, political science, and community studies are all content areas of study within the social studies. They are all appropriate areas for young children to learn, if they are taught in connection with the children's real lives. Now let us look at some of the processes involved in learning social studies.

PROCESSES UNDERLYING SOCIAL UNDERSTANDING

Within the framework of constructivism, the knowledge and processes for understanding social studies include the following: perspective taking and decentering, understanding roles and relationships, making autonomous choices, cooperating with others in a spirit of mutual respect, and developing the symbolic representations for the language of social studies. Each of these will be further described below.

Perspective Taking and Decentering

The ability to take the perspective of others depends on the child's ability to decenter or move away from his or her own perspective. Perspective taking can be a perceptual skill, such as being able to predict what another person can see from a different angle. At its more abstract levels, perspective taking entails understanding another person's point of view or opinion, even when it differs from one's own. The adage "Don't judge another person until you walk a mile in his shoes" taps into the second type of perspective taking.

At both levels of sophistication, perspective taking demands suspending one's own point of view or opinion long enough to consider another way of looking at an object or idea. The first type of perceptual perspective taking taps into experiences with physical knowledge, that is, discovery that objects can look different from different angles. Both types of perspective taking require logical-mathematical reasoning skills because the relationship between the observed and the observer must be considered. The relationship or position of a person to a tree determines the view of the tree he or she sees. On a slightly more abstract level, a child who has spent his entire life living in a large city brings a different perspective to the study of farm animals than a child raised on a farm. The complex, subjective perspectives of persons are relative, depending upon their prior experiences and relationships to the subject studied. Logical-mathematical thinking allows children to shift perspectives and consider more than one point of view simultaneously.

Social-conventional knowledge enters into the learning because learning about other similar and different cultures and ways of life, whether across cultures or time, allows a child opportunities to compare, contrast, and expand his or her cultural knowledge. Understanding that others go about common experiences differently than the child, such as preparing food, shopping, or moving from place to place, develops a child's awareness that there is more than one way to live.

Traditional approaches to teaching history and geography that demand rote memorization of dates, person's names, cities, and states, teach social studies as social-conventional knowledge. The relationships and connections between history and geography and what the child has experienced or already knows are not investigated. Rather, memory devices and rote memorization techniques take the place of logical connections and physical discovery. Social studies knowledge is treated as social-conventional knowledge for students to memorize. Students are treated as passive receptacles of information.

Perspective taking, a process that develops through social studies and becomes a tool for further, more sophisticated social understanding, takes many years to develop to a formal level. Children's firsthand experiences and the disequilibrium created by these experiences provoke further learning.

Understanding Roles and Relationships

Understanding the social world involves understanding that persons have multiple roles and relationships. The same person can be a mother, wife, daughter, aunt, teacher, volunteer, coach, and elected official. Understanding these multiple roles for the same person demands that the child can classify the same objects several different ways. This ability develops in the late-preschool/early-primary years. As children play a variety of roles in dramatic play, such as the big sister, who is also the fairy godmother, who then becomes the queen, they begin to recognize that one's role often depends on the context within which the role occurs.

Similarly, the multiple relationships that persons have to one another are often contextually determined. A person can be a boss and a subordinate at the same time, depending upon which relationship is the focus. A child's understanding of relationships begins with the persons closest to him, such as his parents, siblings, grandparents, and caregivers. As his social world expands, so do his relationship possibilities. He forms relationships with teachers, friends, coaches, teammates, and many others. These relationships are two-way and interdependent. In other words, how one person behaves affects the behavior, thoughts, and feelings of the others. Understanding the interdependency demands that the child use operational, reversible thinking, which develops gradually with operational reasoning.

Making Autonomous Choices

If, as Kamii (1984) contends, autonomy is the goal of constructivist education, children must have practice making decisions that are based on their own convictions and thinking. These opportunities must start with limited, safe choices, such as whether the child wants strawberry or grape jelly on her toast. The important factor is the respect that the adult gives to the child's choices. If the child chooses grape jelly and the parent insists on giving her strawberry jelly, the child's choice was disregarded and the message to the child was that the adult's choice was more important. Allowing children to make decisions is difficult and time-consuming. It is much easier to select the child's clothes for her, pick what soup she will eat for lunch or the book that will be read to her before bed. Yet, if one recognizes that the roots for autonomous thinking begin in these small choices, allowing the child these choices becomes important.

Part of the responsibility of making choices is developing the ability to judge and predict the consequences of these choices. If a child chooses to disobey a clearly defined rule, such as not touching the controls on the stove, the consequences for this choice might be his removal from the kitchen. Not being allowed to stay in the kitchen is a logical consequence for the child's choice to disobey the rules of the kitchen. If this consequence is consistently applied, the child will be able to think ahead to the logical results of his choices, thus contributing to his reasoning skills. Having predictable consequences also gives the child a sense of security. He knows what the results of his actions will be every time. This predictability also adds to his ability to reason logically.

Cooperating with Others in a Spirit of Mutual Respect

Children develop mutual respect, or what Piaget called autonomous moral reasoning, through opportunities to build mutual understanding with others in nonthreatening situations (Piaget & Inhelder, 1969). Children in play situations with other children have opportunities to negotiate and determine rules, remind each other of these rules, and communicate their displeasure when the rules are disrespected. Likewise, children tell each other when they think that their rights have been violated. If Lynn takes a shovel that Geof is using, Geof is going to let Lynn know that he disapproves, probably by verbally telling Lynn that he wants the shovel back and perhaps grabbing it away from her. Young children often communicate their disapproval in inappropriate ways, such as by using physical or verbal aggression, but their message is clear: My rights have been violated, and I do not like it. It is through these social disagreements with peers that children construct an understanding that others have wants, needs, and rights of their own. Children begin to see themselves as part of the social network, wherein one person's actions have effects on all others, and different people may have different perspectives.

Being able to problem-solve and negotiate through the social challenges that inevitably arise when children are together lays the foundation for later abilities to cooperate with others out of mutual respect. Respectful cooperation is a highly developed skill that demands cognitive and social skills beyond the sophistication of preschool children, yet the roots for its later development are firmly planted in constructivist classrooms.

Developing Symbolic Representations for the Language of Social Studies

Like math and science, social studies has symbols germane to its language. Maps, graphs, reliefs, diagrams, and other forms of representing information in the social studies make communicating and recording knowledge possible. Constructivist teachers recognize that understanding these symbolic representations, some of which are abstract and removed from the child's firsthand experiences, takes experiences in less abstract, more concrete forms. For example, a photograph of the playground from an upper-story window is a less abstract form of representing the playground than a map that uses architect's symbols for the bushes, park benches, and swing set. A young child needs to experience levels of representation that fall within her level of reasoning. Road maps are usually indecipherable to four-year-old children. They must learn to "read" the symbols, color notations, and scale, which takes many experiences and a level of reasoning that develops gradually.

Thus, taking others' perspectives, understanding a variety of roles and relationships, making autonomous choices, cooperating with others, and using the symbols and language of social studies are processes that underlie all of the distinct disciplines within social studies. A constructivist teacher recognizes these as the *Big Ideas* toward which she or he must teach.

INSTRUCTIONAL PRINCIPLES

The following are principles for teaching social understanding that follow logically from the "Big Ideas" of constructivism:

1. **Plan for multiple and varied direct experiences with people (adults and children) and opportunities for children to re-enact their experiences.** Preschool and primary-age children are concrete learners who learn best through firsthand experiences. Getting to know and playing with a child from a different culture means much more to a child than listening to stories about children in other cultures. Furthermore, acting upon new learnings about people and cultures by incorporating these learnings into their play allows children necessary opportunities to make this knowledge

their own. They figure out ways to represent (or re-present) their understandings of society and culture in their own terms.

2. **Provide multiple opportunities to engage in perspective-taking activities that help children develop the ability to decenter and perceive events from multiple viewpoints.** The understanding of others is predicated on the ability to decenter or take another perspective. According to Piagetian theory, children learn to decenter as they develop the required cognitive sophistication and social sophistication through meaningful interactions with others. Adults play an important role in the development of decentering skills as they arrange experiences that challenge the child's budding abilities. Yet, other children play an even more important role as they navigate and negotiate through the maze of social conflicts and dilemmas that arise naturally as they play.

3. **Use the languages of culture to explore one's own and others' heritages, allowing children to experience the many dimensions of culture (e.g., the different languages of art, music, dance, play, and writing).** There are many ways to represent cultures that children can understand. Just as many cultures speak different languages, they also enjoy different types of art, music, dance, games, foods, and stories. Children enjoy learning by experiencing these cultural representations firsthand. Tasting a variety of foods, dancing to new types of music, and playing games that other children of other cultures enjoy bring new knowledge to children in developmentally appropriate, concrete ways.

4. **Recognize that children learn rules of convention from adults in their culture and reasons for these rules from their peers.** As will be discussed in Chapter 3, children must learn the culturally determined do's and don'ts from the keepers of the culture around them—mainly the adults. Children come to know if their actions are right or wrong in the eyes of their culture through adults' words and actions. The understanding of the *reasons* for these rules and social mores develops through the children's own development of rules as they interact with each other. Without the deeper level of understanding of the reasons for societal rules, children's respect for these rules will depend on the consequences—rewards and punishments—rather than the realization of the importance rules have for governing civil behavior, a realization that develops much later in life.

5. **Integrate the many areas of social studies whenever possible.** Division of the various disciplines within social studies is often arbitrary and the boundaries are blurred. A culture's geography affects its history and economy. The actions of one culture influences the actions of other cultures. The interdependency and

interconnectiveness of the social and physical worlds must permeate the curriculum. For example, children can come to know how people who live in warm climates or at the ocean's edge provide for their basic needs differently than people living in frigid, landlocked areas.

6. **Assess social understanding by "capturing" the young child's reasoning and behavior in a variety of contexts.** A child's social understanding cannot be assessed by paper and pencil tasks. Children's performance, projects, questions, and reasoning must be tapped in order to understand and assess their developmental level. Placing quantitative grades or scores on their developmental levels creates an arbitrary comparison of children who naturally vary in their levels of sophistication. Assessment in the form of artifacts of the students' thinking (e.g., photos of their block buildings, samples of their questions, projects they have researched and worked on) lead to more authentic portrayals of the child's understanding of the social world.

7. **Allow for child-initiated projects and collection of real data in areas of the children's interest.** Movement away from memorization of a body of facts, such as dates and locations, toward developing the underlying processes involved in social understandings allows constructivist teachers to build in opportunities for children to pursue their own interests. Children motivated by an intrinsic desire to know about their cultural roots, ancestors, or other areas that fascinate them will learn much more from their investigations than children forced to study the same topics. For example, one child may have a fascination for medievel life, another has a fascination for Native American cultures, and another child wants to know about different types of transportation. Many of the same processes that underlie all of the social studies, such as perspective taking and understanding maps and other representations within the social studies, can be developed through explorations of just about any topic. Older primary-age children begin to think like historians or anthropologists as they collect data on their topics of interest. They become autonomous decision-makers as they pursue their own choices, and these choices are valued and respected by their teachers.

8. **Build toward an understanding of others by helping children develop an understanding of themselves.** Children whose cultural and familial roots are respected in a spirit of understanding will come to respect the cultures of others. As children move naturally through the concentric circles of understanding, starting with themselves and their immediate social world, they begin to find the connections and similarities between themselves and others.

As they develop perspective-taking skills, they recognize that others have their own concentric circles, with the multitude of roles and relationships each involves.

9. **Use all three types of knowledge (logical-mathematical, social-conventional, and physical) to contribute to social understandings.** Constructivist teachers recognize that all types of knowledge develop simultaneously and interdependently. Thus, as children use logical skills (such as a sense of time) that allow them to place events within a historical framework, they can study the social conventions of their ancestors and the ancestors of others. Furthermore, they can experience the physical knowledge of the smell of the ocean, the darkness of the coal mine, or the noise of the horses' hooves on the cobblestone streets of long ago if they have opportunities to learn of these physical realities firsthand.

10. **Match symbolic representations of social studies topics (e.g., maps, charts, graphs) to the child's level of understanding of symbols (concrete, pictorial, symbolic).** Preschool and primary-age children are concrete learners who need experiences that follow along the continuum from concrete to abstract, with many stops along the way. Wading in a shallow stream and feeling the current against one's ankles and seeing the movement of a stick as it bobs its way along the water's course is much more concrete than examining a diagram in a book about rivers that shows the direction of its flow using arrows. Making one's own river in the sandbox by watching the water from a hose form a winding path from the highest elevation and working its way to the lowest is more concrete than reading about erosion in a book. Constructivist teachers search for the most concrete, real-life experiences possible and allow time and opportunity for the children to explore these experiences until they are ready to understand more abstract representations of the phenomena.

SUMMARY

Developing an understanding of the social studies involves the deeper, underlying "*Big Ideas*" and concepts germane to an understanding of people, cultures, and environments. Children have a natural interest in and desire to know about other people. This intrinsic interest, combined with the richness and variety of the topics considered to be social studies, lead to an exciting and emerging curriculum that is real—not dusty and distant—for the children.

CHAPTER THREE

Guiding Children's Moral Development

3

A teacher new to constructivism may ask, "How will I ever establish a learning environment that allows children to be active learners *and* encourages them to act appropriately?" Children's behavior, especially inappropriate behavior, can threaten the learning atmosphere for everyone and tempt the teacher to turn to controlling, rigid methods of maintaining order. Yet, one of the distinguishing features of a constructivist learning environment is the sense of shared responsibility for the social order that children and teachers construct together. For that reason, instead of using the word **discipline**, which connotes something done *to* the child, this book uses the word **guidance** to convey that teachers work *with* children to guide them toward moral understanding—an appreciation of the way human beings should treat each other. Morals are universally held rules governing behavior that stem from respect for other people. Furthermore, morals are "structured by underlying concepts of justice" (Nucci & Turiel, 1978, p. 401). A child's morals develop logically from the reciprocal relationships that children have with other children and adults whom they respect. In the same way that teachers guide children's learning in other areas of the curriculum, they guide them toward understanding morals.

CONSTRUCTIVIST THEORIES OF MORAL DEVELOPMENT

Strategies constructivist teachers use to develop and maintain the learning atmosphere are quite different than those used in traditional classrooms. Constructivist classrooms are perceived as minisocieties wherein children and teachers work together to create a democratic community. Teachers recognize that children construct their morality out of their daily experiences during the early childhood years (DeVries & Zan, 1994). They realize that the construction of moral knowledge happens from the inside out; that is, an understanding of right from wrong develops within the child—it is not transmitted by others and then internalized by the child. Piaget contended that just as children construct knowledge of their physical world, they also construct knowledge of their social and moral world. In doing so, children must develop many of the same cognitive processes, discussed elsewhere in this book—logical reasoning, decentering, problem solving—through their firsthand experiences with other people.

In order to examine and analyze a constructivist approach to guidance, constructivist theories of moral development must be understood by the reader. In constructivist appoaches, the long-term goal of guidance or discipline systems is for children to become self-regulated adults who make responsible decisions based on deeply held convictions of right and wrong. During the childhood years, teachers help children become autonomous thinkers in deciding upon the right course of action. This goal guides day-to-day decisions for constructivist teachers, though they realize that achieving self-regulation and autonomous thinking will not be fully accomplished during the childhood years.

Children As Moral Realists

Children develop their understanding of right and wrong in a gradual progression that parallels their intellectual development in other areas. In the youngest ages, through the preoperational period that lasts until approximately seven years of age, children use what Piaget called "moral realism" (Piaget & Inhelder, 1969). Children base most of their judgments of good and bad on what is observable or real to them. At this stage, they do not realize that others have different motives for their actions. If someone spills a gallon of milk—intentionally or not—that person's behavior is bad in the eyes of the moral realist. The more milk spilled, the worse the behavior must be.

Intentional acts of misbehavior are treated the same as accidental misbehavior because the moral realist cannot "see" the person's motives. If a child knocks down another child's small block construction intentionally, this is "less bad" than if the child knocks down a large block construction accidentally. The children judge the act by the observable severity of the damage, not the invisible motives of the offenders.

Moral realists perceive rules as given truths imposed by authority figures. They obey the letter of the law, not the spirit. They have not constructed the reasons behind the rules, thus they take the rules quite literally. For example, four-year-old Kristin develops a habit of stomping her foot whenever she is unhappy. Her mother asks her not to stomp her foot like that anymore. At preschool the next day the class plays "If You're Happy and You Know It." When she hears the verse, "If you're happy and you know it, stomp your feet," Kristin tells her teacher that she is not allowed to stomp her feet anymore. Kristin obviously interprets her mother's rule very literally as meaning that she should never stomp her feet.

During this time of moral realism, children exhibit egocentric patterns in their interactions with others. Their constructions of rules (and the reasons for the rules) center on their own perceptions and needs. When playing with other children, two- to six-year-olds often use impulsive, physical means of meeting their needs (Selman, 1980). At the youngest ages of this stage, if children see a desirable object that someone else is using, they are likely to reach for it, unaware and unconcerned about the current user's rights over the object. Children have not developed an understanding that another person's rights may supersede their own wants. Selman (1980) attributes this egocentric, impulsive behavior to the child's undeveloped perspective-taking skills. Generally, children under six years of age do not recognize that others have inner perspectives different from their own. Thus, they center on their own subjective perspective, which may be, "I want that marker!"

Furthermore, according to Selman (1980), as children begin to decenter enough to know that others have unique perspectives (between the ages of five and nine), they begin to coordinate their needs with others, yet still in a one-way, unilateral manner. Children of these ages may use polite behavior, yet it is usually out of obedience to the rules imposed by adults. Their budding perspective-taking and logical reasoning skills limit their abilities to see the world through the eyes of others. Consequently, they still center on their own points of view. These young children are still developing the understanding of reciprocity, or a mutual understanding of others perspectives.

Children As Reciprocal Thinkers

Selman's research finds that, between the ages of seven and twelve years, children begin to operate out of a sense of reciprocity, or mutual respect, as they begin to consider the feelings or thoughts of self and others. Their developing cognitive skills help them think before acting; they begin to consider others in their thoughts. Children during the elementary school years begin to coordinate their perspectives with those of others. For example, ten-year-old Carla considers the feelings of her best friend before responding to an invitation to a birthday party to which her best friend has not been invited. After thinking about it, Carla decides not to attend the party. Thus, the feelings of her friend entered into her decision and action.

Understanding Conventions and Morals

As children construct their understanding of the rules of right and wrong, they also begin to understand that there are different types of rules. These types of rules vary depending on the type of knowledge they represent. **Conventions**, which stem from social-conventional knowledge, are rules that are culturally or situationally determined. They are "behavioral uniformities which coordinate interactions of individuals within social systems" (Nucci & Turiel, 1978, p. 400). Examples of social conventions in the classroom include procedures that children follow before leaving the room to use the rest room, knowing where and how to hang their coats, remembering to take their hats off inside the school building, and other conventional rules as determined by the teachers in the school setting. Many conventions are determined by the larger culture within which the children live, such as conventions of good manners, dress, hygiene, and speech.

As children learn that others have rights, just as they themselves do, they begin to treat others out of respect for those rights. The rules that govern this mutual respect for others are called **moral rules**. The logical-mathematical thinking that underlies children's understanding of moral rules develops along with children's other logical reasoning skills. In fact, Piaget contended that children's social relations with their peers provide the impetus or disequilibrium for logical reasoning to develop. In Piaget's words, the child "invents nothing without collaboration of his equals" (1965, p. 100). In other words, children's social relations provide the real-life context within which the logical consequences of moral rules are understood and practiced.

Both social conventions and morals govern the relationships of adults and children. For example, when adults travel the speed limit, they may do so more out of fear of receiving a speeding ticket than out of respect for other motorists. Maximum speed limits vary from state to state and country to country because they are locally agreed upon guides for behavior. Thus, they are social conventions enforced by fear of punishment. An example of a moral rule, however, is the law prohibiting murder. All cultures have prohibitions against killing other people except in rare cases, such as self-defense. These universally agreed upon laws are based upon a respect for others' rights. Thus, they are moral rules.

Nucci and Turiel (1978) found that children as young as preschool age could differentiate between social conventions and morals. To determine this, their research team observed ten preschool classrooms. When a child broke a rule, the researchers interviewed witnesses of the violation. They asked the witnessing child what rule was broken. If the child could articulate the rule, for example, "no running in the classroom," then the researchers followed up with another question. They would ask, for instance, "If a child in another school did not have that rule, and he ran in the classroom, would it be wrong?" Through their answers many preschool age children showed that they were able to differentiate between morals and conventions. The children usually perceived that moral rules would still apply at other schools, even if unstated. On the other hand, social conventions would apply only if these rules were stated and enforced. For example, most of the children perceived rules about procedures and conventions, such as where and when it is okay to run or to chew gum, to be contextually bound and only applicable if such a rule were stated. The children considered these rules to be conventions. On the other hand, children perceived rules that prohibited hurting others or taking others' property as applicable and enforceable, whether or not the rule was stated. To them, these universal rules were **morals**. Thus, children as young as three and four years old have constructed an understanding of conventional rules as being different from moral rules.

Furthermore, Nucci and Turiel found that teachers usually pointed out violations of social conventions, not the children. Smetana (1984) found that children responded to moral transgressions by focusing on the intrinsic consequences of such violations, such as their feelings of loss or other emotions provoked by the inappropriate behavior. For example, they would cry or protest loudly. Adults responded to children's breaches in both types of rules with control strategies; they would use for example, commands, warnings, or diversionary tactics.

Children develop their understanding of conventions and morals through different types of experiences and relationships with the adults and peers in their social world. Two other researchers, Much and Sweder (1978), found that adults reminded children to follow social conventions much more than children reminded each other. Yet, children alerted each other to moral breaches more than adults. Adults do most of the teaching of social conventions. They have to because social conventions are not based on logic. They are based on the expectations of the culture and must be memorized by the children. Conversely, children can construct the logic underlying moral rules as they interact with other children and adults. Morals are based on the logic and justice that children experience firsthand in their social interactions.

Deciding the Consequences of Rule Violation

Just as teachers must decide what rules are in operation within the classroom, they must also decide what the consequences of rule violation would be. Traditionally, teachers would use rewards for good behavior and punishments for inappropriate behavior. Yet, Piaget warned against the overuse of controlling tactics such as punishment. He pointed to three unfortunate effects of punishment: mindless conformity, rebellion, and calculation of risks by the children (1965; Kamii, 1984). *Mindless conformity* results when a child no longer makes decisions for herself. Instead, the child adheres to the rules because conformity provides the security of avoiding future punishment. *Rebellious behavior* against controlling authority figures, results when a normally compliant child decides to act for herself and, in order to do so, refuses to conform to adult expectations (Kamii, 1984). The child then *calculates the risks* of getting caught and functions accordingly. Children receive pleasure from performing the forbidden action without getting caught, which further encourages the misbehavior.

All of the unfortunate outcomes of overreliance on adult control strategies, such as the use of punishment and reward, lead children to think heteronomously instead of autonomously. Heteronomous thinkers rely on others to make decisions for them (Kamii, 1984). On the other hand, autonomous thinkers behave according to their reasoning of right and wrong. This reasoning develops in the same way as other reasoning and logical skills, through firsthand experiences and social encounters that challenge their previously held beliefs.

Marion (1981) proposed a related way of looking at guidance systems that provides insight into the negative by-products of teachers' use of rewards as well as punishments. According to Marion, the guidance systems adults use with children usually fall into two main categories: power assertion and inductive reasoning. Although Marion did not relate these categories to constructivist theory, the categories are similar to the Piagetian notions of heteronomous and autonomous reasoning. Marion defined **power assertion** as "a control attempt used by adults who rely on physical or psychological force or threats to elicit behavioral change" (p. 34). The control attempts include issuing rewards for good behavior and doling out threats or punishment for bad behavior. The strategies can be verbal or physical in nature. Piagetian theory would argue that power assertion techniques lead to heteronomous reasoning on the part of children. **Inductive reasoning,** according to Marion, "is a control attempt used by adults who want to help children understand that a given behavior has consequences for themselves or for others" (p. 34). Inductive reasoning appeals to the child's developing logical reasoning skills as the adult helps the child see the connections between behavior and consequences. Piagetian theory would argue that inductive reasoning leads to autonomous thinking by children.

Piaget (1965) and Kamii (1984) contend that autonomous thinkers make decisions about right and wrong based upon their own reasoning, regardless of the system of punishments and rewards. Consider the case of Martin Luther King, Jr. Despite severe punishment, even imprisonment, for voicing his opinions of right and wrong, Martin Luther King, Jr., continued to act autonomously in the face of danger by fighting to end racism in the United States. He was a true autonomous thinker.

The Value of Social Conflict

Another premise that is obvious in Piagetian theory is the value of social conflicts for children's development of moral reasoning. As children experience different perspectives through social conflict, they are forced to compare their individual points of view with those of others. It is through these social conflicts that children come to recognize that others have perspectives different from their own. As children come to recognize and include the perspectives of others, they can begin to cooperate with one another. **Cooperation**, or "co-operation," is a cognitive coordinating of operations (Piaget, 1965). Children cannot cooperate if they allow egocentrism or blind conformity to adult authority to guide their behavior. They must suspend their tendencies to center on their own points of view or an authority figure's control and work with another person to operate in a mutually satisfactory way. Such cooperative efforts lead "to the recognition of the principles of formal logic" (Piaget, 1965, p. 403) because children have to operate according to agreed-upon logical principles, not their own egocentric thinking.

Autonomous moral reasoning and true cooperation take a long time to develop; and they may not develop fully in some children. The roots of autonomous reasoning lie in the early childhood years. The requisite logical reasoning skills necessary for the full development of autonomous reasoning will take many years and experiences before they are firmly in place.

PROCESSES UNDERLYING MORAL DECISION MAKING

There are a number of processes underlying moral, autonomous decision making that constructivist teachers hold as goals for their guidance system. Most of these processes underlie other areas of the curriculum as well. A sampling of these processes follows.

Reciprocal Understanding

Morality based on reciprocity, that is, distinguishing between right and wrong behaviors based upon mutual respect and understanding, is the root of moral reasoning. For example, when children refrain from injuring others with actions or words because they understand how it feels to be injured themselves, they base their actions on a sense of reciprocal understanding. This type of decision making is preferred over a decision based on fear of punishment, which is an example of heteronomous moral reasoning.

Perspective Taking

Requisite to autonomous moral reasoning is the ability to take the perspective of others. Understanding others' perspectives develops over a long time span. It begins with more concrete, direct experiences, such as understanding that a person on the other side of an object sees a different view, and develops into more abstract, less visible forms, such as understanding that people have different feelings and thoughts about the same subject.

Related to perspective taking is the understanding that some actions occur accidentally or without intent. As children come to realize that other people have subjective, internal motives for their behavior, they also realize that intent should be considered when judging misbehavior.

Coordinating One's Actions and Needs with Others'

A corollary to perspective taking is the ability to coordinate several viewpoints at once. Negotiation and compromise are two social skills that reflect a child's ability to coordinate her own and others' perspectives at once. When eight-year-olds Joseph and Alisha negotiate about the rules for their checker game, they must come to a compromise ("co-operate" in the Piagetian sense) in order to play. If Joseph says that players must jump the other's game pieces whenever possible and Alisha disagrees, they cannot continue the game until they agree on the rule. They may compromise and decide that one time they will play according to Joseph's rule and the next time according to Alisha's rule. By resolving the disagreement with compromise, they are coordinating their perspectives and "co-operating."

Knowing the Reasons for Rules

In order for children to construct an understanding of how the laws and morals of society function, they must understand the reasons why there are certain rules. They must begin to grasp the logic underlying society's laws and morals. According to constructivist theory, understanding the reasons for rules develops as children develop their own rules—rules to games, rules in their play, rules that allow a peer group to operate smoothly. As children develop and abide by rules they have constructed, they develop a deep understanding of the function and reason for society's rules.

Establishing Rules Democratically

Marcail Jacobs, a teacher of five- to seven-year-old children, decides to try a more constructivist approach to determining the rules for her classroom this year. She decides to include the children in the development, wording, and displaying of the rules. For the last several years, Ms. Jacobs used a class meeting at the beginning of the school year to generate the children's ideas for the rules. After leading them through a brainstorming session during which the children suggested the rules for the classroom, she had the children illustrate the rules on posters, which hung in the room for the entire year. She was not sure that this was the best way to derive the most relevant rules because sometimes the children suggested rules such as "Don't push each other down a cliff" and "Don't put food in other children's ears." She also noticed that the children did not seem to understand the connection between the rules and their behavior in the classroom.

This year, she decides to allow the rules to emerge from classroom situations and problem areas. Each time a situation arises in which a rule would help in deciding a solution, Ms. Jacobs calls a classroom meeting where children can discuss the problem, propose solutions and rules, and arrive at logical consequences for violators of the rule. As the rules are developed, she writes them on a poster and the children illustrate them. The rule posters take a prominent place on a classroom wall.

Her first opportunity to lead the children through the rule-developing process occurs during the first week of school: Belinda and Chris, two five-year-olds new to Ms. Jacobs's class this year, are playing in the block center when Ms. Jacobs hears Chris crying loudly. She looks over to see him standing in the middle of the ruins of an elaborate tower he had been building minutes earlier. Belinda is pushing a tow truck around the ruins saying, "This is a wrecker truck."

Ms. Jacobs calmly enters the scene and determines that Belinda knocked over Chris's structure as part of her pretending to operate a wrecking truck. Ms. Jacobs calms Chris as she calls the rest of the children together for a rule-forming meeting, which she calls a "Congress." She explains to the children what has transpired, without placing blame on either party. She asks the children, "What is the problem here?" They reply, "Belinda's being mean," and "Chris feels bad." Ms. Jacobs explains to them that sometimes one child's play can hurt another child, even when he or she did not intend to do so. She asks them if they can think of times when this has happened to them. Nearly all of the children think of times when they too were hurt by another child's play.

Next, Ms. Jacobs asks them if they can think of a rule that would prevent this from happening again. As they make suggestions, she writes them on a large sheet of newsprint: "Don't knock down other kids' buildings," "Don't be mean," and so on. After writing down all of their suggestions, Ms. Jacobs reads all of the rules to the children. She asks, "Is there one rule that would include all of these rules?" One child, a seven-year-old, suggests, "Play nicely around your friends." The other children agree. Ms. Jacobs writes this rule in large letters on poster board. Then she asks, "What should happen if someone forgets the rule and doesn't play nicely?" The children suggest consequences that range from "Make them sit in a corner" to "Don't let them play for a week." To bring it closer to their firsthand experiences, Ms. Jacobs asks, "What would be a fair consequence for Belinda after knocking down Chris's tower?" One child suggests that she help Chris fix his building. Ms. Jacobs asks Belinda what she thinks of that consequence. Belinda says that she will get her "building truck" and have Chris's tower fixed like magic.

Ms. Jacobs writes "When we don't play nicely, we need to help the people we hurt" on the bottom of the poster. She asks for volunteers to illustrate the poster. Belinda volunteers, but Ms. Jacobs reminds her that she has something else to do first. "Oh, yeah," Belinda says as she rushes over to get her "building truck" from the shelf.

This year, the rules that emerge from the children's real-life experiences seem to have much more relevance to the children. Ms. Jacobs knows that they are beginning to realize the connections the rules have to the problems they encounter nearly every day. Ms. Jacobs now sees these "problems" as powerful learning situations for the children in her class.

Predicting the Effect of One's Behavior on Others

Being able to predict the effect of one's behavior on another person involves using means-end logical reasoning. Children come to realize that they are part of a social web in which one person's actions affect many other people. They come to this understanding by being part of many social webs and experiencing firsthand how their actions affect others. With experience comes the ability to predict how their behavior will affect others; for example, "If I take Jeremy's crayon, he will get mad at me." Children also become able to predict the reactions of specific people in their social environment: "Mom may react one way if I eat cookies before dinner. Grandma may react in a different way." This ability to think before acting and predict how the actions will affect others develops with operational thinking because it involves logical reasoning. A child must consider an if/then relationship: "If I eat a cookie before dinner, Mom will get mad at me; Grandma won't!"

Social Problem Solving

If the goal of constructivist classrooms is for children to become autonomous thinkers and problem solvers, the social problems they encounter provide endless opportunities for practicing and developing autonomous reasoning skills. Whenever children are together in an atmosphere that allows for peer interactions and group projects, social disagreements *will* occur. Constructivist teachers see each disagreement as an opportunity for children to learn about themselves, others, and the social morals and conventions in operation. As children learn to voice their opinions, listen to others' opinions, compromise, and work out solutions, they are learning the essence of getting along in society at large.

VIGNETTE 3.2

Allowing Children to Take Responsibility

Scott Rosen teaches six- to eight-year-old children in a multi-age first and second grade. He knows how important it is for children to feel a genuine sense of responsibility for the running of the classroom if they are to grow up to be responsible adults. He remembers when he was their age growing up on a farm. He had many real responsibilities, including being in charge of feeding the small animals. If he did not feed them, the chickens and ducks would go hungry. He attributes his keen sense of responsibility as an adult to his early experiences on the farm.

Mr. Rosen knows that nowadays, few children have many real responsibilities around their homes. In his classroom, he tries to build in opportunities for them to practice being responsible. Together with the children he develops a list of all of the jobs they could do around the classroom. These jobs range from "Gardener" to "Coat Closet Checker." They brainstorm about ten jobs, complete with job descriptions. Mr. Rosen posts the jobs and descriptions in a prominent place.

Each Monday, at the opening meeting, the workers are selected. To be fair, Mr. Rosen places all of the children's names in a canister. The children pull names one at a time. The selected children choose their jobs, and put their name cards next to the job titles. This procedure continues each week until all of the children have a chance to select a job, which takes about two rounds. Once everyone has had a job, all of the names go back into the canister again.

Mr. Rosen notices that the children remind each other to "water the plants" or "boot up the computers" more than he does. He smiles to himself as he examines the drowned geraniums or the streaky chalkboards. He knows that these are the by-products of young children learning to take on responsibilities. He realizes that just as the chickens and ducks were patient with him, he must be the same for these children.

INSTRUCTIONAL PRINCIPLES

1. **Use logical reasoning when explaining the rules and consequences governing behavior in the classroom.** When constructivist teachers redirect children's behavior, they clearly state the reasons why the behavior was inappropriate. They do this without attacking the child's dignity. Instead of saying, "How many times have I told you not to carry the scissors with the point sticking up?" a constructivist teacher may say, "If you carry the scissors with the points out, you may accidentally stab someone. What could you do to prevent this from happening?" Furthermore, when a child's behavior warrants it, the consequences should stem logically from the infraction. For example, when children misuse the blocks, they lose their privilege of playing with the blocks for that day. The consequence is a logical extension of the inappropriate behavior.

2. **Keep rules to a minimum and emphasize moral rules over social conventions.** Many rules in a classroom are social conventions or procedures that are necessary for the smooth operation of the classroom community, yet these rules can become overwhelming to the young child. Overemphasizing the social conventions instead of emphasizing a few overarching moral rules leads to a rigid, authoritarian setting where children must rely on the adults to tell them if they are behaving appropriately or not. Children as young as three and four years old recognize the setting-specific nature of these rules (Nucci & Turiel, 1978). Moral rules stem from the child's budding logical reasoning skills. Classroom rules that emphasize others' rights and a sense of justice are universal and can be logically constructed by the child through his experiences with other children and adults. Examples of such rules would be: "Treat your friends gently" and "Ask before taking." These are the important types of rules for children's development of more sophisticated moral reasoning.

   Social conventions are necessary in classrooms. Routines, procedures, and ways of organizing people and materials are essential for a safe and orderly environment. Children and teachers can develop social conventions together so that the children come to understand the necessity and role of social conventions. Examples of social conventions include how to arrange the blocks on the shelves at cleanup time, procedures for using the bathroom facilities, and ways to respond to the teacher's signals.

3. **Avoid using rewards and punishments as the motivating factors for complying with the rules.** Although it is impossible to never use rewards or punishments when working with children, over-reliance on these control strategies leads to heteronomous reasoning on the part of children. When rewards and punishments are used, they should be logical consequences of the behavior. For example, if the children must clean up the room in a reasonable amount of time before outdoor play, and they do so, they will be rewarded with more time on the playground. The children's appropriate behavior—cleaning the room efficiently—leads to the reward of more time outdoors. If the children do not clean up the room in a timely manner, the punishment of less time on the playground follows naturally and logically. Using food or other necessities as rewards or punishments is never an option for constructivist teachers.

4. **Establish rules democratically with the children so that they understand why rules are important.** According to constructivism, a major part of understanding the rule structure of any society is knowing the origins and reasons for the rules. Allowing the children to establish rules in a problem-solving manner gives them the opportunity to be a part of a law-making body. For example, if first-grade children are spending time in the bathrooms socializing when they are on an honor system to use the bathroom then return promptly to the room, the teacher may call a meeting to discuss the problem and arrive at a satisfactory solution with the children. If the children's proposed solutions are respected, voted upon, and enacted, the children learn directly about the *process* of rule making. The same techniques can apply for deciding on consequences for rule violations. The teacher can guide the children through the process of deciding the fair and logical consequences for real-life situations that occur in the classroom society.

5. **Accept that young children will apply rules in an egocentric manner; for example, when playing a game they may change the rules to benefit themselves.** As in other areas of developing reasoning skills, children must go through a series of less-developed reasoning processes before arriving at more-sophisticated reasoning skills. An example of this is when children in the preoperational stage change rules to a game to benefit themselves. When playing kickball, a child may decide that her fly ball caught by the pitcher does

not count because she was not ready for the pitch. Screams of protest from the other players will communicate to the child that she has violated their sense of fairness. This may or may not matter to her, depending upon her ability to decenter and play the game according to the mutually agreed-upon rules. Eventually, she will learn to apply rules in a less egocentric manner when she understands that the same rules apply to all players.

6. **Plan experiences for children so they can establish and maintain rules for themselves (e.g., during dramatic play, block play, and outdoor play).** Children create microcommunities in their play. They establish rules of action, rituals, leadership roles, and so on (Corsaro, 1985). These experiences are important for the child's developing constructions of why we need rules and where they come from. Thus, children need opportunities to play without adult intervention, except of course if they are threatening each other's safety.

7. **Refrain from intervening in social conflicts until it is apparent that the children have reached a stalemate or an emotional level that prohibits them from solving the problems themselves.** Related to the last principle, social conflicts are inevitable in children's play. Constructivist teachers recognize the value of social conflicts in helping the children develop logical-reasoning skills. There will be many times, though, when the children reach a stalemate and they need adult facilitation in helping them solve their social problems. In these cases, teachers can model appropriate stategies that she or he wants the children to use, such as voicing their opinions without using physical force, listening to the other person's point of view, and suggesting a mutually agreeable solution. Social conflicts are viewed as opportunities for learning negotiating and compromising skills.

8. **Allow children to take on authentic responsibility for classroom functions.** Children who are entrusted with responsibilities crucial to the functioning of the classroom will feel a sense of self-worth within that setting. Watering the plants, feeding the class pet, preparing for and cleaning up after snack time, are just a few of the simple tasks that children can do to help the classroom community. Starting with small tasks allows children the chance to practice responsible actions in ways that are safe and nonthreatening, even when they make a mistake. Teachers must expect spills and over-watered plants; and they can build in opportunities for children to correct situations with adult help. For example, if Joey knocks over the plant when watering it and dirt spills on the floor, the teacher can say, "Joey, let's get the dust pan and broom and clean it up together."

9. **Challenge the inappropriate behavior of young children (DeVries & Zan, 1994).** Just as disequilibrium is healthy for challenging previously held ideas in other areas, provoking disequilibrium in the thinking of a child after he has behaved inappropriately motivates him to move toward more sophisticated behavior and thinking. If a child pushes another child to get to the drinking fountain first, the teacher can challenge the child to think about why this behavior is inappropriate through several means: questioning, role-playing a scene in which all persons push their way to the drinking fountain, pointing out the consequences of the behavior. The teacher can also apply logical consequences to the behavior, such as asking the child to wait until last to get his drink so he can practice the correct behavior.

10. **Build in opportunities for children to make restitution for their wrongs.** If inappropriate behavior is viewed as evidence of a child's undeveloped social and cognitive skills, such behavior is used as a springboard for developing these skills. Paramount to this development is the opportunity for children to "right their wrongs." If they act impulsively or egocentrically, they need opportunities to make amends. For example, if a child hurts another child, she can help with comforting the child or getting a bandage or a glass of water. This opportunity for restitution does not take the place of other logical consequences, but it allows the child a chance to make up for a wrong deed. This, in turn, helps the child develop a sense of restitution and justice.

Summary

A goal of a constructivist approach to education is to help children become responsible decision makers and develop autonomous reasoning abilities. Helping children construct moral understandings of right and wrong is a necessary and important part of education. *Discipline* is no longer viewed as the act of controlling children; rather, *guidance* is viewed as the opportunity to assist children in the development of their social and cognitive skills.

As the instructional principles above illustrate, guiding children toward moral understanding occurs throughout the day and throughout the curriculum in early childhood programs. Teachers who follow constructivist theories recognize that children's construction of moral understanding takes much practice, patience, and understanding on the part of the teacher. The importance of moral reasoning in developing reasoning skills ensures it a place in every early childhood curriculum.

CHAPTER FOUR

....

Play and Learning

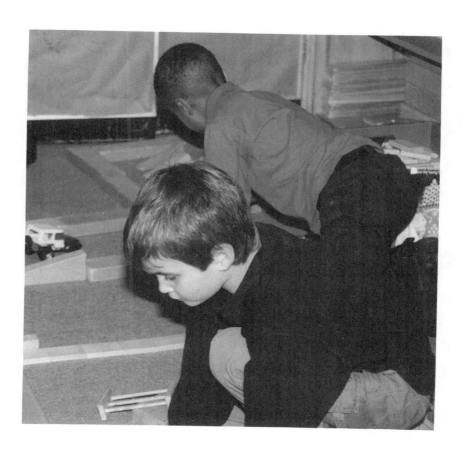

4

Constructivist theory views play as the most natural means for young children to learn and to develop. Much of Piaget's research focused on children as they played, including children from infancy to adolescence. Piaget painstakingly recorded the children's actions and theorized about the accompanying cognitive and social processes that developed through play. Piaget found signs of nearly all of the important processes of learning in children's play. One of his biggest contributions to education is the recognition that play provides the primary way for young children to learn about the world and all of its social, physical, emotional, and intellectual complexities. As we begin to examine the world of children's play, we will start with some basic definitions of play, as proposed by Piaget and others. The remainder of this chapter will highlight some of the many processes children learn through play and the instructional principles constructivist teachers follow when integrating play into the curriculum.

Play is a complex set of actions that most people recognize when they see it, yet have trouble defining. A widely accepted definition of play proposed by Rubin, Fein, and Vandenberg (1983) outlines six factors that characterize play. These factors include the following:

1. It provides intrinsic motivation.
2. It is free of externally imposed rules.
3. It is carried out as if real.
4. It focuses on the process more than the product.
5. It is dominated by the players.
6. It actively involves the players.

In other words, play is an activity that children engage in because they want to, in the way they want to, with seriousness and total concentration on what they are doing. Children are not concerned about the end product of their play; in fact, the play often does not have an identifiable beginning or end. Through play, children explore and experiment with the materials—and people—around them.

Before examining the different types of play, a few words about how play types develop and emerge are in order. Historically, the various categories of play were seen as hierarchical in nature; that is, some types of play were seen as being lower in the hierarchy because they were more commonly engaged in by younger children. Recent research developments indicate that the different types of play overlap and can develop concurrently, with the "less sophisticated" types of play occurring on through adulthood, even if less frequently (Rogers & Sawyers, 1988). In general, play develops from sensorimotor, solitary types of play toward more symbolic, social, and rule-governed types of play. Yet, adults can be found engaging in motor play, such as doodling, once thought to be the domain of infants and toddlers, in very sophisticated ways. With those words of caveat, let's look at some of the widely accepted categories of play.

PIAGET'S CATEGORIES OF PLAY

To differentiate among the types of play, researchers examine the social setting of the play, the type of props the children use, the level of abstraction involved, and the presence or absence of rules followed by the players.

Practice Play

Piaget (1962) labeled the sensorimotor, repetitive type of play that predominates infant and toddler play as **practice play**. Children may practice actions or skills, such as reaching and grasping, pounding on objects, or knocking food off of the high chair tray over and over, with evident pleasure. With time and experience, the child begins to combine several motions, at first by accident and then with intention. For example, a ten-month-old child may shake her bottle of apple juice vigorously, accidentally hitting it on the high chair tray. When the bottle hits the tray it makes a loud noise that surprises the child. She then tries the combination of shaking and hitting the bottle on the tray again, shrieking with joy each time it makes loud contact. Next, she may try new combinations of the actions, perhaps trying the same shaking and hitting actions with her bowl of food. The exclamations she gets from the adults around her, combined with the sound of the pounding of the bowl against the tray, make the activity even more interesting.

Piaget emphasized the importance of practice play for infants and toddlers because, in his view, they were developing mental actions based upon their physical, sensorimotor actions. In other words, these external actions became internalized as the pre-linguistic child's earliest forms of thought. Thinking is evidenced by the way the infant or toddler begins to combine different actions to get results that he seems to have mentally planned and anticipated.

Practice play continues on into childhood and adulthood. The five-year-old who tries to tell a knock-knock joke but fills in the wrong words for the punch line, while laughing heartily, is practicing the question/answer format of the joke without understanding the play on words that make knock-knock jokes humorous (Rogers & Sawyers, 1988). This is a verbal form of practice play. An adult who swings a tennis racket or shoots a basketball over and over, without engaging in a game or competition, also engages in practice play. Thus, the practice play that predominates the toddler's play still has a place in the older child's and adult's play.

Symbolic Play

Piaget labeled the type of play in which players use one object to stand for or symbolize another as **symbolic play** (Van Hoorn, Nourot, Scales, & Alward, 1993). This important type of play emerges when children reach approximately 18 months of age. Piaget theorized that the onset of symbolic play signaled the beginning of a new type of thinking, the stage he labeled **preoperational intelligence**. This type of play predominates the late toddler, preschool, and early school years.

There are two main types of symbolic play, according to Piaget and researchers who continued the study of this type of play, such as Sara Smilansky (1968) and Smilansky and Shefatya (1990). These two types are **dramatic play** and **constructive play**. Each will be considered independently.

Dramatic and Sociodramatic Play

Dramatic play and its social counterpart, **sociodramatic play**, involve the players acting out imaginary roles and characters. Commonly called "pretend play," the players use materials, their voices, and their bodies for imaginary purposes, such as the two-year-old who picks up the telephone receiver and pretends to talk to Grandma in a chatty, adultlike way. At a more abstract level, three- and four-year-olds may use items that do not look like the pretend objects to represent the telephone receiver, such as a rectangular block. They continue to use their voices and bodies to act out half of a telephone conversation. At an even more sophisticated level, five- and six-year-old children pantomime holding a telephone receiver as they pretend to have a conversation with the person on the other end. These sophisticated players may also act out both sides of the telephone conversation, not just their own part. All of these examples of pretend play involve the child's use of objects, voices, or actions—real or pantomimed—to represent other objects, people, or roles.

Also common to dramatic play is using oneself to take on a role, such as a parent, book character, or even a monster. One example is the four-year-old who pretends to be a "daddy dinosaur" as he feeds a plastic dinosaur with a bottle. The child is using himself to represent another object: a father dinosaur. Children role play by taking on the characteristics, dress, voice, and other aspects of the role they are playing.

As children engage in dramatic play, they create their own fantasies. Some of these fantasies are realistic, such as dressing for a party or going on a camping trip. Other themes in their dramatic play fall outside of reality as the children create imaginary plots and scenarios, such as pretending to be Ninja Turtles or space aliens. Symbolic play includes both realistic and unrealistic fantasy play.

Sara Smilansky, an Israeli psychologist whose research on play has spanned the last three decades, differentiated between dramatic play and sociodramatic play. Dramatic play, as defined by Smilansky (1968), is pretend play that children do alone. Sociodramatic play, on the other hand, is jointly constructed pretend play that children coordinate with at least one other person. Sociodramatic play involves several children agreeing on the theme, roles, and script of the play. This agreement usually is more implicit than explicit and is evidenced through the coordination of their actions and roles as the play progresses, such as when each child becomes a different member of a family. Observers of sociodramatic play may witness children negotiating over the materials used, who should do what, and who will play each part (Smilansky, 1968). Children slip in and out of their roles as they talk to each other about the play and its course, almost as if they are both the directors and actors in a stage play.

Children's coordination of roles within sociodramatic play is not always harmonious. Sociodramatic play provides fertile ground for social conflicts and social problem solving as children progress from disagreement toward the consensus necessary for the play to continue.

Constructive Play

Constructive play, another form of symbolic play according to Piaget, involves the child's use of a concrete object to create a representation of another object (Van Hoorn et al. 1993). Children may use blocks, clay, paints and paper, or just about any other material to represent another object or piece of art. As children engage in constructive play, they attempt to represent their own realities. Their block structures look somewhat like the houses children intend them to represent; the clay figure looks like a snowman; the painted sun and sky are recognizable patches of blue and yellow. Smilansky (1968) adds to Piaget's definition of constructive play by adding that a visible end product usually results from the child's play. Thus, the play in the block area that results in a wobbly castle and the play in the sandbox that results in a series of birthday cakes are both constructive play, according to Smilansky, because children use objects to represent other objects and there are visible products of the children's play.

Constructive play involves less abstract thinking or imagining than dramatic play. In constructive play, the child's products resemble his or her mental representations of the intended objects. Dramatic play, on the other hand, moves beyond objects and concrete materials as children use symbolic gestures, language, scripts, and other means to communicate their roles and intentions in a spirit of pretending. Children will take on the verbal and nonverbal characteristics of the "mommies and daddies" as they feed the babies, speak in high-pitched voices characteristic of adults speaking to babies, put the babies to bed, and so on. Children can slip back and forth between constructive play and dramatic play. They create signs for their airport, build roads for the push vehicles, or write out checks at the grocery store, all of which are examples of using constructive play to support the dramatic or sociodramatic play.

Dramatic, sociodramatic, and constructive play dominate children's play between the ages of three and seven, until the next form of play to be discussed, games with rules, becomes more common. But symbolic play does not stop at this point. The open-ended, creative thinking of dramatic and constructive play can be linked to children's understanding of the abstract concepts of literature and social studies, problem solving in math and science, and the divergent thinking necessary for many occupations.

Games with Rules

Piaget (1965) was fascinated with the way in which children negotiated, argued about, and agreed upon the rules of a game as they invented their own games or played an already-known game. As Piaget observed children playing games, such as marbles, he documented the way in which they created and used rules. He found that children younger than five or six years old tended to perceive rules as negotiable and flexible enough to meet their immediate needs.

Children this age generally have not yet developed the more operational, logical forms of thought required to understand the concept of rules. Children in the early elementary school years are beginning to develop this level of thinking. They may accuse their younger peers of "cheating" when they do not apply the rules equitably because the older children see the rules as handed down by a greater authority not to be questioned. Playing games with rules successfully depends upon all of the players agreeing on the rules of the game. Children who still perceive rules as a matter of personal convenience will not fully appreciate or participate in games with rules.

As he watched children develop, negotiate, and enforce rules in their games, Piaget began to see how play could help children develop an understanding of society's legal and justice system. He theorized that as children actively participate in rule making and rule enforcing, they come to understand how and why rules are important for society to function smoothly. Children also come to understand that some rules, which later researchers (Nucci & Turiel, 1978) called **conventions**, are negotiable and socially constructed. They also learn that other rules, which Nucci and Turiel called morals, are not negotiable or subject to change. Examples of conventions are how many strikes a batter gets before being "out" or the location of the safe base for a game of tag. As discussed in the preceding chapter, examples of morals include rules about not injuring others or taking another player's game pieces.

Games-with-rules play predominates the elementary years and continues into adulthood. While earlier theories placed this type of play higher in the hierarchy of levels of play, Smilansky and Shefatya (1990) have shown that symbolic play, including dramatic, sociodramatic, and constructive play, remains important as well. Constructivist programs continue to encourage and provide the environment for all types of play to thrive.

PARTEN'S CATEGORIES OF PLAY

Since Mildred Parten first proposed it in 1932, teachers and researchers have also categorized play according to the social involvement of the players. Parten presented a continuum of social participation in play, starting with solitary behavior and progressing to cooperative play (Parten, 1932; Van Hoorn et al., 1993). Since the terminology that Parten first used remains important and useful today, her main types of social play will be briefly defined. Keep in mind that Parten was classifying play along a social continuum, whereas Piaget classified play according to its cognitive, representational dimensions. Thus, although the two theorists were both analyzing play, they did so from different, yet complementary, perspectives.

Solitary Play

Quite simply, **solitary play** is play that is done by oneself. A child who pretends to fill up her tricycle with gasoline as she plays by herself exemplifies solitary dramatic play. Parten viewed solitary play as being rather unsophisticated because of its limited social demands. More contemporary notions of solitary play acknowledge that it can be rather complex and engaging for the player. Consider a child experimenting with a model train set. He may put the track together in different configurations, change the incline of the track, vary the speed of the track at different points, all the while testing hypotheses and changing his actions according to his findings. This child is engaging in very sophisticated thinking. However, he is not playing with anyone else; in fact, he may prefer to engage in this type of play by himself. Socially, the play may be unsophisticated, but cognitively it is very complex.

Young children often talk aloud to themselves when they play alone. They may narrate their actions, speak for their doll figures, or sing to themselves. This type of speech is usually not directed at anyone else, yet it seems to be important for directing the thinking that accompanies the play (Vygotsky, 1962). The distinguishing characteristic of solitary play is that it is conducted by oneself.

Parallel Play

According to Parten, when two or more children play alongside each other, using the same materials in similar ways, yet not interacting, this is **parallel play**. Children may engage in conversation, imitate each other, and watch each other closely in parallel play; yet they do not coordinate their efforts or share materials in a cooperative way. The play has a give-and-take quality to it. Picture two three-year-olds sitting on the carpet in the block area building their own block towers. They may speak to each other intermittently, use some of the same materials, even take some materials from each other. Though they may argue at times, they interact very little. Parallel players are not working toward an agreed-upon goal, nor do they negotiate or compromise their own wants for the sake of the other person. Therefore, according to Parten's classification system, these three-year-olds are engaging in parallel play.

Associative Play

Parten called the last two forms of play **group play** because they both involve groups of two or more children engaging in the same types of play. The first of these two types of group play, **associative play**, involves children doing similar activities, sharing materials, and speaking to each other about their play, such as children using the same funnels and measuring cups at the water table. Associative play involves more give-and-take between the players than parallel play, yet it lacks coordination of the players' efforts toward a mutual goal. It also lacks specific assignment of roles. In the water table example, all of the children work on their own ideas: one pretends to make a birthday cake, one pretends to be a chemist, and one watches the movement of the water as it travels through the funnels.

Cooperative Play

The second type of group play, which falls at the social end of Parten's continuum, is **cooperative play**. Cooperative play is the most sophisticated type of social play, according to Parten. Children coordinate their efforts as they share the same materials, play various roles, or follow the same rules to a game. Individual needs and wants are often compromised for the sake of group cohesion and sustaining the play. As children speak to each other, the conversation involves constant negotiation, explanations, and compromising. Several researchers (Scarselletta, 1988; Waite-Stupiansky, 1987) have found that children move fluently back and forth between associative and cooperative play, as defined by Parten, making the boundaries between these types often blurred and fleeting. Therefore, some contemporary theorists and researchers combine associative and cooperative play into one category called **social play**.

PROCESSES LEARNED THROUGH PLAY

Piagetian theory contends that play is the natural, central medium for young children's learning. Yet, what are the players learning while they play? Although children's play may lead to learning of many concepts and facts, such as the color that results from mixing yellow and blue play dough, constructivist educators are even more concerned about the underlying thought processes that children learn through their play. Constructivist teachers would take interest in the logical thinking engaged in by the child while mixing the yellow and blue play dough: the hypothesizing, testing of ideas, reformulating of earlier ideas, and drawing conclusions that the child does as she plays with the colors. The constructivist teacher would watch, ask questions, and listen to the child's reasoning, all the while provoking the child to push herself to think a little harder and stretch her ideas a little further. The constructivist teacher teaches toward the *Big Ideas*, or the processes that underlie many of the knowledge disciplines. Let's examine some of these processes found in children's play.

Operational Thinking

Paramount to operational thinking is the ability to reverse one's reasoning. For example, if $x = y$, then $y = x$. Or, at a more complex level, if $5 - 3 = 2$, then $2 + 3 = 5$. Reversible thinking also involves being able to reverse an operation mentally and return to the starting point (Athey, 1988). During play, children experiment with reversible thinking. The child who fills up her bucket with sand and pours it out again will be able to mentally reverse these two operations and be able to picture in her mind what will happen even before she performs the actions with the sand and bucket. On a more complex level, the seven-year-old child who regularly plays a strategy game such as checkers can mentally move his and his opponent's pieces several moves, hence making mental manipulations and changes when moves do not lead to his benefit.

Another example of reversible thinking involves understanding cause-and-effect relationships. The child who tries rolling a toy car down inclines of different slopes and lengths in the block area develops an understanding of the cause-and-effect relationships between the slope and length of the incline and the reaction of the car. Within sociodramatic play, children who act out commonly known scripts, such as family role play with a mommy, daddy, and baby, act out cause-and-effect relationships. When they comfort the crying baby, clean up the dishes after pretending to cook a meal, or pay "money" to have the car repaired, they act out a series of related, logical sequences in which cause-and-effect relationships are embedded. Predictable sequences of behavior occur when all of the children playing agree on the logical progression of events to follow.

In another example, the child who puts together a puzzle experiences the process of taking a whole entity apart and putting it back together again. A child playing with clay experiences a medium that maintains the same mass but takes on different shapes and configurations. A child playing with blocks may build them into a tower, knock them down, and build them up again. All of these play experiences help the child develop logical, reversible thinking. This type of reversible, operational thinking underlies just about all later logical thinking requisite for mathematics, science, and the interpretation of history and literature.

Developing a
Play-Centered Curriculum

Bertha Wilson, a teacher of three- to five-year-old children in a full-day child care center, schedules maximum opportunities for play in the children's day. Ms. Wilson knows that the types of play she wants to occur must be carefully planned for and facilitated by the adults. Thus, she sets her room up with distinct play areas: a block area, sand and water area, dramatic play area, puzzles and math area, reading and listening area, and so on. The children are free to move from area to area in a natural manner. Ms. Wilson keeps many of the same materials available every day, such as the wooden blocks, child-size kitchen equipment, and painting easels. She also adds new materials to accompany the thematic units they are studying, such as shoe store equipment to the dramatic play area after a trip to the local shoe store, or aerial maps and photographs to the block area after a trip to the airport. She believes that children need the continuity of having much of the same equipment, as much as they need the surprise and novelty of adding new, theme-related materials.

Setting up the environment for the children's play is just part of Ms. Wilson's challenge. The next part of the challenge is to facilitate the types of play that she would like the children to engage in. She starts by being an active play partner herself. She sits on the floor with the children in the block area, constructing her own buildings and inviting the children to join her. She accepts invitations to take part in the dramatic play center, enthusiastically "drinking" the tea that the children pour for her and "eating" the pancakes served on her plate. Ms. Wilson demonstrates a playful attitude herself, displaying her sincere enjoyment of participating in the children's play. She tries not to dominate or dictate the play, which would be easy to do because the children look to her as an authority figure. Sitting on the floor or in the small chairs diminishes her size. Waiting for the children to invite her or tell her what to do in the play allows them to lead her in the play.

The benefits of using a play-based program have been many. The children follow their natural rhythms, selecting solitary activities when needed and social types of play when preferred. Ms. Wilson knows that the children are learning. They use materials in ways that stretch their thinking ever so gently. For example, she notices that as time progresses the block constructions are becoming more elaborate, and children are constructing them together more often. Children even ask if they can keep the structures standing from day to day, instead of pursuing the ritual of knocking them down at cleanup time. Ms. Wilson interprets the children's desire to save their constructions as a sign that the children are putting more planning and careful thought into them, so she enthusiastically agrees to let them stay up for a day or two. The language use of the children is flourishing as they communicate with each other and with her as they play. Physically, the children naturally practice their fine and gross motor skills as they roll the play dough, dab paint with a brush, pour sand back and forth from container to container, stack large and small blocks, "cook" dinners, and wash the dishes. All of these activities help the children gain coordination and strength in the muscles they will need for future activities.

Best of all, Ms. Wilson knows how relaxed and happy the children are when they are playing. The positive tenor of the room with the constant buzz of children's voices and activity make this a place where children feel valued. Parents report that the children love going to the child care center because they have so much fun there. These words make Ms. Wilson know that this is a good place for children and their development. She is sure that the play-centered curriculum is the key.

Perspective Taking and Decentering

Another process central to reasoning is the ability to take the perspective of others. Such perspective taking requires suspending one's own point of view temporarily to take on the point of view of another person. Sociodramatic play allows children natural opportunities to take on the roles and perspectives of others (Athey, 1988). Symbolic play allows children the opportunity to suspend their own realities and create new and imaginative roles and contexts. Both of these types of pretending develop the processes required for understanding the deeper meanings of literature and the interpretations of history and social studies. In fact, understanding science has been described as being able to understand stories about nature and natural phenomena (Rose, as quoted in Fisher, 1992). Thus, play provides opportunities to practice the perspective taking that many forms of abstract thinking and reasoning require.

Using Symbolic Thinking

Children engage in symbolic actions as they take on pretend roles, build replicas of castles, and paint flowers and rainbows. Accompanying these actions is the thinking that allows them to engage in such symbolizing. In constructivist theory, acting and thinking are inextricably intertwined. Actions with objects stimulate mental actions and vice versa. That is why symbolic play is so important to symbolic thinking and reasoning. Play *is* thinking in action.

Problem Solving

Through play, children have opportunities to solve problems in a relatively risk-free environment. Social problems to be solved present themselves almost every minute that children play with each other. These problems must be solved in a satisfactory way for all of the players for the play to continue. Cognitive problems are inherent in play as children make decisions, try solutions, and analyze the results. These cognitive problems may be as simple as which block to select next for the wobbly skyscraper or as complex as what rules should be enforced for a game of kick-ball. All of these problems are real and important for the children to solve. They all involve tapping into the children's logical reasoning, negotiating, and compromising skills.

Flexible, Creative Thinking

Related to the process of problem solving is the ability to think flexibly and creatively. The society within which children will operate when they become adults will require much more than rote memorization and linear, step-by-step thinking. These adults of the future will have vast amounts of information available to them at the touch of a computer key, much more information than they can memorize. Their challenge will be to ask good questions, sift through information, and use it creatively and flexibly. Play provides the opportunities to practice these processes. Play provides a myriad of possibilities, countless choices, and opportunities for creative, divergent thinking.

VIGNETTE 4.2

Using Play to Develop Autonomous Thinking

Jasmine Cooney teaches five- to seven-year-olds in a combined kindergarten/first-grade class. Of the 18 children in her class, some have never been to school before, whereas several others have been in child-care and preschool programs since they were toddlers. Thus, some of the children are still learning how to go to school, whereas others have already adapted to a full-day program. Additionally, the range in academic abilities is wide; for example, some children can read and write independently while others are just learning how to write the first letters of their names. Ms. Cooney is convinced that the mixed-age grouping benefits all of the children because it creates a natural environment for learning that allows children to progress at their own rates. Yet, facilitating that environment takes much planning on her part.

To start the day, Ms. Cooney uses a play-centered curriculum so that children can make choices about activities, playmates, and challenges. Ms. Cooney has ten centers set up around the classroom each day. These include a listening center, reading center, dramatic play center, block center, art center, science and math center, writing center, computer center, cooking center, and sand and water center. The children have basic materials available to them each day at each of the centers. Additionally, she introduces new activities, such as an experiment in the science center or a new art media in the art center. She posts the center choices for each day and "today's specials" in pictures and words on a prominent bulletin board.

As the children enter the classroom each day, they prepare their own planning sheets. They draw or write the activities they would like to pursue that morning. As they finish their planning sheets, they hang them on a bulletin board for quick reference by teachers and children. If the children change their minds as the morning progresses, they can return to their planning sheets and alter them.

For approximately one hour, the children choose activities around the room, according to their plans. The children who enjoy dramatic play and all of its social negotiations choose the dramatic play center nearly every day. Children who prefer solitary, quiet activities usually go to the listening or reading center. Ms. Cooney only enforces one rule about children's choices: some of the activities must be done by everyone sometime during the week, such as the science experiments. Ms. Cooney and her assistant sometimes make a concerted effort to invite particular children to centers, but their intervention is definitely in the form of an invitation, not a command. This is the time of the day for children to make choices.

At the end of the hour, Ms. Cooney calls all of the children together to clean up and then meet together in small groups, one led by her and one led by her teaching assistant. Before discussing their activities, the children may add to or revise their original planning sheets to accurately reflect what they did during the preceding hour. Next, they share their planning sheets and comments with the other children and adults in their small groups. The adults take notes on what each child did each day. By recording the children's activities, the teachers have a record of which children participated in the various activities. The children take the planning sheets home with them each day so that they can share them with their parents. This way, communication with the parents is improved. Ms. Cooney knows that this is much better than having children answer their parents' queries about what they did at school that day with the pat answer, "Play."

The planning sheets not only record what the children did during the center time, they also record the child's representation of the activities, in drawings and words. The beginning readers and writers use more pictures and simple words to record their activities. The more advanced readers and writers use whole sentences, complete with invented spellings, to record their activities. No matter what their level, the children are able to engage in the whole process: planning, engaging in the center activities, and reviewing their plans.

Other parts of the day consist of large and small group activities led by the teachers. The play-center part of the day is led by the children.

Autonomous Reasoning

According to Kamii (1984), autonomy is the goal of education. Autonomous reasoning involves making decisions for oneself, based upon what one knows at a deep level of understanding. Autonomous reasoning is the opposite of heteronomous reasoning, which is controlled by others. During play, children make countless decisions for themselves. They are free to operate within the boundaries limited only by safety and respect for others and property. Play provides the setting wherein they can determine the courses of action they will take. They feel safe to make decisions, change their minds, and learn from their errors, all of which are necessary for autonomous thinking.

INSTRUCTIONAL PRINCIPLES

1. **Provide the context, materials, and time for children's play.** Setting the environment for children's play takes time and planning. Play that leads to the processes described earlier does not happen by chance. Instead, teachers communicate that children's play is valued and important for learning by creating a rich physical, social, and cognitive learning context that invites children to play. The environment is safe and organized and has attractive materials that stimulate children's play. Space for building, creating artwork, dramatizing, and other types of play must be large enough and protected from disturbances. Children cannot be rushed through play activities, so time allotments that allow for play themes to develop and persist are crucial. Teachers' active participation encourages and sustains children's play when the play stagnates or takes unhealthy or unacceptable directions. Teachers do this by becoming part of the play, offering encouragement, or making suggestions to keep the play on track. In an environment like this, children will usually begin to do what is most natural to them: play!

2. **Teach children to play by having a playful attitude yourself.** The sincere enjoyment of play that teachers model for children communicates the importance of play for all. As adults play with children, on the children's level and taking the children's lead, they experience the world of childhood again. The ways of "teaching" children

to play range from participating as a play partner to setting the context and framework for the play, such as suggesting, "Would you like to build a spaceship with me? We can pretend to fly it to the moon!" Teachers who play with the children teach them that play is not frivolous or extraneous; it is central to the learning environment.

3. **Integrate the curriculum through play.** Just as play provides the natural context for play, it also provides a natural means for integrating the curriculum. For example, math, science, language arts, and social studies blend together as children create homes for their toy dinosaurs in the sand. They use one-to-one correspondence as they make sure each dinosaur has a home. They explore their knowledge of dinosaurs as they use their scientific names and decide what foods the dinosaurs will eat. Children practice language skills as they describe what they are doing and search through books on dinosaurs for more information. They use social studies as they create a dinosaur community with the basics of food, water, and shelter. Knowledge is not divided into content or subject areas when children play. Knowledge is interconnected and integrated at its deepest levels.

4. **Extend children's thinking through play.** Vygotsky (1978) contended that when children play, they operate in the zone of proximal development for children, which is the zone that is one step ahead of where the child is currently functioning (Berk & Winsler, 1995). In other words, well-designed play situations provide the right amount of challenge and motivation for children to extend their thinking into more sophisticated realms. As children select materials, seek out problems to solve, and try their own solutions, they challenge themselves to be "a head taller" (Vygotsky, 1978).

5. **Refrain from imposing too many rules and constraints on the children's play.** If children are to practice autonomous reasoning in their play, they must be allowed to develop some of their own ground rules and resolve their own conflicts. In this way, play provides the context and the motivation for children to learn the reasons for society's rules. When adults provide a long list of do's and don'ts, children are denied the experience of thinking and acting autonomously. This is not to say that children should be allowed to hurt one another or treat others disrespectfully in their play. The teacher's role is to establish the limits for the children's behavior and help children realize that hurtful or disrespectful actions are wrong and will not be allowed.

6. **Communicate to parents and other professionals about the value of children's play.** Oftentimes adults see play and work as being on opposite ends of the continuum. An extension of this thinking is

that in a work-driven institution, such as school, play is out of place. In the constructivist view, play and work are inseparable for children. Children apply themselves fully to the problems embedded in their play, without having to be rewarded by others for their hard work. They regard activities that they enjoy as play, yet they work very hard at these activities. Unfortunately, schools that divide play and work create an atmosphere where work is defined as activities that the children do because the teacher assigns them or rewards the products with grades or points. The intrinsic, self-directed nature of the activities that children consider to be play are relegated to the playground or after-the-work-is-done status. A constructivist classroom continues to build into the learning environment the playful, intrinsically rewarding, self-directed aspects inherent in play. For example, when older children have opportunities to make choices as part of their day, they may choose to write and illustrate their own books. They work hard on their books because they have chosen to do so, not because they have to. If asked if they were working or playing, they would probably answer, "Both."

7. **Use play to assess and document children's social, cognitive, emotional, and physical development.** As children play, they tell us much about their social, cognitive, emotional, and physical development. They use social skills to negotiate through peer conflicts, motivate others to do things their way, and voice their opinions when events or classmates are unfair. Cognitively, they think through problems, try solutions, and evaluate the outcomes. Children's minds are engaged as they challenge themselves and each other. Adults can learn about children's cognitive development as they observe the way the children problem solve. They can ask questions like, "What would happen if . . . ?" or "Why do you think . . . ?" while playing with the children. Children's language becomes the medium of their play as they communicate about things that really matter to them. Recording children's use of language gives insight into the level of their language development and functioning. Play also provides insights into how children are doing emotionally; feelings, insecurities, and fears become manifest as children play. Observant adults can learn much about a child's emotional development by watching and listening closely. Physically, most play incorporates constant movement. Children stack, knock over, pound, stir, pour, and engage in many other movements that let us see the development of their fine and gross motor control and coordination. Although teachers cannot possibly take notes on each child's play every day, oftentimes, recording one or two observations for each child every week will provide an

interesting portrayal. An advantage of using the play-sampling method of describing a child's language, emotional, physical, and other areas of development is that teachers capture the child's best and most natural behavior.

SUMMARY

Using play as the framework and medium for learning sets the tone and foundation for the processes underlying all learning. As children learn through their play, they experience the joy of learning how to learn. They direct their own learning and form habits of thinking that, if allowed, will stay with them throughout their lives.

CHAPTER FIVE

Young Readers and Writers

Constructivist teachers view language and literacy in fundamentally different ways than teachers using traditional approaches to teaching reading and writing. Traditionally, reading has been viewed as decoding written symbols and translating these symbols into their auditory equivalents. Writing is viewed as the reverse of reading: translating sounds into their written symbols. Teachers stress the mechanics of text deciphering, starting with recognizing isolated letters of the alphabet and then identifying the sounds associated with individual letters or groups of letters. Writing instruction, often treated as a different subject than reading, stresses spelling, punctuation, capitalization, and penmanship (Ferreiro & Teberosky, 1982). This view of reading and writing has been labeled as "reductionist" (Taylor, 1989) because it reduces reading and writing into the simplistic learning of a coding system that matches sounds to symbols. The assumption underlying such reductionist approaches is that understanding the meaning of the text will follow as soon as the child becomes a skillful "decoder."

CONSTRUCTIVIST APPROACHES TO READING AND WRITING

In opposition to the reductionist model of reading and writing, constructivist approaches to the teaching of reading and writing consider language a complex representational system that makes the communication of meaning possible between and among people. Reading and writing are parts of this communication system, as are speaking and listening.

Constructivist researchers and teachers plan their instructional strategies in reading and writing by first attempting to understand the natural ways children learn to read and write. Although Piaget did not study how children learn to read and write, other researchers and theorists have taken his basic theory and expanded upon it to investigate and explain literacy learning (Ferreiro, 1991; Harste, Woodward, & Burke,

1984; Manning & Manning, 1991; Siegrist & Sinclair, 1991). The ideas of these more recent constructivists will be reflected in this chapter.

Understanding Reading and Writing As Representational Systems

To understand how children construct their reading and writing skills, we must start by defining the nature of the skills to be learned and how children come to master them. Reading and writing, according to constructivist thinking, are representational systems that people use to communicate an almost limitless body of information, including thoughts, emotions, descriptions, and much more. It is one of many languages that humans use to communicate. Other modes of expression natural to children include, "movement, drawing, painting, building, sculpture, shadow play, collage, dramatic play, and music" (Edwards, Gandini, & Forman, 1993, p. 3). Written language joins drawing, painting, and other visual art forms as graphic representations that can be returned to at a later time.

Inherent in this theory is the idea that communication does not occur in a vacuum; it occurs in a rich context that includes the relationship between the communicants, the setting of the communication, the history of the discourse, the anticipation of the communicants, and so on. Take, for example, the exclamation, "That's great!" These words could communicate a genuine compliment or a sarcastic remark. If the compliment came from a person who compliments often, it would mean something different than if it came from a person who rarely offers compliments. Understanding the meaning of these two words involves much more than being able to decode and recognize the individual sounds.

A six-year-old child who writes, "THTS GRAT" on a picture she draws conveys her own meaning with the written words. Perhaps she is complimenting her own work. Or she may be taking on the role of a teacher who routinely writes compliments on her work. She did not use the conventional spelling, but she demonstrated a well-developed understanding of how the English sound-symbol system is used to communicate meaning. She is using the words in her own meaningful, communicative way. The child is learning the communicative possibilities of written words in a natural, self-directed manner.

Understanding Language As an Open System

Another characteristic of language is its openness as a system. Humans have an infinite number of combinations they can use to communicate their messages to one another. Meaning is not embedded in each sound, as is common to nonhuman species, such as dogs and birds.

Meaning in language is embedded in the combinations of sounds, words, and contexts.

If learning to read and write involves becoming an active participant in the communication between author and reader, and using a complex, open language system within a context that influences meaning, how can young children become partners in this "grand conversation"? According to several of the researchers who have spent the last several decades studying the ways that children learn to read and write, we must allow each child to "inform" us of how he or she comes to understand and use the written language; we must listen, hear, watch, and follow the child's natural way of learning (Ferreiro & Teberosky, 1982; Harste, Woodward, & Burke, 1984; Manning & Manning, 1991). Although there are global patterns in learning to read and write, each child makes sense out of written language in individual and unique ways and on their own timetables.

Understanding Reading and Writing As Evolving Processes

Children enter school, even preschool, with the ability to use oral language in sophisticated and meaningful ways. In most cultures, they also come to school with a myriad of prior experiences with print. Children in most societies are surrounded by print—print on the boxes of food products, signs along the road, books, newspapers—so they develop a wealth of hypotheses about the meaning of this print. Constructivist approaches to reading and writing start with the children's knowledge of the language and include them immediately in meaningful events with print. Children try out, refine, and test their hypotheses about how the written symbol system works. Four-year-olds may "read" pictures and "write" marks to record their shopping lists. They may know that most fairy tales start with "Once upon a time," so they start their stories the same way, even though it may look like "WASAPANATAEM" (Harste, Woodward, & Burke, 1984, p. 96). As evidence that children bring meaning to their writing, researchers have found that preschool-age children use different forms of writing, depending on its purpose. Stories, lists, letters, and other genres take on different forms early on in the child's writing (Harste, Woodward, & Burke, 1984). Thus, children already know much about how the different forms of writing function. Furthermore, Harste, Woodward, and Burke (1984) found that preschool children already make marks that have the characteristics of the written language of their culture, such as straight lines and circle figures in English and curlicue figures and dots in Arabic.

These *are* reading and writing events as defined by constructivist teachers. The children are bringing meaning to the pictures; they are recording their meaning in their writing, even if it is undecipherable to us. Just as the toddler begins speaking with one- and two-word utterances that only the parents can understand, such as saying, "Ahhhh" to communicate "more milk," the four-year-old brings his understanding of how the written system works to his first attempts at writing different types of messages. His "writing" may look like unrecognizable marks on the paper, but these marks convey meaning in his mind. In fact, he could probably "read" the message embedded in his marks with conviction as, "Thanks, Grandma, for the bat and ball."

Allowing the children to experiment with the way they hear the words is much more meaningful than forcing the children to copy a "correct" model or writing the story for the child. By experimenting with their own spellings, children test their hypotheses about the written language. They must make many "constructive errors" along the way (Ferreiro & Teberosky, 1982). Just as in other types of learning, constructivist teachers consider these errors as necessary and important for the child's learning to read and write. As they correct their own errors, children learn much more about the written language than if they copy someone else's error-free models.

Thus, in the constructivist view, children are "reading" the first time they bring meaning to print. Children are "writing" when they use marks to represent their ideas. Reading and writing are evolving processes that take years to refine. The myth of a "magic moment" when reading or writing begins fails to take into consideration the years of language learning that children begin at birth. Constructivist teachers focus on the fascinating and complex processes that all children bring to each reading and writing experience.

To make sense out of the seemingly chaotic, limitless system of symbols that represents the written language of their culture, children must learn the language's functions, structures, and conventions. They learn the relationships of the sounds and symbols (the graphophonemic system); they learn to combine words into sentences and phrases in a way that makes sense to them (the syntactic system); and they bring meaning to the words and combinations of words (the semantic system). All of these relationships in the written language are learned as children become active participants in its use. Just as they learn the complexities of spoken language through talking, they learn the rules of written language through writing; and they learn to read through reading and being read to.

As children learn to read and write, they must reconstruct for themselves the written symbol system with all of its properties. Children must experiment with different ways of putting the symbols together, to write words and convey messages. They must "read" pictures, groups of words, and entire books in a way that makes sense to them. They must watch adults use the language in its written forms to experience the communicative power of the written word. Standardizing reading instruction into a series of hierarchical steps that all children must follow denies children the opportunity to experiment with language as the open system that it is (Goodman, 1986).

Understanding Individual Variations

Children do not absorb the meaning embedded in the written words, they must construct the meanings themselves, in their own way, in their own minds. Learning to read and write are not linear processes that start with step one and proceed in an orderly, invariable progression common to all learners. Children may jump ahead and start to read independently without warning. Or they may progress and regress over and over, especially children who have learning disabilities specific to learning to read and write.

Just as instruction of reading and writing must allow for individual variation and focus on what a child knows, rather than on what he does not know, assessment must do the same. By nature, the "one-test-fits-all" standardized test cannot provide an accurate picture of a child's current reading patterns. Teachers' written observations of children engaged in meaningful reading and writing events, samples of the child's reading (on audiotape or videotape), the child's own thoughts about the reading, and samples of the child's original writing all provide more authentic, valid data for describing what the child knows about print for the child's portfolio (Engel, 1991). Collecting data directly related to the individual prevents the tendency to compare and grade children on a preconceived definition of what a "first grader" or "second grader" should be able to do. Such comparisons lend themselves to focusing on what some of the children cannot do, or a deficit model, instead of looking at each child as an individual striving to make sense out of the printed word in his or her way. Test scores often serve the purpose of comparing children with each other on surface-level skills involved in decoding and encoding the written language. Tests often measure comprehension skills through literature extracts that interest some children and not others. These types of assessment ignore the last 20 years of research and constructivist theory of how children learn to read and write. The recent developments emphasize the deeper-level, individually constructed processes that all readers, even very young ones, use whenever they bring meaning to text.

If teachers accept the constructivist approach to reading and writing instruction, there are certain processes that they encourage. These are the *Big Ideas* underlying reading and writing instruction. Unlike isolated facts or memorized procedures, these processes cannot be taught directly. The learning environment and classroom climate can be conducive to the children's active use of the processes germane to learning to read and write in a natural, fulfilling way. Let's examine some of these processes underlying learning to read and write.

PROCESSES OF LITERACY DEVELOPMENT

Bringing Meaning to Print

In order to understand the messages conveyed in print, children must assimilate these messages into what they already know and have experienced (Goodman, 1986). Therefore, the wider and deeper the child's knowledge and experiential base, the more meaning the child can bring to the print. The same principle holds true for writing. Writers must have something to write about. Their knowledge base allows them to convey their own meanings through print. Teachers of young children help them build their knowledge base by providing direct experiences, such as visiting people or places, or exploring the properties of science phenomena, or tasting new foods. Indirect experiences, such as reading about people and places, writing to pen pals from another community, and watching video presentations, allow children to vicariously experience others' lives and feelings. The younger the children, the more direct the experiences need to be. These direct experiences have been described elsewhere in this book as "concrete experiences," which are the principle means of learning for preoperational and concrete operational thinkers.

VIGNETTE 5.1

Planning Print Activities with Three- and Four-Year-Olds

Martin Clarke, a teacher of three- and four-year-old children, was given the opportunity to set up a classroom for a newly added preschool program at a public school. As he went about setting up the environment for the new program, he kept in mind that he wanted children to have many natural opportunities to use print.

Print was a natural part of all of the learning centers Mr. Clarke created. He set up the dramatic play center with many household items, such as a stove, refrigerator, table and chairs, dishes, pots, and pans. Then he added many items that could be found in homes and used print: telephone books, memo pads, checkbooks, cookbooks, magazines, and labeled food boxes and cans. In the block center, he provided road signs, road maps, builder's blueprints, and books on castles and other architectural designs. He also left paper and markers so that the children could create their own blueprints, signs, and written messages.

As Mr. Clarke set up the reading center, he provided a display-type bookshelf that was low enough for children to reach. He put on it a variety of books, ranging from nonfiction to scientific books and familiar fairy tales. Mr. Clarke also put comfortable pillows, beanbag chairs, and a child-size sofa near the books. Not far from the book corner, he set up a writing center. Paper of all different textures and sizes, pens, markers, pencils, and crayons were all within an arm's reach of the center. He also added blank books, which he made by stapling pages together within a construction-paper cover, for the children who wanted to write books at the center.

In another corner, Mr. Clarke set up a listening center. He put a tape recorder with multiple headphones, comfortable floor pillows and a variety of story tapes with corresponding books that were color coded in individual zip-lock bags. On the tape recorder, he put a green sticker on the play button, a red sticker on the stop/eject button, and a yellow sticker on the rewind button. The stickers would enable the children to use the tape recorder independently.

Throughout the room, Mr. Clarke placed message boards and wipe-off markers, an announcement board, and a sign-in clipboard, so that the children could write each other messages and sign in when they arrived at school.

As Mr. Clarke planned how he would engage the children in meaningful events with print, he decided to spend time the first several weeks developing simple posters and signs with the children's help to be posted around the room. He would write down their suggestions for rules for the room, names for the various centers, and reminder signs, such as how many children could use the blocks or listening center at a time. Mr. Clarke decided to make these signs with the children so that they would be part of the process of deciding what to write and how to write it.

As Mr. Clarke stood back to look at his new room, he felt satisfied that the children would know right away that reading and writing would be a natural part of what happened here. He knew that as the year went along, the children would add many more signs and artwork to make the room theirs.

Authentic Authoring and Using Print to Convey Meaning

Children learn the power of print by using it to convey their own meanings. They dictate their thoughts to a person who can write it down for them; they write their own messages, lists, and signs. In other words, they experience the authoring process firsthand. As children begin to want to share their written works with a larger audience, they can engage in revising and editing their drafts to make them more understandable, just as all authors do.

Risk Taking and Problem Solving with Print

Children must feel comfortable and confident about their abilities to actively engage in reading and writing activities without fear of failure. Children usually enter school with confidence that their writing says something, and it does to them. Constructivist teachers are careful not to stifle this confidence in their haste to correct the child's errors or judge the child's efforts against a predetermined standard. Teachers do not pressure the child to produce perfect copies of someone else's writing. They realize that children must feel free to test their own hypotheses about how the written symbol system works. When children approach print with a problem-solving attitude, they gain power over the print. They use printed symbols to convey *their* meanings and when they read, they bring to others' writing *their* meanings.

Problem solving with print includes children's correcting their own errors when they experience disequilibrium between what they think the print says and how it is written. Children develop strategies for making sense out of print, including anticipating what it will say, the context of the print, and the sound-symbol relationships. When children solve problems of communicating meaning through print, they learn more than the sound-symbol system. They learn how to make the words their own.

Planning a Center-Based Program for Five- and Six-Year-Olds

Responding to a request from the principal, Lee McFadden, an experienced first-grade teacher, volunteered to teach an experimental kindergarten/first-grade class the following year. She spent the summer reading the current literature on multiage groupings, the integrated curriculum, and literacy theories. She set about planning for the new year with newfound excitement. Ms. McFadden decided to revise her curriculum to reflect constructivist theories of how children learn to read and write.

For the past five years, she had been using a basal and workbook series as the core of her reading instruction. Her writing instruction consisted of daily journal entries, which the children copied from the chalkboard exactly as she modeled. She corrected the children's journals for sloppiness, misspellings, and other errors. She had divided the class into three reading groups. As she worked with one reading group, the children in the other two groups did silent seatwork, which usually consisted of rereading a story from the basal text and doing workbook pages based upon the text. She noticed that the children did not enjoy reading and writing instruction, although she knew that they loved hearing a story read aloud, writing their own stories (that were full of misspelled words!), and acting out stories. She had wondered why the children were not showing the same enthusiasm for the basal reading and writing activities.

When planning for this year's multiage class, Ms. McFadden decided not to use reading groups, basal texts, or workbooks. Instead she used her reading budget to buy multiple copies of well-written children's books, big books, blank books, and lots of writing materials. She rearranged her room from rows of desks and chairs to clusters that would be work spaces for groups of children. Since she was integrating kindergartners and first graders, she knew that she would have to plan for a wider span of developmental levels. Ms. McFadden decided to organize the curriculum around learning centers, the children's play, and projects. She set up a science center, dramatic play center, block center, math manipulative center, writing center, reading corner, listening center, and a sand and water center, all of which used reading and writing. Ms. McFadden decided to try the center-based organization of her class for the entire year, after which she would evaluate the effectiveness of the model.

Ms. McFadden also decided to change her methods of assessing the children's progress. The skills checklist and multiple-choice tests she had given in previous years were inappropriate for the age range and methods she was using this year. In their place, Ms. McFadden started a portfolio for each child on the first day of school. She collected writing samples, artwork samples, audiotapes of the children's oral reading, records of her conferences with the children, and stories that the children dictated to her to type on the computer. She dated everything in the portfolio and made the materials accessible for the children to inspect their own portfolios whenever they wanted to do so. Along with the portfolios of the children's work, Ms. McFadden completed a profile of the children's progress and wrote a narrative description of their development in reading and writing in October, December, March, and May. Copies of the profiles and narratives were shared with the children and their parents.

Although Ms. McFadden was a respected teacher, other teachers were watching her closely with open skepticism about her "newfangled" ideas and techniques. Fortunately, the principal, Ms. Sheerer, had an early childhood background and understood the theoretical foundation of what Ms. McFadden wanted to do. Ms. Sheerer gave Ms. McFadden her wholehearted support, which was important because many concerned parents, school board members, and other teachers made their way to the principal's office throughout the year to express their concern about Ms. McFadden's sudden change in methods.

As the year progressed, Ms. McFadden found herself and the children filled with excitement about their work. She coordinated the children's literature with the topics they were studying in science and social studies. For example, when they were observing the metamorphosis of the cater-pillars into chrysalides and then into butterflies, Ms. McFadden found as many fiction and nonfiction books she could about butterflies and cater-pillars. The children wrote stories about butterflies, acted each other's sto-ries out, painted pictures of butterflies, sang songs about butterflies, and so on. Some of the children even wrote letters to the butterflies after they let them loose on a warm May afternoon.

When parents and other teachers asked Ms. McFadden whether the chil-dren were really learning or just having fun, she was able to document their growth with the portfolio samples. These questions soon subsided, espe-cially from the parents, because the children came home full of new dis-coveries they wanted to share. The children started to ask for writing mate-rials at home so that they could compose stories, letters, and journals. But the main difference the parents noticed was in the children's attitudes toward school. Children actually complained about not being able to go to school on weekends and holidays! They willingly got ready for school each day. The parents became Ms. McFadden's biggest supporters—next to the children.

Needless to say, Ms. McFadden continued her constructivist program the next year. She even had a head start because the kindergarten children stayed with her for their first-grade year. She was able to integrate the new five-year-olds right into the routine with the help of the "veteran" six-year-olds. She was impressed with the community atmosphere that developed that second year of implementation. Discipline problems subsided; "on task" behavior skyrocketed as children pursued their own projects and interests. Ms. McFadden knew that she would not go back to the more tra-ditional modes of teaching reading, writing, or any subject the way she had in the past.

Representing Meaning
Through Expressive Modes of Communication

As children sing, dance, draw, dramatize a play they made up, or make music with instruments, they are expressing and communicating their thoughts and feelings through a variety of symbolic systems. These acts of expression help children increase their abilities to communicate, which in turn helps bring meaning to the symbolic systems of reading and writing. All of these modes of expression, and many more, expand the means by which children can communicate. Oftentimes these modes, referred to as the creative arts, receive emphasis in preschool programs, then diminish in emphasis in elementary schools as the chil-dren begin to read and write with printed symbols. Print provides one means to communicate, while music, art, dance, and dramatics, provide others. All of these forms of communication are important for representing and conveying meaning. Constructivist programs encourage children to use more than one mode of communication whenever possible.

Using a Constructivist Approach with Seven- and Eight-Year-Olds

Joy Brown, a new teacher at the same school as Ms. McFadden, had recently graduated from a teacher education program that taught her how to use constructivist approaches. She student taught in the campus laboratory school where she had worked with whole language, hands-on math, inquiry-based science, experiential-based social studies, and an integrated curriculum. When the principal of her new school asked her if she would like to teach the experimental second/third grade class, she willingly agreed. The principal provided time for Ms. Brown and Ms. McFadden to plan related units together, observe in each other's classrooms, and attend workshops on relevant topics. Since this was the first year for both of them to implement a multiage, constructivist program, they used the time together primarily to problem solve and plan. One day a week, each of the teachers had a regular substitute, so that the teachers could spend time together.

After going back through her books and materials from her teacher education program, Ms. Brown decided to organize her reading and writing curriculum around a literature-based, individualized program. Here is what one day in her classroom was like. The day started with a whole-group meeting when current events were discussed, special projects shared, and announcements made. The meeting concluded each day with Ms. Brown reading a piece of literature to the children that related to their current thematic unit. Next, the children had 30 minutes of quiet reading and writing time. They kept literature response journals in which they recorded their summaries and impressions of the literature. Children chose the literature Ms. Brown had read to them or selected their own, with Ms. Brown's guidance. Ms. Brown thought this was important because the children were at all different levels of reading and writing development. Ms. Brown wrote back to the children in their journals every day, embedding comprehension and higher-order thinking questions in her responses. The children responded to Ms. Brown's comments in their next entry. Some of the children needed assistance reading Ms. Brown's comments, which they obtained from their classmates or teacher. The morning would end with time to read with partners, write to pen pals, illustrate and write stories, conference with the teacher for individual skills lessons, and many other options relating to reading and writing.

The afternoons began with another whole-group meeting, at which the children and teachers presented new information relating to the thematic unit. They also discussed the procedure for the upcoming science experiments and math activities. Then the children participated in the math and science learning centers. The children rotated through the different centers, carrying their science and math journals with them in which they recorded (in diagrams or words) their reflections from the center activities. Before rotating to a new center, Ms. Brown gave the children five minutes of sustained writing and recording time. After an hour of center time, the children reconvened for a whole-group sharing time. They listened to each other read from their journals, asked questions of each other and Ms. Brown, and shared their new discoveries.

The last hour of the day was spent on the children's contracted projects, which ranged from writing a class newsletter to designing computer software. The children worked alone or in small groups on their projects. At the end of project time, they had ten minutes to record their progress for the day and plan for the following day. Ms. Brown looked over the contracts after school. The next day she would return them to the children with comments, questions, and suggestions.

Along with the daily routine described, Ms. Brown convinced the principal that her class needed to have as many real-world experiences relating to the thematic units as possible. She asked for and received permission to go on at least one field trip per month. She used the field trips to spark interest in the new thematic units. For example, when studying local history, she took the children on a steam-powered train ride through the early oil well sites so that they could experience firsthand what life was like in their community in the late 1800s. She also took the children to a Native American museum that re-created the long houses and lifestyle of the original inhabitants of the local area. Ms. Brown was convinced that the more real-life experiences she could provide for the children, the deeper their understanding would be of the concepts and information they learned from more abstract sources, such as books and videos.

INSTRUCTIONAL PRINCIPLES

1. **Provide many contexts for spoken and written language to develop and expand.** Constructivist teachers provide a balance of contexts within which children can practice and expand their communication skills. As children play, work on projects, write stories, draw pictures, and pour water at the water table, they use language in context. They may talk to themselves, make their own charts, explain what they're doing, or negotiate with a peer for a desired toy. All of these experiences using language enhance their competencies as communicators.

2. **Build in multiple, varied opportunities for children to use print in meaningful ways as they explore and learn about the world around them.** As children use print to communicate with others, such as writing "checks" in the dramatic play area or making signs in the block area, they encounter print in meaningful ways. As adults use print to record the lunch orders, to find a song on a record or tape, or to write themselves a reminder, they model for the children the many ways that print assists them throughout the day. Furthermore, providing the props and tools, such as paper, markers, telephone books, cookbooks, and other appropriate materials, encourages children to engage in the adultlike uses of print.

3. **Read to children from all types of books (fiction and nonfiction literature, informational and resource books, etc.) based on their interests.** If we approach reading as a way of accessing information on limitless topics, children will become questers of knowledge as well. As adults read to children from many types of literature and include them in the search for new knowledge contained in books, children will start to seek out books on topics that interest them. They will go to the library and ask if there are any books on bats or rockets or dinosaurs. They will discover authors that they enjoy. In other words, children will begin to tap into the wealth of information written materials offer. Children need countless opportunities to experience the wide world of print. With each experience, they will be able to build upon the meanings they have created already.

4. **"Litter" the environment with print (Harste, Woodward, & Burke, 1984).** Children and adults can make signs, label parts of the room, post rules, share favorite stories or poems, and surround themselves with meaningful print in other ways. The key to making the environmental print meaningful for the children is to include them in the process. If the adults have the room already labeled and decorated with posters, charts, and labels, the children will probably not pay attention to the print. However, if they make or help to make the signs for the restaurant in the dramatic play area and the rules for the reading loft, these signs become meaningful for them.

5. **Invite children to take ownership over their reading and writing.** Children learn to take responsibility for their own attempts to read and write. When a teacher hangs up five-year-old Olivia's stop sign on the tricycle course, written as STP, Olivia feels a sense of ownership over her writing. She has written for a purpose, which the teacher acknowledges and honors. When the other children abide by her stop sign and bring their tricycles to a squealing halt in front of the sign, Olivia experiences the power of her printed message. She will probably be motivated to write more signs for

the tricycle course. If her signs are not clear enough for the other children to understand, she will make revisions, for as a writer with a purpose, she must communicate in a way that makes sense to her audience.

6. **Set the environment for risk taking and hypothesis testing.** Children who know that it's fine to write a word the way they hear it or make a sign for their block structure that only they can read develop the confidence to keep writing and reading. If children's attempts to read and write are constantly corrected or if children are encouraged to copy "correct" writing, they're likely to become dependent upon others to tell them if their writing is "right." Similarly, if children's early attempts at writing emphasize letter formation and writing on the lines, fluency and content will be sacrificed. On the other hand, if the adults in the child's life show enthusiasm and interest in the child's writing and reading attempts, the child will develop the confidence to be a risk taker and keep communicating through print.

7. **Use assessment to guide instruction.** Assessment should guide instruction; and, instruction should guide assessment. In other words, information gained from any and all assessment events, which ideally occur within the natural course of the learning environment, should provide information that helps the teacher make further decisions about the best learning experiences for the child. Attempts to convert children's reading and writing abilities into quantifiable scores rarely help the teacher or child know the best next steps for instruction; instead teachers collect samples of children's work—drawings, first attempts at writing, and tape recordings of early reading—upon which to base assessment decisions. Feedback to parents takes the form of narrative descriptions, descriptive profiles of the children's progress, and sharing of the children's work.

8. **Plan for many opportunities to interpret stories using a variety of representational systems (e.g., story acting, drawing, music, puppetry).** One of the most exciting dimensions of literature is bringing one's own meaning and interpretation to each story. Children will identify with different characters in a story. They bring their own background experiences, cultural groundings, and developmental levels. Thus, each piece of literature has a different meaning for each child. Allowing children to interpret their understandings and communicate their interpretations through other means, such as acting out the story themselves or using puppets, drawing pictures to highlight their favorite parts, or putting the story to music, encourages children's creative expression. When teachers accept multiple interpretations instead of promoting a single

"right" one, children become less inhibited about bringing their own understandings to literature.

9. **Allow children to use the many languages that are natural to them.** Children have many "languages" with which to express themselves. They use music, movement, art, and, of course, speech and print. All of these languages are developing rapidly in a preschool or primary-age child. The greater the opportunities for them to use the languages, the more sophisticated they will become in all forms of communication.

10. **Invite children to illustrate their writings with a variety of media.** Children move gracefully between writing and drawing in their early attempts to use print. Unfortunately, once the children become more accomplished in using the printed words, illustrating their writing is often seen as an "extra," unnecessary step of communicating. Yet, expressing the meaning of a story through art remains important for the children. As evidence of this importance, consider the way children (and adults) marvel at the beautiful illustrations found in many picture books. The illustrations convey a message and tone that the words cannot. Some children and some compositions lend themselves more easily to communicating through words, whereas others are more suited to communicating through illustrations. Providing a wealth of materials and media so children can choose how to illustrate their messages conveys to them that all forms of communication are valuable.

11. **Use child- and teacher-selected books and materials over prepackaged basal programs whenever possible.** Prepackaged basal and workbook series often assume that all children follow the same linear path to literacy. Such series also assume that all children will be interested in the same selections of literature and limit children's opportunities to bring in their own experiences and construct their own understandings of how print works. Basals that use controlled vocabulary and simple sentences for the sake of the children's emerging phonetic skills can lose the appeal that rich language and complex sentence structures offer children. When teachers and children select literature that interests them, they approach the literature with a hunger to untap its meaning. The literature used in constructivist classrooms is a combination of teacher-selected and child-selected books on a wide variety of topics and at many different reading levels. Many excursions to the library fulfill the self-directed readers' appetite to sample as many types of books and print as possible. Computer-assisted access to information, such as through encyclopedias on disks or through the Internet, represent another source of information now available to children.

12. **Take advantage of opportunities to help children construct an understanding of sound-symbol relationships.** As children attempt to write new words or bring meaning to printed words, teachers can find many opportunities to help them construct the logic of the graphophonemic system. For example, when six-year-old Bryan wants to write "blocks" on his sign, instead of simply telling him how to write it, his teacher asks him to think of a word he knows how to write that starts the same way. After several attempts ("mom," and "stop"), Bryan thinks of his own name. Without even asking his teacher for more help, he confidently writes BKS on his sign, which is acceptable to him (and his teacher). Bryan used his prior knowledge and his beginning understanding of the graphophonemic system of the English language to write a new word. Thus, he is constructing an understanding of the written and spoken symbol system through his teacher's guidance. Opportunities like this arise naturally in classrooms that allow multiple experiences for children to interact with print.

13. **Offer strategic skills lessons that focus on the children's emerging literacy needs.** Rather than teaching the same skills lessons to all of the children, teachers can address skills one-on-one or in small groups of children who have common needs. For example, if several children consistently attempt to write words without the silent "e" on the end (e.g., cak for cake), a teacher can gather these children for a skills lesson on the use of silent "e." Furthermore, the teacher can use words following the pattern in the children's journals, point out the word patterns when reading with the children, and work with the children to generate charts of words using the targeted word pattern. Children who have not reached the point of trying to use the word pattern or who already use it correctly need not be included in the skills lesson. Such focused skills lessons require constant assessment and monitoring of the children on the part of the teacher. Yet, the rewards of such focused instruction for both the teacher and students are many, including less time wasted and more timely and meaningful instruction.

SUMMARY

Reading and writing are part of a much larger system of communicating. If we engage children in all aspects of this communication system, they will become part of the human race's "grand conversation." Learning to read and write happen naturally with most children if they are surrounded by multiple opportunities to interact with print in meaningful, communicative ways.

CHAPTER SIX

Making Math
Meaningful for Young
Children*

* This chapter was written with Nicholas G. Stupiansky.

6

As children explore the physical world, they formulate the foundations for math. As they think about their explorations, they invent strategies for imposing order on the world (Kamii, 1982b; Van de Walle, 1994). Meaningful math experiences involve children in constructing the logical connections among objects and the events around them. Once these concrete connections are constructed by children, the more abstract relationships can be built. In the words of the National Council of Teachers of Mathematics (NCTM):

> Knowing mathematics means being able to use it in purposeful ways. To learn mathematics, students must be engaged in exploring, conjecturing, and thinking rather than only in rote learning of rules and procedures. Mathematics learning is not a spectator sport. When students construct personal knowledge derived from meaningful experiences, they are much more likely to retain and use what they have learned. This fact underlies teachers' new role in providing experiences that help students make sense of mathematics, to view and use it as a tool for reasoning and problem solving. (1989, p. 5)

Piagetian theory tells us that as children develop cognitively, they experience a series of shifts in the way they think about and order their experiences. The thinking of preschoolers and primary-age children is closely connected to their experiences with the concrete world. They think about relationships as they explore concrete objects. As they experience order and relationships among objects firsthand they are developing internal thoughts about these relationships. When trying to decide how best to build a tower of blocks, they ask themselves, "Should the flatter blocks go on the bottom or top?" "Should a cylinder block be placed on its rounded side or on its end?" Their thinking is connected to active, concrete experiences with physical objects.

Much of what we ask children to do when solving mathematical problems is to think about the relationships between objects, such as whether the objects are more, less, or equal in number or to perform addition and subtraction operations using the objects. Understanding these relationships involves order in children's thinking that can be imposed on their physical worlds. Constructing these relationships takes time and multiple experiences. The understanding of mathematical relationships actually involves predictable changes in the cognition of young children. We cannot see these shifts in children's thinking, but we can observe the signs as we watch and listen to children as they manipulate physical objects and solve mathematical problems. Mathematical relationships that are meaningful to a child are based on the child's active involvement with mathematics (Bredekamp, 1987).

BASIC MATHEMATICAL PROCESSES

Creating and implementing a meaningful mathematics curriculum depends on knowing what basic math processes children develop as they actively think about their experiences. Some of these processes include conserving, comparing, classifying, seriating, patterning, constructing one-to-one relationships, and estimating. Knowing the characteristics and developmental expectations of each process helps teachers set the stage and ask the right questions for children's active use of these basic math processes. All of these processes are developed by extensive explorations with concrete objects or firsthand experiences. Let's look at some of these processes and some of the strategies teachers can use to facilitate development within each one. It is important to note that these processes are not directly teachable; yet there are many educational experiences that help children learn.

Conserving

A preschool child playing with play dough will say that two balls of play dough are the same size when they are the same shape. Yet, when one ball is rolled into a snake or flattened into a pancake, the child changes her mind and decides that the long and skinny play dough is now larger. This familiar scene demonstrates that many preoperational children have not developed the ability to conserve. The child is responding to her direct sensory experience with the play dough. The snake *looks* bigger than the ball; therefore, it must *be* bigger. She is unable to mentally manipulate the qualities of the mass of play dough in the two different configurations. Thus, she relies on her immediate and latest direct observation of the play dough to judge the size relationship, which she will most likely continue to do until she is around six or seven years old.

Just as children under seven years old may not be able to conserve quantities of mass, such as the play dough, they do something similar when conserving volume (e.g., beakers of different shapes appear to hold different amounts of liquids) and number (e.g., rows of the same number of objects spread over varying distances appear to have different amounts). Conservation cannot be taught in the traditional sense, but it must be learned for later mathematical reasoning to be possible. Children must construct understandings of conservation when experiences and cognitive development allow.

The environment naturally offers many materials that change shape and configuration but remain constant in amount, thus allowing children to use them to develop the notion of *conserving*. For example, sand and water tables with multiple containers for pouring and filling, play dough and clay for pounding and shaping, and objects that can be arranged and rearranged, such as milk carton tops and plastic game markers or chips, all allow children to experience the same amounts of objects in different configurations. Cooking and measuring activities also provide experiences that help children experience the same amounts in different forms. Asking children to compare and to predict whether amounts have changed or have remained constant after altering their appearances can give teachers insight into the children's conservation abilities. The reasoning that the children give for their answers can reveal what qualities (e.g., physical appearances of height or length) the children are using to arrive at their answers. Teachers must be open to the answers and reasons that children give for their responses; after all, their answers are developmentally right for their level of cognition.

Conservation is requisite for later mathematical problem solving, such as whole number operations. Piaget and Szeminska summarized this importance when they specified that "conservation is a necessary condition for all rational activity" (1952, p. 3). Without the ability to conserve, children will not be able to understand other math concepts such as equivalence and nonequivalence (Piaget & Szeminska 1952; Leeb-Lundberg, 1988). Thus, conservation is a basic prerequisite for most mathematical problem solving. Its presence signals to a teacher that a child will begin to use logic to override judgments based upon immediate physical appearances, an important ability for logical-mathematical reasoning. We can usually expect to see signs of a child consistently applying conservation around six or seven years of age.

Classifying

Sorting and **classifying** objects according to common qualities are also basic for logical-mathematical reasoning. Preoperational children may classify according to one quality but have difficulty reclassifying objects according to a different quality. For example, a child classifying various fruits may sort them according to color. When asked if he can find another way to put fruits that are alike together, he may say no. As children develop cognitively, they become more flexible in their abilities to classify according to several different qualities. A child who has developed classification flexibility may propose sorting the fruit according to the texture of the skin (e.g., pineapples and coconuts are rough; apples and bananas are smooth) or the way that the fruits grow (e.g., grapes grow on vines; apples and oranges grow on trees). Classifying is an abstract way of imposing order on just about any set of objects. Experiences, practice, and cognitive shifting are necessary to be able to see many different ways to classify one group of objects.

Opportunities for classification occur throughout the day. When cleaning up the room, blocks of various shapes and sizes are sorted and shelved together. Clothing and accessories are sorted in the dramatic play area. Crayons and markers are grouped by colors. Other opportunities for classification can be planned into the day. Just about any collection of objects—from bottle caps to shoes—can be classified and sorted by various dimensions. Teachers can encourage children to classify by the questions they ask; for example, "Can you put all of the shoes that are alike into one row?" If we watch and listen closely to the way children classify objects, we will find signals that they are becoming more creative and flexible in their thinking, a sign of a cognitive shift in the development of their logical-mathematical reasoning abilities. The child's thinking about the relationships among what is being classified is more important than the sorting activity.

Seriating

When ordering objects along one dimension, for example, height, weight, or color, children are **seriating** or imposing a logical relationship among the objects in a group. For example, when children see the order of the heights of a group of children as progressing from shortest to tallest they have taken the dimension of height and seriated the group accordingly. Young children will begin ordering by trial and error, usually taking two members of the group at a time and dichotomizing the two members into tallest and shortest. Older children will use a more logical system in their ordering, for example, putting all of the members together and selecting the tallest each time until all members have been chosen. When planning seriation activities for young children, it is best to provide small groups of objects and work up to larger sets as children develop the logical means for placing the objects in serial order.

Many different objects and events can be seriated. Notes played on the piano or bars on the xylophone can be ordered from highest to

lowest pitch. Paint chip samples from paint supply stores can be seriated according to color hue. Measuring cups can be ordered according
to size. Cars can be ordered according to speed. And, of course, people can be ordered according to many characteristics: weight, height,
age, or length of hair, to name a few. Importantly, teachers can use
words such as smaller, younger, lighter—and their converse, bigger,
older, and heavier—throughout seriating activities. What is crucial for
the development of logical-mathematical reasoning is not the child's
sorting of the objects, but the mental relationships imposed on the
objects. An important shift in thinking occurs when children realize
that the same group of objects can be ordered from largest to smallest
and smallest to largest. This is a logical, reversible operation and a sign
that concrete operational thinking is emerging.

VIGNETTE 6.1

Providing Sorting, Classifying, and Graphing Experiences

Tamara Harris, a teacher of four- and five-year-old children, knows the
importance of integrating many natural opportunities for children to
engage in math processes such as conserving, classifying, seriating, and
patterning. As she plans activities for her classroom, she considers all of
these math processes.

For example, one week she plans a series of activities around the children's shoes. She noticed that the children expressed interest in each others' shoes, especially as the seasons changed and the children started
wearing boots and other cold-weather shoes. She begins her series of
activities by asking each child to take off one shoe and put it in the middle
of their meeting circle.

"What could we say about our shoes?" she asks the children.

"They're all different," "New and old," "Different sizes," were some of
the responses the children offered.

"What if we had to sort this big pile of shoes into two piles, how could
we do it?" Ms. Harris asked.

After a series of suggestions from the children such as, "Put a line down
the middle," and "Take turns putting them into the piles," the children
come up with some ideas that focus on the characteristics of the shoes:
boots/not boots, ties/no ties, shiny/not shiny, old/new, and big/small.

Ms. Harris leads the children in selecting a way to sort the shoes. They
decide on the ties/no ties sort. She and the children divide the shoes into
two piles accordingly. As they work, they talk about each shoe and where
it should be logically placed.

The next day, Ms. Harris asks the children to remove one shoe again. This
time, she sorts them into two piles without telling the children what crite-

ria she is using for her sort. She asks the children to figure out what she is using to conduct her sort. After many tries, the children figure out that she is using a sneakers/not sneakers sort.

The third day, Ms. Harris decides to introduce graphing into the activity. She wanted to use a real graph because the children's level of symbolic reasoning was still undeveloped. She began by asking the children to suggest ways to sort the shoes. They offered a number of ways, but finally arrived at a consensus to do a one-color/multicolor sort. After sorting the shoes into two piles, Ms. Harris asks the children how they can tell which pile has more shoes. The children suggest counting, which they do together. As they count, Ms. Harris lays the shoes toe-to-heel in two lines: one line with one-color shoes and one with multicolor shoes. When they are done counting, she asks them if they can tell at a glance which line of shoes has more shoes. The children enthusiastically say, "Yes!" Several say that the multicolor shoes were "longer" or "bigger." Ms. Harris then takes out a large piece of plastic that has two rows of equal-size boxes on it. She shows the children how they can put one shoe in each box with the one-color shoes in one row and the multicolor shoes in the other. She allows the children to place the shoes in the boxes. After they place all of the shoes, she asks them to step back and look at what they have made. She tells them that they have just created a graph.

The next day, Ms. Harris continues the shoe activity. This time, she begins with the question, "Is there some way we could put all of these shoes into some kind of order?" After several minutes of discussion, one of the children suggests the most obvious way, which is according to size. Together, Ms. Harris and the children make a long line of shoes ranging from the shortest to the longest. When they are all done, she asks, "Can you think of another way to order the shoes?" (She was thinking of the number of lace holes or color hue.) "No," the children reply in unison. Ms. Harris decides then that extension of the activity would have to wait until a future date.

Later, Ms. Harris repeats the sorting, classifying, and graphing activities using a variety of materials (e.g., hats, coats, buttons). She knows that through these experiences, the children will be constructing an understanding that the same processes can be applied to all different types of objects. She also knows that understanding the processes of sorting, classifying, and graphing without objects could not be expected of four- and five-year-old children. Full understanding was still several years away. But activities such as these are the ways in which the children will experience firsthand the logic underlying the abstract relationships represented in classification systems and graphs.

Patterning

Patterning is an underlying theme of mathematics. Children need many different opportunities to develop the concept of patterns. Children can find patterns using many senses; they can explore visual, auditory, and physical patterns. Patterns are everywhere. **Visual patterns** appear in the bricks in the sidewalk, the designs on the rug, and the stripes on sweaters. **Auditory patterns** can be found in the melodies of music, rhythms of clapping games, and repetitive language or sounds of predictable books and fingerplays. **Motor patterns** are embedded in dance and exercise sequences. Children construct patterning abilities from their experiences identifying existing patterns, repeating patterns, and extending pattern sequences. Children can create patterns of their own. The identification and re-creation of repetitive patterns around them helps children understand and appreciate that sometimes the relations of elements can be predicted indefinitely (Baratta-Lorton, 1976). Some items that can be used for visual patterning include beads, small manipulatives, stamp pads and rubber stamps, dry macaroni of different shapes and colors, and just about any other type of material that can be ordered in recurring patterns.

One-to-One Corresponding

An important shift occurs when children can perform **one-to-one corresponding** tasks between related objects or between objects and the numbers we use to count objects. As children solve real-life problems, such as making sure that each child at the table has a cup or each person has a car in the block area, they are employing one-to-one correspondence in meaningful, child-initiated ways. Games that use dice, spinners, and cards with numerical directions motivate children to use one-to-one correspondence as they move the game pieces one space for each number they count.

Children who are still developing one-to-one correspondence will probably go through a series of trial-and-error solutions to problems they encounter naturally, such as making many trips to the cupboard for one cup at a time until they have enough for everybody. Furthermore, until children grasp conservation of number (around the age of six or seven), they are not likely to count objects ahead of time to match the number of objects needed (Copeland, 1984). Children need many trials and errors when attempting to solve these real-life problems before adults ask them to solve problems requiring one-to-one correspondence. The mental processes required for one-to-one correspondence cannot be taught directly, but they can be practiced with the help of an adult. With multiple experiences, the child begins to construct the concepts necessary for one-to-one corresponding.

Counting

Counting involves learning the sequence of number names and using the number names to identify quantities of objects. Counting is often taught as a type of social-conventional knowledge to be memorized without connection to the mathematical concepts the number words represent. The logical-mathematical connection between the number words and the number concepts must be emphasized by counting real objects and events.

There are various levels of sophistication in counting (Labinowicz, 1985; Reys, Suydam, & Lindquist, 1992). The least sophisticated type of counting is rote counting. Some young children can orally recite numbers in sequence. They may have an understanding of the order of the sequence. However, knowing a string of number words does not mean that the child has an understanding of the concept of number. Number word recitation merely involves memorizing a string of words in order. A child may be able to say the number words from one to ten and still not be able to associate these sounds with the concept of quantity or to use this sequence to count groups of objects. Rhymes, fingerplays, and songs are appropriate to reinforce the counting sequence, as long as teachers realize that memorization of the counting words is more of a verbal skill than a mathematical skill.

At a more sophisticated stage, the child assigns successive counting words in a coordinated way to the items being counted. At first, children will over- or undercount sets with more than three or four objects. As children gain one-to-one correspondence, they will begin to match a number word for each object counted.

Children reach the stage of rational counting when they realize that the last number counted represents the total amount of objects in the set. In other words, if you ask children, "How many objects are there?" after they have finished counting a set of objects, they do not have to count the objects again before replying.

A more sophisticated stage of counting incorporates the notion of conservation, as discussed earlier, in which the child realizes that the arrangement of a group of objects does not vary the quantity being counted. The objects can be changed, rearranged, and counted in different orders or configurations, yet the child recognizes that the number of objects remains constant. It is at this stage of counting that children are able to count with understanding and have constructed the concept of number. Children need multiple experiences with counting activities to develop one-to-one correspondence, conservation of number, and the meaningful construction of number.

Estimating

Estimating involves projection of a number concept onto objects or relationships. For example, when estimating how many jelly beans are in a jar, a child must apply the concept of number (e.g., 100) to the jelly beans in the jar. This process involves mental manipulation of numerical concepts and thus is rather difficult for preoperational and early concrete operational children to perform. That is why an estimating task such as the jelly bean example may generate estimates ranging from 10 to 1,000 from young children. Children who have not grasped the concept of number, particularly of numbers in the higher ranges (i.e., over 20), will obviously have difficulty estimating with numbers.

An easier way for children to estimate is to use concrete objects to represent their estimates. For example, when estimating the circumference of a pumpkin or a tree, the children can represent their estimates with a piece of string or yarn. By doing so, they do not have to translate their estimates into abstract units of measure such as inches or centimeters. They can use concrete representations of their estimates in the form of lengths of string. Furthermore, to check the accuracy of their estimates, they can wrap their pieces of string around the circumference of the pumpkin or tree and experience for themselves how well they were able to estimate the distance (Baratta-Lorton, 1976).

As children develop the ability to impose numerical concepts, such as the number of jelly beans in a jar or inches in the circumference of a pumpkin, they demonstrate that they are able to mentally impose numerical order on physical objects. If we go back to the jelly bean example, most adults would base their estimates on a logical way of segmenting the jelly beans into smaller groups or sets, for example, groups of ten jelly beans, and estimating how many of these sets occupy the jar. This process involves imposing a relationship of number (10) on a group of jelly beans and then estimating how many of these groups there are in the entire jar. Children need opportunities to do the same type of estimating by means of smaller units of measure. Before asking children to estimate how many jelly beans are in a jar, the teacher can help the children count out a subgroup of ten to determine how much space this amount occupies, then project how many of these units are in the jar.

Common items can be used as estimating and measuring tools. Examples of using concrete, meaningful ways of estimating and measuring might include the number of footsteps to get from one end of the room to the other, the number of hand-widths to cross a tabletop, and the number of cups of water to weigh the same as a rock.

Comparing by Graphing

Graphing is a problem-solving tool that applies and integrates counting, classifying, and comparing. Children are naturally interested in comparing groups of objects. Graphing can help children see these comparative relationships as they organize their data in ways that help them discover quantitative relationships (e.g., more, less, and equal).

Children can begin by comparing two groups of concrete objects. The number of groups can be gradually increased as children become comfortable with more comparisons. These activities should be arranged in a sequence progressing from concrete to pictorial to symbolic. Mary Baratta-Lorton (1976) and Marilyn Burns (1992) suggest three types of graphing activities that reflect this developmental sequence:

- *Real Graphs.* Concrete graphing experiences provide the foundation for all future graphing experiences. Children can lay out objects such as shoes, color cubes, favorite toys, types of food, and so on in rows to visibly compare the amounts of real objects. A variety of objects encourages flexibility in math thinking.
- *Representational or Picture Graphs.* Representational graphing experiences encourage children to use pictures or models to stand for real objects. Photographs, magazine pictures, models, or drawings can be used at this stage. An example of developing a meaningful picture graph is placing photographs of children on a graph to represent their favorite foods or colors.
- *Symbolic Graphs.* The most abstract level of graphing is experienced when children use symbols to stand for real things, for example, using colored squares on a bar graph to represent groups of ten people in a population survey. At first children might use one colored square to represent one person on a graph before moving on to more abstract concepts.

Many opportunities for graphing experiences evolve naturally and spontaneously. It is important for teachers and children to use graphing to visually represent numerical comparative relationships so that children can begin to actually see the mathematical relationships that graphs represent.

Measuring

Children develop ideas about measuring as they interact with their environment. Concrete experiences with comparing, classifying, and seriating lead to developing concepts about measurement.

Comparison of objects of different sizes is the first step in constructing concepts of measurement. Noticing that one car is longer than another, that one rock weighs more than another, and that one cupcake is bigger than another involve children in making direct comparisons in terms of height, weight, size, shape, and so on. These informal experiences provide a rich environment for students to construct and refine their concepts of measurement.

Children begin **measuring** by using nonstandard units of measurement (e.g., hands, feet, blocks, etc.) to help bring meaning to distances. Instead of merely comparing two objects or distances and realizing that one is longer than another, the use of nonstandard units (e.g., it takes 12 footsteps to go from the sand table to the door) allows the child to determine "how much" in familiar units.

As students use nonstandard units of measure, they eventually see the need for standard units of measure, such as rulers and scales, so that common units can be used to make comparisons.

VIGNETTE 6.2

Providing a Real-Life Experience with Measurement

Ms. Harris, the teacher of the four- and five-year-olds introduced earlier in Vignette 6.1, wants to extend the math activities she has started with the shoes. She sets up a little "shoe store" in the dramatic play area, complete with shoes and shoe boxes, a cash register, play money, receipt pads, foot stools, and rulers. The children seem to know just what to do. Taking on the roles of shoppers and shopkeepers, they begin measuring each other's feet and "selling" each other shoes.

"You wear a size 7," one child informs a "shopper." After measuring all of the shoes on the shelf, this shopkeeper informs her customer, "We don't have any shoes in that size today. Would you like to buy a size 8?" The customer eagerly takes out his wad of money, hands it to the shopkeeper, who writes up a receipt, boxes, and bags the size 8 shoes for him.

Ms. Harris knows that the children are applying their measuring skills to a real-life situation that they have experienced—purchasing shoes. They are reading the numbers on the rulers, matching the measurements of the feet and shoes, and having fun at the same time.

Adding and Subtracting

According to Piagetian theory, **adding** and **subtracting** are reversible operations. Children begin combining objects at a very young age when they find one shoe and look for its mate, gather all of their toys together when cleaning up, and put handfuls of cereal on their plates. They subtract as they take the shoes off, take the toys off of the shelf, and eat the cereal. When they start to add and subtract as numerical operations, they build on all of these previous experiences, as well as all of the processes described above. They must have a sense of number (e.g., "five-ness"), equality, and one-to-one correspondence. To understand addition and subtraction, children should have developed reversible, operational thinking, which means that after solving 6 – 3 = 3, they can reverse the thinking and know that 3 + 3 = 6. At first, children of five or six years of age can solve these types of problems with objects: "If Jeremy had six pretzels and he gave three to his sister, how many does he have? If his sister gives the three pretzels back, how many does he have now?" After multiple experiences with addition and subtraction problems using real objects, children can begin to attach the symbolic notation for the operations. Writing 3 + 3 = 6 is much more difficult conceptually than adding three and three pretzels. Now the child must bring her understanding to the symbolic level. Constructivist teachers can help children make the transition to the symbolic level by encouraging children to represent number sentences with pictorial symbols, counters, and other less-symbolic means than numerals.

Unfortunately, when children are rushed to represent number operations with symbols before they have had adequate experiences with concrete representations of the operations, they may resort to memorizing the answers and distrusting their own logical reasoning in attempting to solve the problems (Kamii, 1989). Careful observation of the children as they solve number operation problems with objects and symbols inform the constructivist teacher about their level of reasoning and when the children are ready to attach symbols to the operations.

Introducing Mathematical Symbols

André Sherman, a teacher of five-, six-, and seven-year-olds in a multi-age kindergarten/primary class, works with the same group of children from the time they enter his class at age five and leave at age seven. This two-year span gives him the opportunity to follow each child's mathematical development. He arranges many activities that all of the children can participate in, such as estimating tasks, graphing activities, and using math in dramatic play, block areas, the cooking area, and during science experiments. Yet, he has found that the conceptual range in his class necessitates flexibly grouping the children so that he can challenge them at the appropriate level.

When the children are five and six years old, he leads them in many problems that use discrete objects to count, measure, estimate, and so on. When they begin to show signs of using operational thinking and conservation in their reasoning, as well as a firm understanding of number (e.g., five ants is the same number as five elephants), he slowly introduces them to the symbolic representations for the number operations of addition and subtraction (e.g., 5 + 5 = 10).

In order to introduce the children to numerical symbols such as +, −, and =, Mr. Sherman uses materials that the children can count, add, and subtract, while noting their actions in their own symbols. Six-year-old Veronica usually uses penciled dots to represent her work. Ian, who is seven years old, uses a series of dashes. Mr. Sherman shows them how to write numerals for their dots or dashes: . . . . . = 5. He also introduces other models for the children to "see" the addition and subtraction problems. He uses linear rods called Cuisenaire Rods™ that vary by size and color. He also uses bean sticks that he and the children make by gluing one to ten beans on wooden popsicle sticks. Each stick has the numeral written on it in permanent marker. Mr. Sherman uses plastic cups with a numeral label matching the number of beans inside. He also uses cubes that fit together. With all of these materials, Mr. Sherman helps the children connect the physical actions they perform with objects to ways to note these actions in symbols or pictures. Eventually, they get to the point where they can read and write number equations with all symbols. For some children this may take several weeks, for others several months. Mr. Sherman is careful not to push the child to the symbolic notations before they understand what the symbols represent in concrete terms.

Conserving, classifying, seriating, patterning, counting, estimating, comparing, measuring, and adding and subtracting objects all actively engage children in the construction of their own logical-mathematical knowledge. Children develop cognitively as they actively explore and impose order on their physical environment through these processes. To say that any of these processes can be taught directly is a misconception. Teachers can teach *for* mathematical reasoning. The children have to try out and invent their own reasoning; teachers cannot do it for them (Kamii, 1985b; Piaget, 1973).

The following are some principles to keep in mind when planning for a mathematics curriculum that allows for active mathematical learning.

INSTRUCTIONAL PRINCIPLES

Knowing the way children learn math provides the foundation from which developmentally appropriate math programs for young children should be developed and delivered. The following principles are based upon the ideas of Piaget, as interpreted by Kamii (1982a, 1982b, 1985b) and Leeb-Lundberg (1988). They provide guidelines for planning and teaching math based upon the basic processes described earlier.

1. **Encourage children to be aware of and curious about objects, actions, and events around them.** Children construct logical-mathematical knowledge as they explore and observe the physical world they encounter through their senses. Adults can facilitate this process by pointing out the intricacies of the objects and events all around us and by asking questions that stimulate curiosity. For example, patterns in the floor tiles, configurations of windows in nearby buildings, shapes and sizes of trees, and different kinds of trucks are all around awaiting children's notice. Asking questions such as, "Do you see any patterns in the tiles on the floor?" guides the children's observations of their physical surroundings. Adults can encourage a curious, questioning attitude by modeling curiosity about the environment themselves.

2. **Plan for the children's construction of relationships between and among concrete objects.** Once children have developed curiosity about their environment, the next logical step is for them to seek relationships among the objects they observe. Logical-mathematical knowledge is not inherent in the objects themselves; it is based on the relationships imposed upon the objects by the child. Children can use classification skills to group objects that are alike, according to their thinking. They can extend patterns that they have identified. They can graph objects and visually compare quantities of items. All of these are examples of ways that children can impose relationships upon objects around them.

3. **Use objects that are meaningful to the child.** Preoperational and concrete operational thinkers need to have objects that they can experience directly—through touch, manipulation, hearing, taste, or smell. They do not learn well from someone else's experiences with objects; they learn through their own experiences. Math concepts are constructed through the child's natural and everyday explorations of the physical world. Objects in this physical world provide the tools for meaningful math learning. Mass-produced paper-and-pencil tasks such as workbook pages or dittoed sheets that require children to bring meaning to pictorial or symbolic representations of objects and numerals are not as meaningful to the children as experiences with objects that they can physically manipulate, order, rearrange, and count (Kamii, 1985a).

4. **Match the level of abstraction with the developmental levels of the children.** As preoperational and early concrete operational thinkers develop cognitively and have multiple experiences with concrete objects, they begin to be able to understand representations

of objects and relationships in more symbolic forms. Experiences with the objects themselves are on the concrete level. Pictorial representations are on the semi-concrete or representational level. Words and numerals are abstract symbols of what they represent. Representations of objects and relationships among objects can only be as symbolic as the child is ready to understand. The level of abstraction for which the child is ready depends upon the child's prior experiences and cognitive development. Children cannot be rushed to levels of symbolic abstraction but need to be allowed to progress at their own pace.

Children operating at the concrete level of abstraction need to have experiences with many sets of objects—objects that they can count, manipulate, arrange, and rearrange—before they can bring meaning to symbolic representations of these objects. A case in point is their understanding of the abstract notion of number and the symbolic representations for number called numerals. With concrete experiences, children will discover that number concepts, such as "five-ness," transcend the type, size, and arrangement of the objects. Five kernels of corn and five chairs both represent the same number; five pennies spread over a large surface is the same number as five pennies that are neatly stacked in a column.

As children master the concrete level of representation, they can begin to bring the concept of number to pictorial representations of the objects, for example, drawings of five ducks or five teddy bears. Finally, at the symbolic level of abstraction, they can bring meaning to the Arabic symbols used to connote number, for example, 5. The numerals are the symbolic way of representing the concept of number. Children should not be expected to memorize rotely or practice writing numerals for correct penmanship until they have proceeded through the first two levels of abstraction, and only then will the symbolic numerals have meaning for them.

5. **Stress relationships between and among objects rather than the symbols that represent these relationships.** Symbols such as +, −, and = are representations of relationships among sets of objects. A number sentence such as $5 + 1 = 6$ not only uses abstract numerals for the concepts of 5, 1, and 6, it also uses symbols to represent additive and equivalent relationships between the numbers. A child who has not had multiple experiences with manipulating sets of actual objects in groups of five, one, and six and has not developed an understanding of the concepts of five-ness, one-ness, and six-ness cannot abstract the operation involved when adding five and one. To solving this problem logically, the child needs to have developed concepts of the numbers involved, equivalence, and addition.

When a child has developed these concepts, adding and subtracting will be performed as logical, reversible operations. A child will logically reason that if $5 + 1 = 6$, then $6 - 5$ must equal 1 because addition and subtraction are logical inverses of each other. Children who have not constructed the operations of addition and subtraction or are unsure of their abilities to reason will continue to count objects—usually fingers—when confronted with addition or subtraction problems. Counting concrete objects is developmentally natural and necessary for them. They still need to connect their mathematical thinking to concrete objects. Children will be able to manipulate relationships among objects "in their heads" sometime in their primary school years if allowed to do so naturally. This internalization will be a natural process when the children are cognitively ready.

6. **Encourage children to problem solve and think flexibly about math concepts without fear of arriving at incorrect solutions.** The processes children use as they seek solutions to math problems are as important as the solutions they reach. Logical-mathematical knowledge is constructed as children try out solutions that work and ones that do not work. The children's mistakes are just as important as their correct responses for the development of the logical systems that are basic to mathematical reasoning. If children operate in an environment where they feel pressured to arrive at the "right" answers, without regard to how they constructed the answers, they will not develop the creative fluency and problem-solving capabilities that higher-order mathematics requires.

   Teachers can gain insight into the methods that children use to arrive at their solutions if they encourage children to share their reasoning. Oftentimes, this reasoning is illogical to adults; for example, a child might say that six pennies spread apart is more than six pennies in a stack. Yet, to the preoperational child, basing the solution on the physical distance that the pennies cover rather than on the number of pennies, is reasonable. A teacher who accepts the children's solutions and reasoning will have students who are willing to try out new theories without fear of adult disapproval. Risk taking should be encouraged and valued, not discouraged or shamed.

7. **Support verbalization of math concepts.** If children feel comfortable "talking math" (NCTM, 1989, p. 26), they will test their ideas against those of their peers and teachers. Consider two children playing at the water table who disagree about which container holds more water. Through their disagreement, each will probably try to convince the other of the validity of his or her claim. In order to do so, they may try to prove their contentions, for example, by

pouring the contents of each container into a third container. They may need a little guidance in arriving at such a means of solving the argument, which is where an observant teacher can help. By articulating the problem and orally proposing various solutions, the children are "talking math" in connection with experiences with real objects. Furthermore, they are developing logical means to solve problems. Verbalization helps children construct, order, clarify, and conceptualize math concepts.

8. **Integrate math concepts throughout the day and curriculum.** Children construct math concepts as they explore and manipulate their environment whenever and wherever they may be. Teachers can make the whole day and the whole environment "math rich." For example, by providing funnels, shovels, containers, and measuring cups of several sizes in the water or sand area (indoor or outdoors), teachers can help children begin to compare and to contrast the amount of material each holds. If children have a questioning, curious attitude, modeled by the teachers, they will begin to draw relationships between the objects and use comparison words such as *more, less, biggest, smallest,* and *same,* all of which are important concepts for later math development.

   Thinking mathematically should not be restricted to a particular time of the day or area of the classroom. Teaching for math concepts can be integrated into just about all areas of the curriculum. As these principles demonstrate, mathematics for young children involves the way they explore and order their physical world— everywhere and all of the time.

9. **Seek to understand children's thinking and build experiences based on this thinking.** Marilyn Burns suggests that the answers provided by students provide a "window" into their thinking (1992). "Mistakes" are opportunities for learning about the child's reasoning. The five-year-old child who says that a penny is worth more than a dime is telling us about her logic: the penny is bigger, so it must have a bigger worth. In other words, things are as they appear. This is developmentally appropriate reasoning for a five-year-old. A seven- or eight-year-old who reasons the same probably has the conceptual understanding to realize that worth is not determined by size; yet he probably lacks experiences with pennies and dimes, much like the experience of an American confronting a foreign currency for the first time. Usually several opportunities using the currency will lead to an understanding of its relative worth.

10. **Design learning experiences that allow for and encourage students' interactions with others.** According to constructivist theory,

children need interaction with others as well as with their physical world in order to construct knowledge and meaningful relationships.

The ideas and relationships derived by one child may be different than those constructed by her peers. It is through sharing varied ideas that students can verify, refine, and modify the relationships they have constructed.

The value of social interactions cannot be overstated. As children exchange ideas with one another and their teachers, they revise their thinking in light of others' comments and ideas (Burns, 1992; Rowan & Bourne, 1994).

SUMMARY

The love of math is contagious. If children are to feel successful in math, teachers need to communicate to children that math is exciting, that math is necessary, and that math is meaningful in their lives. They can help children make math exciting and meaningful through playing, manipulating, and talking about the relationships among the objects around them.

Children must be allowed to do their own inventing. Teachers can aid in this process by arranging a math-rich environment of concrete materials that can be used for active, meaningful learning by children. Constructivist teachers use open-ended, nonjudgmental conversations with children to convey an awareness of and respect for their levels of thinking. Teachers who are alert to math processes and development understand how children construct the operations that will become the basis for understanding later math concepts. Through concrete experiences, children naturally begin to develop key mathematical processes such as conserving, classifying, seriating, patterning, counting, and comparing, all of which are basic for later mathematical reasoning.

Young children have a natural curiosity about the world and a natural need to impose order on the world around them. Constructivist teachers draw upon this curiosity and help them with the process of imposing order. They don't expect children to think like adults before they have had a chance to think like children first.

CHAPTER SEVEN

Becoming Scientists

7

Probably no other area of the curriculum reflects constructivist teaching more vividly than science education. Science is no longer perceived as a set of facts and figures to be memorized. Constructivist science education challenges children to think and act like scientists. Children observe, question, seek answers, compare results, reflect, and record, engaging in many of the same activities as scientists. Scientists are curious about the world and act on that curiosity in analytic ways; they question in order to understand how things work. Science involves "attempts to study and understand the physical processes that touch upon human experience and imagination" (Fromberg, 1995, p. 118). The world of science provides a constantly evolving story, a story that gets better with each new scientific discovery (Rowe, as quoted in Fisher, 1992).

GOALS OF CONSTRUCTIVIST SCIENCE TEACHERS

The goal of constructivist teachers is to include children in the unfolding story about how the world works—not as observers, but as active participants. Children become questioners, data collectors, analyzers, and theorists as they construct their understandings about the physical and biological worlds. This is not to say that facts and concepts are not important to scientific understanding. It *is* to say that understanding these facts and concepts involves more than simple memorization; understanding involves thinking about, questioning, and figuring out the answers to one's own and others' questions.

There is a core of knowledge common to science. The difference between teaching science in a constructivist way and a traditional way is that children discover and construct the core knowledge themselves as they engage in scientific processes. Explanations for scientific phenomena arise from their own explorations and experiments. The teacher guides the explorations, poses probing questions, models the scientific process, answers questions, and helps children put their thinking into words. In other words, the teacher provides the scaffolding or framework for the children's experiences (Berk & Winsler, 1995).

Constructivist teachers understand that children must progress through a series of incomplete or even erroneous explanations for phenomena before they arrive at more accurate conclusions. Telling children that their ideas are incorrect and giving them the "correct" explanations does not promote understanding; and it may undermine children's confidence in their own observations and explanations. When teachers use a didactic approach, children become dependent upon others to give them the "right" answers instead of becoming independent, autonomous thinkers. Science becomes a series of facts to be gleaned from teachers and textbooks, memorized, and then reported back through single-answer questions on paper-and-pencil tests. The constructivist view of science as an evolving story becomes lost in this type of approach.

Constructivist teachers understand that it takes more than a strong conceptual base to make a person a scientist—values, attitudes, and skills, along with a strong conceptual base, are just as important. A report by the American Association for the Advancement of Science (AAAS) states, "Once people gain a sense of how science operates—along with a basic inventory of key science concepts as a basis for learning more later—they can follow the science adventure story as it plays out during their lifetime" (AAAS, 1993, p. 3).

Piaget emphasized the process of discovery involved in learning about physical knowledge (Kamii, 1985b). Much of science involves a physical knowledge of the world—the visible properties of matter, the feel of cold and hot, the sound of thunder or wind or musical pitch. Such physical knowledge must be taken in directly through the senses. And much of science is logical-mathematical knowledge, such as the effect of combining two colors, the heat produced by light passing through a magnifying glass, the consequence of watering, or not watering, the seedlings. A great deal of science is also social knowledge that must be learned from persons who already have the knowledge: the words used to describe the phenomena under study, rules about how to treat the natural world, and the culture and accepted practices of behavior in the scientific community. Thus, all three types of knowledge—physical, logical-mathematical, and social—contribute to learning science.

Now that the ever-expanding knowledge base of science is more accessible than ever before through technology, where do we begin to teach science to children who will live most of their lives in the next millennium? The American Association for the Advancement of Science gives this advice:

> For students in the early grades, the emphasis should overwhelmingly be on gaining experience with natural and social phenomena and on

enjoying science. . . . By gaining lots of experience *doing* science, becoming more sophisticated in conducting investigations and explaining their findings, students will accumulate a set of concrete experiences on which they can draw to *reflect* on the process. (1993, p. 4)

Doing and reflecting must both be emphasized. Science is not only "hands-on," it is "minds on," too. To paraphrase the great American educational philosopher John Dewey, we do not learn from our experiences, we learn from *reflecting* on our experiences.

Let us examine some of the **scientific processes** and experiences that teachers should emphasize in the early school years.

SCIENTIFIC PROCESSES

Observing

Much of science involves looking closely at a subject, whether it is a butterfly landing lightly on a flower petal, a cloud forming overhead, or a snowflake melting under a microscope. A common characteristic of all scientists is the ability to observe carefully and accurately.

Teachers provide the opportunities, motivation, and models for such careful observation. Games such as "I spy," where the "spy" gives hints about what she or he is looking at helps the children sharpen their visual observation skills. Auditory games which challenge the children to identify objects or animals by their sounds sharpen auditory observation skills. Constructivist teachers take advantage of everyday opportunities to point out the changes in the environment. Making efforts to notice the smells, sights, and sounds that are all around will help teachers sharpen their own observation skills as well as the children's.

Describing

Related to observing scientific phenomena is the ability to describe what is observed in clear, detailed, and accurate ways. In the early childhood years, descriptions can be given in words, art, music, poetry, dance, or just about any medium. A simple event like watching popcorn pop in a clear popper can lead to descriptive words such as "exploding," "jumping," "popping," "changing." Children could draw what happens to a popcorn kernel. Some of the drawings may look like fireworks, others may look like sequential depictions of the stages of the kernel. A musical reenactment of the noises created by the popping corn, accompanied by a dance where the children move like popping corn, would be another way to describe what they experienced. These are just a few ways that children can describe scientific phenomena.

Making Predictions

Formulating hypotheses that use an if-then format engages the budding scientists in applying what they already know and what they think will happen. Science consists of many hypotheses and theories about what and how things will work. "If I plant the seed a foot under the ground, then I think it will not grow," or "If I drop the penny in a clear glass of water, then it will look the same," both involve making predictions or forming hypotheses that can be tested through scientific inquiry.

Children's predictions are taken seriously in a constructivist approach to science. Most predictions should be proven or disproven by firsthand experimentation or observation, if possible, not by hearing the information from someone who already knows. Recording predictions such as how much rain will fall in the month of April or how high the balloon will go, testing the predictions with real data, then reviewing the information and predicting again, allows for children to engage in the hypothesis-testing-and-revising cycle of the scientific method.

Classifying

Science has classification systems or frameworks for just about everything. These classification systems provide the logical schema for placing individual objects or specimens. As simple as living/nonliving or plant/animal, classifications help us generalize about an individual specimen. For example, if a child is able to classify a rock as nonliving, she probably would not expect it to breathe, eat, or have offspring. Further ideas on classification concepts are found in Chapter 6: "Making Math Meaningful for Young Children."

Identifying

Knowing that the bright red bird with a crown on its head is a cardinal or the puffy white cloud that looks like cotton is called a cumulus cloud reflects the ability to observe and classify individual cases within a larger framework. Thus, identifying individual scientific phenomena by giving each one a name that others recognize allows one to communicate more clearly with others about the different phenomena. As teachers use resources such as bird identification charts and books, encyclopedias, experts, and other sources, children also will learn how to use these to find answers.

Designing Investigations

When a child has a question about a natural phenomenon, acting on the question by designing an investigation is a natural next step. For example, the seven-year-old child who wonders if fish close their eyes and go to sleep could help design an observational study to try to figure out the answer to the question. He might devise a schedule to check the fish at designated times to find out. He might have to use a video recording of the fish to collect data when he is not present. Potential investigations are everywhere, from the very simple one-time data collection type to the long-term investigation that may last a week or longer.

Collecting Data

After designing an investigation, the young scientist must learn to collect data in a careful manner. Collecting data often involves measuring, counting, timing, and other mathematical skills. For example, after counting the seeds in the watermelon they eat one day for snack, the children can plant the seeds and plot their growth by posting lengths of string on the calendar on the dates the measurements are taken. Simple activities that the children can perform with a minimum of adult help give them opportunities to collect their own data.

Interpreting Data and Making Inferences

After the data have been collected, scientists then look for patterns, interpret the data, and bring meaning to it. Different ways of manipulating the data, such as graphing or plotting it on a matrix, assist scientists in this process of interpretation. Consistent patterns found in the data lead child scientists to formulate conclusions that can be further tested.

Communicating Results

When the investigation has been completed, data interpreted, and findings derived, the next step is to communicate the results in a way that others will understand. Photographs, puppet shows, movement and musical presentations, displays, models, drawings, and written reports are all ways that the results can be communicated. The young children will need help with writing the words to label their displays, but they can dictate the words that they want to use.

The difference between the processes of describing and communicating results lies in the timing and the scope of the audience. Describing scientific phenomena occurs throughout scientific explorations and investigations. Communicating the results occurs after results and conclusions have been reached and the scientist is ready to share the findings with a wider audience. Young children can share their findings with other children in informal ways such as at sharing time during a class meeting. Older children could share their results at an open house or schoolwide science fair.

Values and Attitudes Basic to Scientific Study

Just as the above processes enable new and experienced scientists to approach the study of scientific phenomena in fruitful ways, there are underlying values and attitudes basic to scientific study. These values and attitudes, although hard to quantify, are as important for scientists to develop as the processes described in the previous section.

Curiosity

Lilian Katz (1988) pointed out that children's dispositions to learn are as important as the knowledge they are learning; if the disposition to learn has been squelched or discouraged, children lose their motivation to learn. Curiosity is one such disposition that contributes to learning, especially when learning about scientific phenomena. It is hard to imagine a successful scientist that is not driven by curiosity about how the world works. Constructivist science education must nurture and build on the children's curiosity, which means building experiences around their questions and interests.

Openness to New Ideas

Because science provides an ever-evolving story, scientists must be open to the new twists and turns the story takes. Scientists who become "stuck" in old theories or paradigms will be resistant to new chapters of the science story. Children can experience the changes in their thinking that accompanies new discoveries as they revise their original predictions and change their minds. Teachers who are open to the new ideas and demonstrate willingness to accommodate and modify their thinking provide models for the type of openness the budding scientists will need.

Informed Skepticism

To balance their openness to new ideas, scientists must also act as informed skeptics, wary of new ideas and discoveries until adequate verification data have been collected. Scientists must continually question and test new ideas before accepting them. The teacher can lead the way in questioning the validity of new ideas by questioning the children in supportive, thought-provoking ways.

Scientific Concepts and Knowledge Base

Along with the processes involved in doing science, there is a knowledge base that children must begin to understand in order to establish the foundations for later scientific concepts. During the early years, these subjects should be approached with a sense of awe and wonder. Children's curiosity and questions about these topics are more important than their being able to explain them.

The following set of content areas is adapted from the Project 2061 reports of the American Association for the Advancement of Science entitled *Science for all Americans* (1990) and *Benchmarks for Science Literacy* (1993).

The Universe

The **universe** of stars, galaxies, and space is so large that all people struggle to conceptualize its vastness. Our fastest rockets would take thousands of years to reach the star nearest to our sun (AAAS, 1990). Constructivist approaches to studying the universe start with the children's firsthand experiences: the cycle of day and night we experience as the earth turns, the phases of the moon, the seasons of the year. All of these phenomena result from the effects of the light and heat of the sun. Experiences and simple experiments with light and heat lead to an understanding of how elements of the universe work and help children build a base for later concepts involving the universe.

Observations through telescopes, photographs, videotapes, and the naked eye are important for the young scientist, too. For example, observing the changes in the moon over the course of a month and being able to record and describe those changes are more important than being able to explain the reason for the moon cycles. Discovering the pattern to the cycles of the moon and realizing that the whole moon is still there, even if we can only see a slice of it, matches the child's developmental level. If a child asks, "Why does the moon do that?" a constructivist teacher would ask her what she thinks, interjecting some probing questions like, "Where does the moon's light come from?" and "Do you think the moon stays in the same place or moves across the sky?" The teacher must make the judgment about when the child is cognitively ready to understand an explanation that includes lunar and planetary orbits, solar reflection, and visual angles.

It is most important for children up through second grade to notice and describe what the sky looks like at different times (AAAS, 1993). Explanations will come later when their conceptual and experiential development allows.

Earth and Ecology

A child's understanding of the earth and all of its **natural phenomena** will take years and countless experiences to develop. The full picture includes concepts such as "temperature, the water cycle, gravitation, states of matter, chemical concentration, and energy transfer" (AAAS, 1993, p. 66). Understanding grows slowly as children experience these phemonena in a variety of contexts and as their cognitive skills develop.

The emphasis in the preschool and primary years is on the repeating patterns in nature, such as the cycle of seasons and the transformation of water into a solid, liquid, and gas. Children's explanations for these phenomena are not as important as their observations and descriptions. Children can plot temperatures, precipitation (amounts and types), and other seasonal changes (such as changes in the trees and animals). They come to know that some patterns are predictable, such as it is warmer in July than January (if they live in the northern hemisphere). Such understanding lays the groundwork for later, more complex concepts about the cycles of nature.

Also important for understanding the earth is knowing about the processes that shape the earth. These processes include natural phemonena such as earthquakes, volcanos, and floods, and human-influenced phenomena such as using up the earth's resources and modifying its ecology (AAAS, 1993). Investigations into the geology of the earth can start with observing and classifying rocks according to their shape, size, color, and other characteristics.

The youngest scientists should become familiar with the many changes in their environment and investigate the causes of these changes. Some changes happen quickly, such as the accumulation of rain or snow during a severe storm. Others happen too slowly to see, such as the gradual change in a river's course. Simulated experiments using models of rivers in the sand table and rainfall in the terrarium can bring these phenomena within the child's experience and thus lead to understanding.

The Structure of Matter

The **structure of matter** as explained by atomic theory is too sophisticated and abstract for most young children to grasp. Vast conceptual knowledge and a scientific imagination are essential for understanding that matter is made up of moving atoms that one cannot see. Thus, the Association for the Advancement of Science recommends introducing the idea of atoms at the end of eighth grade (AAAS, 1993). The preschool and primary-age scientists can experiment with a variety of materials by "mixing, heating, freezing, cutting, wetting, dissolving, bending, and exposing [them] to light to see how they change" (AAAS, 1993, p. 76). All of these processes involve reactions that the children can see and describe. They can use descriptive words to communicate what they observe, such as "The ice cube is turning into water," or "The sugar is part of the water now."

Furthermore, many experiences with constructing things out of materials that have similar small parts, such as blocks or connecting toys, gives them firsthand knowledge of how the same materials can be arranged and rearranged into different products. They also begin to discover that properties of combinations of objects may react differently than the individual materials they are made of. For example, the tower made out of connecting blocks is more stable than one made from loose blocks.

VIGNETTE 7.1

Dissolving Crystals

Ms. Nel Kraft, a teacher of four- and five-year-old children, planned cooking activities for the children several times a week. She noticed some of the children's fascination with stirring sugar into wet ingredients when they were making carrot cake one day. Several of the children wanted to put more sugar in because they said that it "disappeared" after they stirred it. Ms. Kraft decided that the children would benefit from some experiments designed to discover the properties of these everyday crystals.

She started by consulting a scientist she knew to ask her if she would like to help. The scientist, Dr. Dawn Alexander, a biology professor at a local university, said that she would gladly participate. The two women worked together to set up a series of experiments wherein the children would discover a variety of the properties of sugar.

The first day, the children worked in groups of four. Each group poured two glasses of water, into which they measured a teaspoon of brown sugar. Dr. Alexander instructed them to stir one glass, but leave the other glass unstirred. She asked them to describe what they observed happening in the two glasses. The children said that the stirred water looked like iced tea. The other glass looked like the sugar was melting at the bottom of the glass. Ms. Kraft asked the children if they drank the first glass if they thought it would taste like iced tea. The children laughed and said, "No-o-o!" Dr. Alexander asked the children what would happen if they were to leave the glasses of water on the windowsill for several days. The children offered several theories, including, "It will dry up," and "Nothing." Dr. Alexander poured the contents of the glasses into a flat pan and set it on the windowsill.

The next week, when Dr. Alexander came back, she started by asking what happened to the pan of brown water they had left on the windowsill. The children excitedly went to retrieve the pan, which to their surprise now had splotches of brown crystals on the bottom of the pan. Dr. Alexander asked, "What is this on the bottom of the pan?" The children excitedly replied, "Sugar!"

Dr. Alexander set up another experiment in which the children put a spoonful of sugar into a square of paper towel, then closed the paper towel around the sugar with a rubber band. She instructed the children to attach the bundle to a straw and dangle it over a glass. She showed them how to carefully fill the glass with water until it was just touching the sugar bundle. Then she asked them to watch and describe what happened. To the children's delight, a barely visible swirl of less transparent liquid started to come out of the paper towel. The children watched in amazement as the swirl danced slowly in their glass of water. Dr. Alexander came by and dropped several drops of food coloring into the glasses, which joined the swirl and made it more visible. She advised the children to gently move the glass around in a circular motion, which they did (with only one spill!). The color slowly swirled and eventually mixed into the water, creating a consistent color in the water.

Dr. Alexander asked the children, "What happened?" The children used descriptions like, "The sugar got out of the paper towel and swirled around in the glass," "The food coloring followed the swirl," and other vivid descriptions. Dr. Alexander refrained from explaining to the children why this phenomenon occurred, although she whispered to Ms. Kraft that the color attaches itself chemically to the denser sugar molecules in the water. She knew that such a chemical explanation was beyond the children's experience and understanding.

ENERGY AND MOTION

The concept of energy is mysterious and abstract, even to many adults. Yet, an understanding of the basic ideas of energy will be important to later understanding of many scientific theories. At the youngest ages, children can conceptualize **energy** as what is "needed to make things go, run, or happen" (AAAS, 1993, p. 81). They can get in the habit of searching for the source for events, such as the application of heat to make steam or wind to make the flag wave. By the end of the second grade, children should know that the sun warms the land, air, and water.

Related to the concept of energy is the concept of **motion**. Young children should be cognizant of all kinds of moving things, from themselves to the insects, birds, balls, bicycle wheels, and trees around them. They should observe and record how things move, such as in a straight line, fast, slow, all at once, or in spurts. Musical instruments use motion to make sound: drums, bells, stringed instruments, xylophones, even their own voices. Experimenting with and describing the sounds and their variations is enough for the young children. Understanding how and why will come later.

Forces of Nature

Two forces important for children to experience are **electromagnetism** and **gravity**. At young ages, the children can focus on the motion these forces create: magnets can make things move without touching them, and balls fall to the ground if nothing holds them up. Children can experiment with magnets and different materials to discover that some metals respond to magnets while others do not; they can try using magnetism through different types of materials, such as cardboard, paper, and water. Children can also try to magnetize various objects by rubbing them on the magnets. The explanations for why magnetism works the way it does, including atoms and poles, is not comprehensible for most preschool and primary children.

Multiple experiences with gravity are important. These can include dropping objects of different sizes, weights, and shapes from various heights and observing what happens, exploring how objects move down inclines of various slopes, and throwing objects into the air to see what happens. These types of activities allow children to experience the force of gravity firsthand.

The Living Environment

Most young children have a natural curiosity about other living things. The natural world provides an abundance of **living species**; over one million have been identified. Familiarity with living things through observation should move naturally toward classification of these things by the attributes that connect them. The teacher's task is to help children note the characteristics that connect species to each other, such as the type of skeleton they have or the way their offspring are born.

Children who have limited opportunities to interact with nature need to have the opportunities provided for them. Trips around the neighborhood, classroom pets and plants, excursions to the zoo, parks, or streams are all important. Observing living specimens is important, but observations should not be for their own sake. Students' and teachers' questions provide purposes for the observations: "How do the animals eat?"; "Where do they live?"; "How do they care for their young?" These are all questions that can be answered through children's observations. The teacher knows that some characteristics are more important than others for classification systems that will be introduced later, such as the way animals bear and feed their young.

Some teachers have concerns that children's literature often gives animals characteristics they do not have, such as the ability to carry on conversations in English or cook meals on a stove. These humanlike depictions may confuse young children. Teachers and other adults can guide children toward distinguishing between realistic depictions of animals and fictional depictions by talking about what is realistic and what is not.

Another topic related to living organisms is the concept of heredity. Preschool and primary children learn early on that animals reproduce their own kind; that is, they know that people have human babies and cats have kittens. Offspring within a species are much alike, but there are variations. Building the observational base for concepts of heredity can occur in the early years. Studying the offspring of plants and animals, such as different types of seeds and eggs, can involve comparing them to each other, matching them to their parents, and watching them grow and develop to look more and more like their parents.

The Human Organism

Although the **human organism** has much in common with other animals, humans' ability to use language and thought set them apart. Furthermore, human beings have much in common with each other; yet they also have many differences. Children in the younger levels should concentrate on external, observable characteristics of people, such as color of hair, eyes, and skin; the roles they play within their families and communities; and their common needs for water, food, air, and waste removal. They can develop ideas about how people and other animals live, grow, feed, move, and use their senses (AAAS, 1993). The life stages of humans, from infancy to old age, are evident to children. Learning about their parents' experiences as children or projecting what they would like to do when they are adults help the children understand that humans go through a series of life stages.

Learning about the functions of different body parts, such as eyes for seeing, noses for smelling, mouths for breathing and eating, helps children lay the groundwork for understanding body systems, which will come at a later time. Another important aspect of the human organism is how it stays healthy. Young children can learn that certain eating and living habits contribute to good health, whereas other habits are unhealthy. By the end of second grade, children should know that some diseases are caused by germs that spread from other people, whereas other diseases are not spread this way. Similarly, some things eaten or breathed in from the environment are harmful and can hurt them (AAAS, 1993).

VIGNETTE 7.2

Learning About Families

Mr. Enrico Gonzolez, a teacher of six-, seven-, and eight-year-olds, planned the integrated unit on children's families to include several areas of the curriculum, including language arts, science, math, and social studies. He wrote a letter to the parents of the children in his class and asked them to be part of the unit by answering questions and providing information for the children.

He introduced the unit with a series of children's books that portrayed life in a variety of families, some with customs similar to the children's and some that were different. Books included families with several generations living together and families that lived in a variety of types of homes and ate a variety of foods. Consistent in the stories was the respect and warmth that members of a family feel toward each other.

Next, Mr. Gonzolez introduced the idea that the parents and grandparents of the children in the class were children at one time, too. To do this, he invited parents and grandparents to come to the class and share a story about when they were six or seven years old. Several of the parents volunteered to do so. The children were mesmerized by the stories of bike accidents, mischief making, and potty accidents at school. The children realized that these grown-up people they see every day had experiences similar to theirs. They also realized that some parents spoke different languages, lived in different types of houses, and ate different foods.

For the science part of the unit, Mr. Gonzolez and the children developed a series of questions that would allow them to collect data on the different families. They came up with questions like: "What type of pet(s) do you have?"; "How many people live at your home?"; "How do you get to school?"; and "Where were the people in your family born?" The children set out to collect their data. As they brought the results back to school, Mr. Gonzolez helped them put the information onto large graphs, which the children helped develop. The graphs had to go through several revisions because the children realized that they needed new categories or more space. Mr. Gonzolez let them make the revisions because he knew it would help them understand how graphs were constructed. When they were done collecting the data, Mr. Gonzolez led the children in a discussion of what the graphs said. He asked them if they saw any patterns in the graphs.

With the help of Mr. Gonzolez's questions, the children learned from the graphs that dogs were the most popular pets, that more families had five people in them than any other number, that more people were born in their state than any other single location, but that as many people were born in other places if they were added together. They used a world map to mark the locations from where members of the children's families were born.

Mr. Gonzolez was satisfied that the children had used their language arts skills when writing the questions and recording the answers, mathematic skills and science skills when collecting, graphing, and interpreting the data, and social studies skills when learning about how families were the same and different.

An often overlooked aspect of the human organism is mental health. Helping children accept their emotions and those of others, ranging from pleasant to unpleasant, and learning healthy ways of dealing with these emotions leads to understanding that all people—including themselves—have feelings.

Agriculture, Materials, and Manufacturing

Many children do not know the origins of the foods, clothing, and other products they use every day. Young children can begin learning by hearing stories and seeing pictures about life on the farm and what happens to food and crops between the farm and the store. They can study the machines used in planting and harvesting foods and the means of transportation needed to move crops and animals. They can analyze the products that they eat and wear to determine what they are made from and where they come from.

THEMES UNDERLYING SCIENCE CONTENT AREAS

The American Association for the Advancement of Science has identified four themes that underlie all content areas of science, as well as other domains such as mathematics, economics, and law (1990, 1993). These are the *Big Ideas* in the constructivist sense because they connect the curriculum at the deepest levels. Teachers who are aware of these four themes can teach toward them throughout the study of scientific phenomena.

Systems

The notion of a **system** as separate parts related to each other within a whole is understood through higher-order thinking skills. The concept of a system is beyond expected levels for the typical preschool or primary child (AAAS, 1993). Young children tend to see the parts as separate entities. Their science experiences should lead them to see how the parts work together to perform functions within systems that influence them in their daily lives. The solar system, sewage system, government system, and digestive system are all examples of systems. In these systems, each part affects the other parts, and they work together to perform a function that the parts could not perform separately.

Children begin to understand the notion of systems as they take things apart and recognize that the whole cannot function if it is missing parts, such as the radio without a battery or the toy truck without one of its wheels. As children "dissect" simple machines, they discover the many individual parts that make it up. As they play with dolls and doll houses, wheeled vehicles, and blocks, they put together systems that work together: families with various roles, roads and houses for their cars and trucks. They enact the roles of the individual "parts" in relation to the whole system they have created.

As the children become more sophisticated thinkers, they will come to understand that sometimes the whole that the parts create is very different than the individual parts. For example, sugar is sweet, but the elements that form sugar (carbon, oxygen, and hydrogen) are not sweet by themselves (AAAS, 1993).

When a smoothly operating system has a change in one of its parts, the whole system has to adapt. For example, when a member of a family becomes ill, the whole family has to adapt to this new condition. Similarly, when a new part is introduced to the system, the system must adapt, such as when a new baby enters into an already established family system. The same principles apply when a new chemical is introduced into the earth's environment, a new animal enters an established ecosystem, or a meteorite breaks through the earth's atmosphere.

By the end of second grade, children should know that things are made of parts, that some things may not work if some of the parts are missing, and that when parts are put together, they can do things they could not do alone (AAAS, 1993). More sophisticated thinking about systems will develop as the children mature cognitively and build their experiential base.

Models

Models can come in physical, conceptual, or mathematical forms. Physical models that replicate the real world are the first type that chil-

dren understand. They are familiar with play objects that look and sometimes function like the real thing: miniature trucks, dolls, and tea sets are
physical models of the real things. Children can also come to recognize
that these objects are different from the real objects and have limitations.
For example, most real trucks do not need someone to push them to
make them go and real babies cannot be put away in the toy chest.

Conceptual models require a level of abstract thinking that most
young children are not ready to perform. Yet, through literature and
the arts, they can explore imagery, metaphor, and analogy, which are
the precursors to later conceptual models that will require imagination
and abstract connections. Mathematical models, which are usually
more abstract than physical and conceptual models (AAAS, 1993), are
often taught separately from the real problems they represent. Most
children can logically solve a real problem such as "If you have one
cookie and your mom gives you two more, how many will you have?"
before they can solve $1 + 2 = 3$, which is the mathematical model of the
same problem. Unfortunately, when the model is introduced separately from the real-life applications, children do not make the connections
between the new problem and what they already know. Further discussion of constructivist approaches to mathematical understanding
can be found in Chapter 6, "Making Math Meaningful for Young
Children" in this book.

Constancy and Change

A common theme in science is understanding how **constancy and
change** occur in the natural world. Animals prepare for winter, day
changes to night, and water changes to ice or steam. Yet, when looked
at in a broader sense, all of these changes reflect a constant pattern:
winter follows autumn, night becomes day, water changes to a solid or
gas and back again. The theme of constancy and change occurs
throughout science.

As children gain maturity, they can begin to study constant versus
varying rates of change, change and constancy at the same time (such
as a rock whose chemical composition remains constant even when it
changes shape and size), or change that is constant but looks quite different in different circumstances (such as oxidation occurring in the
form of rust or the form of fire). Ecological systems can undergo more
noticeable gradual changes that are almost imperceptible when examined in the short term or they may undergo short-term changes that
have neglible effect over the long term. Mathematical models such as
graphs help scientists understand and represent these changes.

By the end of second grade, children should know that things
change in some ways and stay the same in other ways; some changes

are fast and others are slow; some are large, others small. People can track changes by making observations and measurements over time. There are many ways that things can change, including size, weight, color, and movement (AAAS, 1993).

Scale

Two major ideas surround the concept of **scale** in science. The first and most obvious is that of magnitude. The world of science encompasses phenomena that are so small that we can only see them with the most powerful microscopes and so large that our earth is like a speck in comparison. The second idea within the concept of scale is that phenomena do not always act the same when they differ in scale. For example, a large cup of hot water will take longer to cool than a small cup of water of the same temperature. A star more massive and larger in scale than the sun can collapse into itself and not even allow light to escape (AAAS, 1993). Both of these concepts are difficult for young children to understand. Their understanding of scale should be within their first-hand experiences and comparisons, such as, "Point to the biggest tree you see," "Show me the smallest flower," and so on. They can also use technology such as telescopes, microscopes, and videotapes to "see" things closer than they could without assistance. Similarly, they can use stethoscopes to hear their own hearts or lungs at work. Many opportunities to compare and measure sizes, weights, ages, speeds, and other aspects that vary in scale help them to experience the ranges possible.

INSTRUCTIONAL PRINCIPLES

The following principles highlight the ways in which teachers can implement a constructivist approach to teaching and learning science.

1. **Allow children to propose and test their own questions and ideas about scientific phenomena.** Young children are full of questions about the natural world. When they ask questions like "Why is the sky blue?" a constructivist teacher would probably ask the child what she thinks first. The child might say that the sky is blue because someone painted it blue. A follow-up question could be, "Then why do you think the sky is gray on a cloudy day?" This may provoke the child to reason that the blue and gray colors of the sky have to do with how the sunlight reaches us, which is enough of an explanation at this point. Understanding that the blue color has to do with the color spectrum and the bending of light waves is hard for most children to understand because they cannot see light

waves. Experiments that use light to make rainbows and shadows, refractions through water, and intense heat through a magnifying glass build on the child's natural curiosity about the properties of light and would be an appropriate follow-up to the original question about the blueness of the sky.

2. **Model an inquiry-based approach to learning about the world.** Teachers who ask questions about the world and use the questions to guide their discoveries provide models for the children. For example, when a new noise comes from down the hall, the teacher might ask out loud, "I wonder what that noise could be?" She could go on to hypothesize, "It could be a lawn mower, or maybe an electric drill. I wonder how we could find out." At that point, the children could offer their hypotheses and their suggestions about how they could find out where the noise is coming from. Together, the children and teacher could pursue the children's suggestions and discover the source for the noise. Although this is a simple activity that might take less than five minutes, the teacher has modeled for the children how to find answers to their own questions.

3. **Build in opportunities for children to investigate and find the answers to the teacher's questions.** Children are rarely without questions, but oftentimes the teacher may want to steer the thinking toward a particular topic, which can be done with carefully worded questions. For example, if the teacher wants the children to realize the amount of water they are wasting when they leave the faucets on in the bathroom, she may ask, "How much water do you think comes out of our water faucet when we leave it on?" After the children have made estimates, they can devise an investigation to find out the answer. They may propose using buckets from the water table (or the water table itself) to measure how much water comes from the faucet in a minute. When they discover how much water comes out in a minute, the teacher can show them how much water would come out in the time that they are eating their lunch or out on the playground. By connecting the results to the children's daily lives, the teacher hopes that the children realize the consequences of leaving the faucets on. And all this started with a question.

4. **Keep science as concrete and observable as possible.** Children who are preoperational and concrete operational thinkers need to see firsthand the phenomena that they study. They need to see the pull of a magnet or the eggs of the robin. Children will probably not understand explanations that include phenomena they cannot see or touch, such as molecules or atoms. There are so many topics that children can see, hear, feel, touch, and taste. These topics should be the focus of science investigations for preschool and primary-age children.

5. **Provide a purpose for the observations and experiments.** When children have a purpose for their observations, such as "Find as many types of leaves as you can," or "Which toy car gets to the finish line faster, the one on the flat surface or on the hill?" they enter into the activity with a goal in mind. When a teacher introduces an experiment with a purpose, such as "Do you think my hand will look bigger if we look at it through this glass of water?" the children make an investment in the outcome by predicting "Yes" or "No." Their curiosity has been piqued.

   Another strategy that constructivist teachers use is to introduce the activity with a connection to a real life experience. For example, the teacher may say, "On my way into school today I noticed lots of worms on the sidewalk. Did anyone else notice the worms? Why do you think they were on the sidewalk?" This might initiate an investigation into the habits of worms. The teacher may learn as much as the children through this type of investigation.

6. **Ask open-ended questions.** Too often adults ask children questions that have one right answer that the adult already knows. "Is the ice hot or cold?" is an example of this type of single-answer question. Conversely, the question could be worded in a manner that allows for more than one right answer, such as "How does the ice feel to you? Can you think of something else that feels similar?" The children may use words like "frosty," "cold," "slippery" and "popsicles," "ice cream," and "icicles." The teacher did not know what the children would answer when he asked the question because many answers could be considered "right."

   Once in the habit of formulating divergent, open-ended questions, teachers are amazed at the creative responses the children give. And the more practice the children have in answering open-ended questions, the more creative their answers will become.

7. **Use resources and scientific equipment daily.** Scientists use all kinds of tools and equipment to find out more about the natural world. They use computer-based information sources, such as those found on CD-ROMs or the Internet. They use hard copy resources such as encyclopedias and information-type books. And, of course, scientists use magnifying glasses, rulers, timers, microscopes, binoculars, magnets, droppers, and much more. Much of this equipment is readily available to teachers or inexpensive to purchase. If the children get used to using scientific tools, they will think to use these tools to answer their questions. Children often need time to explore the uses of the equipment. The first time they use a pocket microscope, for example, they will probably want to look at everything they can think of, from the cloth of their pants to the skin on their thumbs. Having the equipment readily avail-

able and a natural part of the classroom will allow the children to explore for as long as they need to.

8. **Take advantage of naturally occurring events as a source of scientific investigations.** When a bee flies into the room or a spider dangles from the light fixture, the moment is right to think like scientists. Instead of swatting the bee or the spider because they are nuisances, constructivist teachers would take advantage of the natural specimens that just arrived unannounced. "Where do you think bees live?" or "How does a spider do that?" could spark impromptu investigations into the living habits and habitats of these species. The message sent to the children is that nature is fascinating, not something to be frightened by. Of course, we need to use caution around stinging insects or biting spiders, but when caution is followed, we can make them a source of study.

9. **Make caring for the environment a part of the classroom culture.** Showing respect for the environment by recycling and reusing as many products as possible introduces the children to the habits of caring for the environment. Bins for recycling paper, glass, aluminum, and plastic; compost piles for food scraps; and cautious use of energy such as the lights and other electrical appliances can become part of the daily routine. Children are forming their lifelong habits as they go through their early childhood years. Caring for the environment can become a habit and a value that they will carry with them into adulthood.

10. **Become part of science yourself.** Probaby the most important principle of all is for the teachers to become excited about the emerging science story around them. As new discoveries about dinosaurs or stars or the ozone layer become known, the teacher who shows genuine interest and excitement as she shares the new knowledge with the children teaches the scientific attitude, as well as the scientific knowledge. The children may not remember the specific facts the teacher shared. But they will remember that their teacher loved science enough to get excited about it.

SUMMARY

Science is everywhere and touches everything. Children are naturally fascinated by scientific phenomena, so learning about science is quite natural for them. Constructivist teachers build science curriculum on the processes, themes, and content that the natural world offers. This is an area of the curriculum that children and teachers can experience the thrill of learning together.

As children engage in discovering about how the natural world works, they become part of its story. Our task as constructivist educators is to help them develop their abilities to interpret the story, appreciate the story, and tell the story. We do this by helping them develop the thought processes necessary to learn the concepts that underlie science. Overall, the best example we can set is to be part of the science story ourselves.

CHAPTER EIGHT

The Arts—Basic in a Constructivist Curriculum

8

The first time children make marks on paper, move their heads to the beat of a song, or dramatize talking on the telephone, we see the possibilities for artistic expression awakening inside of them. Participating in artistic expression is what makes people human (Fromberg, 1995). The arts open up new ways of knowing the world. Moreover, the arts provide another means of communicating knowledge. As the adage says, "A picture is worth a thousand words."

The arts highlighted in this chapter include *visual arts*, including drawing, painting, sculpting, and other two- and three-dimensional art forms; *music*, including singing, playing musical instruments, and listening; *movement and dance*, including learning to move and express oneself kinesthetically with one's body; and *dramatic arts*, including sociodramatic play, puppetry, and story acting. Although there are other means of artistic expression, these four areas represent important and essential areas of the early childhood curriculum.

CONSTRUCTIVIST NOTIONS OF ARTISTIC EXPRESSION

Implications of Piaget's theory when applied to the arts curriculum must come indirectly from an understanding of the basic tenets and philosophy underlying constructivism. Although Piaget recognized the importance of children's drawings, dramatizations, and other art forms as ways to understand the children's thinking, he never suggested ways of developing artistic knowledge. Thus, we start with his ideas about representational thinking to gain insight into constructivist notions of artistic expression.

According to Piagetian theory, as children pretend to drive cars, they use their actions of steering the wheel and making car noises to symbolize or represent driving a car. This simple level of representation or symbolism is soon followed by more sophisticated forms, such as representing ideas through drawing, which uses written marks to symbolize what the child is thinking. As children move further toward

144

abstract ways of representing reality, they become more symbolic in their thinking. The arts provide a number of means for children to represent reality, from the concrete, literal level to the abstract, nonliteral level.

Children not only use representations to express their understandings of the world, they interpret others' symbolic representations and, in doing so, bring their own meanings to pictures, music, and other art forms. Thus, art has expressive and receptive communicative values. The meaning that children bring to the art forms they create or interpret stems directly from their experiences. Seefeldt states, "Art is basic. Its value lies in the contributions it makes to the individual's experience with and understanding of the world" (1987, p. 196).

The arts provide a way for children to link their newly discovered social and physical worlds with their previous knowledge about these worlds. The arts provide a way of knowing about the world and a way of expressing that knowledge. In the words of the contemporary writer, Barbara Kingsolver, "The artist deals with what cannot be said in words" (1995, p. 233).

Although Piaget emphasized the cognitive and symbolic/representational nature of art forms and the degree to which these representations matched reality, today's constructivist educators also acknowledge the aesthetic value of artistic expressions, which may or may not closely resemble reality in its concrete forms. Art forms may communicate abstract, fantasy-filled interpretations of the world as well (Zellich, 1994; Winner, 1986). Interestingly, the early, less realistic art forms of children contain imaginative, free forms that usually disappear in middle childhood and may not reappear again except in the most accomplished artists, dancers, and musicians.

> Because preschool children are unconcerned with realism, their drawings are free, fanciful and inventive. Suns may be green, cars may float in the sky and complex, irregular forms in nature are reduced to a few regular geometric shapes. They produce simple, strong pictures that evoke the abstractions found in folk, "primitive" and contemporary art.
>
> The older child's drawing may be more realistic, neat and precise. . . . Suns are now appropriately yellow and placed carefully in the corner of the picture, and cars now rest firmly on the ground. (Winner, 1986, p. 35)

Yet, constructivist teachers want children to develop the imaginative, inventive side to the arts, along with the reality-based side. They strive for divergent, inventive thinking in the arts, just as in other areas of the curriculum. The focus is on the children's development of the thought processes underlying art as much as the products children create.

The processes that children use as they explore, manipulate, create, and communicate with art media and their bodies are important as they learn the power of artistic expression. Constructivist teachers realize that there are many languages children use as they express themselves artistically, and they recognize that multiple experiences using these languages allow children to become more fluent and confident (Edwards, Gandini, & Forman, 1993). Early emphasis on and evaluation of products the children create can stymie the creative processes. The teacher's role, then, is to encourage the development of children's artistic processes. As with other areas of the curriculum, the beginning point for constructivist teachers is knowing and understanding each child, then building the expressive arts curriculum upon this knowledge. As Seefeldt advises, "Once teachers understand children's thinking, they can provide children with alternatives that will expand their frame of reference and can build opportunities for children to act on their environment with their present state of knowledge" (Seefeldt, 1987, p. 206).

THE BIG IDEAS IN ART

This chapter will highlight some of the processes and content teachers can emphasize as they teach children to express and understand themselves and their world artistically through music, visual arts, movement, and drama. Each of these areas will be examined for the *Big Ideas* that teachers teach toward. These *Big Ideas* are the important elements for artists in the respective art fields. This chapter emphasizes a generalist approach to artistic development within the context of the broader early childhood curriculum. Specialized instruction in specific areas of the arts (e.g., programs provided by the art, music, or physical education teachers) is assumed to occur in most school settings by specialists in their fields. Ideally, these specialists would coordinate with the teachers responsible for the rest of the curriculum. This chapter will discuss practical, meaningful ways for the regular classroom teacher to naturally infuse the arts into the day-to-day curriculum of the preschool, kindergarten, and primary classroom.

THE VISUAL ARTS

When we think of art, we usually think first of **visual art** forms, such as painting, drawing, and sculpting. These visual art forms are essentials for early childhood programs. They represent the "languages of children" (Edwards, et al., 1993), important means by which children can communicate and record what they know. Visual art forms give children ways of expressing themselves without words. In Piagetian terminology, children's drawings are a way to represent their thinking about and understanding of the world. Their art gives us insight into their perceptions and conceptions of the physical and social objects and events around them. An early childhood program without the arts is impossible to imagine.

Early childhood literature is rich with thorough investigations into the milestones of children's artistic development. The works of several of the researchers have become "classics" in tracking the development of children's visual expressions (see Brittain, 1979; Kellogg, 1969; Gardner, 1980; Golomb, 1973; and Lowenfeld, 1947). The research has been evaluated, replicated, and synthesized to reveal a series of stages that categorize children's progression from scribbling to more representational art. Knowledge of these stages and milestones is important in helping teachers understand children's art.

However, the belief that children will progress through the stages of artistic development with minimum adult guidance and maximum exposure to art media has prevailed in early childhood education. This belief has strongly influenced the practice of teaching art to young children, mainly the tradition of allowing children to express themselves in any way they want, using a variety of media, with a minimum of adult intervention (Thompson, 1995). Early childhood educators came to believe that because children's artistic expression would progress naturally, there was little need for intervention of any sort.

More recently, theories such as those proposed by Vygotsky (1978) and the practices of the Reggio Emilia approach (Edwards et al., 1993) include important, interventive roles for teachers. In the words of Thompson (1995), "Vygotsky believed that a child's actual developmental level should be the starting place for teaching rather than a limitation that teachers are obliged to respect" (p. 84). The role of the teacher as stimulater, questioner, and coresearcher in the quest for new ways to use the visual arts is quite different from traditional teaching methods that either followed a "do as I show you" approach or a more laissez-faire approach of providing materials and little instruction. Teachers in a constructivist program help the children get to know the subject of their art by taking the children to the subject, such as an animal at the zoo, or bringing the subject to the children, such as the pumpkins they want to draw in the fall. For further reading about the role of the adults in the Reggio Emilia programs that integrate art into all aspects of learning, based upon the theories of Piaget, Vygotsky, and others, see *The Hundred Languages of Children* (Edwards, et al., 1993).

Elements of the Visual Arts

Knowing how the children represent their ideas through the visual arts and what they are thinking as they create their artwork is as important as knowing the common milestones of development. Further, knowing the *Big Ideas* within the visual arts, as perceived by accomplished artists in each discipline, helps the teacher build learning experiences for the child that incorporates the essential elements. These *Big Ideas* start with the type of media selected, then move into the use of color, line, shape, texture, pattern, space, and contrast in children's visual expressions.

Media

The **media** or materials that children use to create their visual art forms, whether paints or chalk, clay or fabric, torn or cut paper, determines what they can create. The media influences the artist as much as the artist influences the media. This interaction is part of what differentiates a craft from an art. The craftsperson is product-driven and often produces multiple copies of the same product. A craftsperson knows what he or she is going to make before starting. An artist, on the other hand, engages in a dialogue with the media (Thompson, 1995). The texture of the paints, the absorbancy of the paper, and the pliability of the clay all enter into the creation process. The artist negotiates his or her ideas as the creation progresses. Creating art is an emergent process, especially with young children, that is very much influenced by the media used.

Color

One the most obvious elements in visual arts, next to the media, is **color.** Some colors are bold and full of energy, while others are muted and soft. Children experiment with using colors. The colors influence the child's art as much or as often as the child purposely chooses colors to fit emerging ideas. The colors children choose at young ages are often unrelated to the realistic colors of the objects they portray. Suns may be green, faces purple, and hair fuchsia. As children become more interested in portraying objects realistically, often around the age of six or seven, they select colors accordingly. Yet, realism should not be forced on the children. If they want to make purple bunnies and blue grass, their autonomy over their creative expressions allows them to do so. As children gain more control over their visual expressions as a way to communicate emotions, they may choose unrealistic colors once again, just as accomplished artists do.

Line

A child's creation of **line** drawings begins very early, from the first scribbles she makes on the page to covering a page with endless lines.

The scribble lines may be curved, zigzagged, looped, spiraled, circular, or dotted (Haskell, 1979). The early scribbler (1½ years to 2 years) engages more in the muscular process of putting crayon to paper than the resulting marks. The sheer joy of putting marks on paper becomes a "dance" that the toddler engages in as he experiments with the lines and colors that result from his motions. As he gains eye-hand control and interest in the lines created, he may start to create structures, often by accident. The use of a line to outline an object enters in at around age three (Winner, 1986). Prior to the use of an outline, the child may draw a face as a loose arrangement in space of eyes, nose, and mouth.

Another type of line creation comes with the child's use of a baseline, which may appear around the ages of six or seven years. The child may draw the ground, upon which sit the houses, trees, and people, or the skyline, which many young children draw as a line across the top of the picture. The use of a baseline is more of a cognitive concept than a visual one. The child seems to be applying the knowledge that houses and trees sit on the ground and the sky is above our heads. So she makes a baseline to represent the ground and a skyline to represent the sky. It is not until later that she will match what she sees when she looks at the houses, trees, and sky around her to her representations of them in her drawings. Thus, if she continues to progress in her drawing, she will eventually move away from using such distinctive lines to depict the ground and the sky.

Shape

Visual art forms provide opportunities to use **shape** in all possible configurations, combinations, and sizes. Children's concepts of shapes can be interestingly represented by their use of different shapes in their two-dimensional drawings and three-dimensional sculptures. After lines, circular shapes usually appear. A little more difficult for the child are shapes that have angles, such as rectangles and triangles. Piaget found that preoperational children might represent triangles as squares with points on the top. They might be able to recognize the shape and describe some of its features, but draw it in a way that reflects some but not all of the features.

Texture

All art forms have **texture**. The paint strokes may be muted and soft or bold and visible. The clay may be smooth and shiny or rough and gritty. Chalks and pastels have different textures than crayons and markers. Children explore textures before they begin to use them purposefully for artistic expressions. They often surprise themselves when the textures remind them of something they had not thought of, such as the airy texture of shaving cream reminding them of clouds or the sandy texture of a paint and sand mixture reminding them of streets after a winter thaw. Experimentation over a long term, not just once or twice, allows children to progress from exploring to creating, using materials of different textures.

Pattern

Children often use **patterns** in their visual art. They may repeat one shape (e.g., a dot or line) over and over within their drawings. The pattern may be more a result of the repeated movements they used to create the shapes than of an interest in the resulting marks on the paper. Many children become comfortable with a shape or figure and use it repeatedly, such as the house with a pitched roof or a pine tree that looks like a triangle perched on a block. Young children may draw their way through a large stack of paper, making what looks like the same marks over and over. Children may have a "signature" design that they make over and over, such as a particular dinosaur or animal. Thus, patterns may appear within one piece of children's art or throughout a number of their creations.

Space

Artists use positive and negative **space** to communicate a feeling or a mood. Children may fill in most of the space of their papers, covering over earlier marks in their enthusiasm. They often arrange their figures as if they were floating in space, particularly before they begin to use a baseline or skyline in their drawings and paintings. Young children draw objects with their own expressions of size relativity; for example, the dog may be larger than the house. Perhaps this is because the dog is the important object in the drawing; adding the house may have been a second thought. As with other logical reasoning skills, representing size relationships develops over time. Accordingly, depicting objects that are farther away as smaller than those that are close involves the same type of relative thinking. Most art teachers refrain from directly teaching children specific techniques for showing distance relativity before the children begin to try their own strategies.

Contrast

The visual arts are full of **contrasts**. Contrasting colors, light and dark, rough and smooth, angular and curved—all of these are contrasts used in visual arts. Children in the preschool and primary years are not too young to start to describe and recognize contrasts in art. Thompson (1995) uses the example of six- and seven-year-olds commenting on the qualities of dour determination in the faces of the couple in Grant Wood's *American Gothic* painting and the soft, lace curtains hanging in their farm house. Finding contrasts in others' art can lead to finding and using contrasts in their own art.

The visual arts are a natural part of a constructivist early childhood program. Children seek to communicate their perceptions and conceptions of the world in a variety of ways, and art forms give them "languages" to use in this process. The role of the teacher is to stimulate the "dialogue" and to provide the means and the framework for such expression.

VIGNETTE 8.1

Integrating the Visual Arts for Three-, Four-, and Five-Year-Olds

Toni Manuel, a teacher of four- and five-year-olds, decided to build in a year-long study of the children's sense of self into her preschool program. She introduced the study by taking black-and-white photographs of each child at the beginning of the year. If they wanted to participate in the activity, she provided the photographs for the children to use to help them draw pictures of themselves using black markers. She also provided a large mirror for the children to use. As they worked, she heard the children commenting on the shape of their noses, the expression on their faces, and other distinguishing characteristics of themselves. She purposely used black and white photographs and drawing media because she wanted them to look beyond the color of their eyes, clothes, and hair. After the children had completed their drawings to their liking, she hung them alongside the photographs in a special location in the room.

Several days later, Ms. Manuel provided potter's clay for the children to sculpt busts of themselves, using the photos and mirror images as guides. Once again, the children commented to each other about the shapes of their ears, eyes, and type of hair. They worked for several days on their sculptures. When done, Ms. Manuel displayed their busts next to the photos and the earlier drawings.

Ms. Manuel repeated this cycle of photographing the children and asking them to draw and sculpt themselves later that year. She added the drawings or sculptures to the display in the classroom. Not only did the children become more sophisticated in their representations of themselves, they became their own critics, commenting on the inadequacies of their earlier works and the improvements in their second attempts. They also critiqued each other's work, usually with compliments on the improvements and likenesses.

Ms. Manuel was pleased with the insights she and the children gained into their understandings of themselves through the project and the way in which the children's growth and development was evidenced throughout the year. Not only did the children grow physically, they grew artistically in the way they portrayed themselves through the art media. She decided to continue this project each year, especially since many of the children stayed with her for several years. She knew that she was gathering important samples of the children's growth and development. When the children left her class to go to kindergarten, she packaged and sent home their self-portraits and sculptures, sure that they would become important mementos for the children's families.

MUSIC

Children are natural music lovers. Perhaps this is because they are surrounded by music from before they are born. The mother's heartbeat and voice as well as other sounds outside the womb introduce the unborn child to the world of sounds and rhythms. After babies are born, lullabies soothe them to sleep, jingles come over the radio and television, and the sounds of nature become a part of their world at a very young age. Even the voices of the people close to them become recognized and soothing for infants. Children whose hearing is blocked or impaired learn rhythm through other means, such as gentle pats to the back to bring up a burp, rocking in a cradle or chair, or being carried to a walking cadence. The vibrations of their caregiver's voice introduces them to the rhythms of speech.

By toddlerhood, most children start to use rhythm and music as they engage in repetitive song/chants like "Peekaboo" or "So big." They associate melodies with games or activities, chant their favorite words while performing particular motions, and create their own rhythmic patterns and tunes. All of these developmental milestones lay the groundwork for the musical experiences of the preschool, kindergarten, and primary years. During the preschool years, children begin to sing and move in unison (Haines & Gerber, 1996). They may all sing in several keys, but they enthusiastically unite their voices in song. Preschoolers may engage in chants, rhythms, and songs spontaneously as they play alone or in groups. They may make up their own songs or words to a song. Four-year-olds start to imitate sounds, tones, and rhythmic patterns both vocally and with simple instruments (Haines & Gerber, 1996). Fingerplays, simple songs, and chants are easily memorized by four-year-olds, who revel in the repetition of the familiar melodies and words day after day. Five- and six-year-olds have the motor control and cognitive ability to coordinate their bodies with music in simple dances, coordinate their voices and instruments to create simple orchestrations, and create their own musical melodies. Seven- and eight-year-olds bring their reading skills to the task of understanding simple musical notations. They match tones more precisely and can sing rounds or songs with several parts. Self-consciousness may inhibit the primary-age child's spontaneity when singing or moving to music. But, overall, the five or six years from toddlerhood to the end of the primary years show a remarkable development in the coordination of the child's cognitive, physical, and musical skills, especially in an environment where these skills are encouraged with planned, rich musical experiences.

Elements of Music

If teachers of young children are aware of the elements essential to music, they can incorporate these elements in the musical experiences they provide for children. The following elements of timbre, form, melody, dynamics, rhythm, and harmony are important for beginning and accomplished musicians.

Timbre or Tone Color

We distinguish sounds from one another because each sound has distinctive tonal qualities (Rozmajzl & Boyer-White, 1996). The sounds of a vacuum cleaner, rustling paper, and violins all differ in recognizable ways. In music, **timbre** includes the way the same note can have a different quality (e.g., C) when played on a variety of instruments or come from different sources. A piano and a flute can play the same note, but the source of the sound makes them vary in tone color.

As young children use rhythm instruments to rattle, rub, drum, and scrape, they experience a range of tone colors. The materials the instruments are made of affects the sounds they create. For example, hitting a stick on a wood block sounds quite different than using the same stick to hit a bongo drum, cymbal, or metal drum. As children listen to recordings of voices ranging from soprano to bass, they begin to recognize the tonal colors of human voices.

Instruments come in families, including strings, brass, woodwinds, and percussions. Each family has distinguishing characteristics and tone colors. Children can learn to put common classroom instruments into "families" as well, such as the sticks and wood block into the "woods" family, triangles and cymbals into the "metals" family, and maracas and other instruments that shake into the "rattles" family.

Learning to identify and use tone color takes years to develop and happens gradually as children create tones with their voices and musical instruments. Multiple experiences with a wide variety of tonal qualities, such as listening for the sounds of the various animals in *Peter and the Wolf* or identifying instruments from their sounds, help children develop an ear for the range of tonal colors available.

Form

Musical pieces have **form**, or order. A chorus or refrain may follow each verse. A melodic phrase may be repeated several times, such as in "Three Blind Mice." As children first begin to learn about form, they recognize that some parts of music are the same and others are different. Young preschoolers begin to discriminate the distinctive parts of music as they sing repetitive songs or recognize familiar tunes. Four- and five-year-olds become more adept at recognizing distinct phrases in music. They can share this knowledge by matching actions with parts of a song that share the same melody, such as playing the rhythm 1-2-3, 1-2-3 with a wood block, each time they sing "Three Blind Mice." Primary-age children can begin to represent the different parts by labeling them "A" or "B" and matching these symbols to the appropriate phrases.

Children's understanding of the form of music develops as their sense of patterning, logical reasoning, and use of symbols increases. The preschool, kindergarten, and primary years are full of opportunities for children to learn to recognize, reproduce, and create their own songs, which will be full of different forms and arrangements that they will learn to write in symbolic form later.

Melody

Whenever we think of singing, we think of melodies. Music is full of patterns of notes that comprise melodies. The words that accompany the melody may change, but the melody remains. Take for example, "Twinkle, Twinkle Little Star." Once the child knows the **melody**, or the pattern of the notes, she can put all kinds of words to it. She may sing, "Here I go to take my bath," or "This is how I brush my teeth" to the "Twinkle, Twinkle Little Star" melody. She is following the rising and falling of the notes. Melodies can progress in short steps or great leaps, skipping several notes at a time. The notes of a melody can be high or low, in one key or another. Yet the pattern of the notes is recognizable and repeatable for the young child.

Most young children begin to match their voices to the pitch of the notes and follow the patterns of the melody at a young age, usually by preschool age. Some children may have difficulty with these skills. The more opportunities they have to hear themselves and sing along with easily repeated melodies, the more progress they will make.

Dynamics

The **dynamics** of music refers mainly to the contrast in the volume of the music, that is its loudness or softness. The change in volume may be gradual or sudden. Single notes may be accented or groups of notes or phrases may increase in volume gradually (Haines & Gerber, 1996). Toddlers use the dynamics of sound as they lower their voices to a whisper or raise them in squeals of delight. They may respond to loud noises by covering their ears or crying. Preschoolers gain more control over the dynamics of their own voices, using quiet voices to share a secret or loud voices to express anger or frustration. Kindergarten and primary-age children can recognize the dynamics of music and the expressive qualities the loudness or softness of the music communicates. Understanding the abstract quality of the music's intensity as represented by changes in volume will develop later. During the preschool and primary years, the children's control of their own dynamics when singing and playing instruments and the recognition of the dynamics in music they hear will build the foundation for the abstract uses of dynamics that will follow in later years.

Rhythm

The temporal quality of music, including the beat, duration of sounds, tempo, and rhythmic patterns, are considered its **rhythm** (Haines & Gerber, 1996). Rhythm is one of the most important of the musical elements for children to experience and to express (Rozmajzl & Boyer-White, 1996). Rhythm exists in nature, such as the rhythm of heartbeats, rainfall, and breathing. Rhythm serves as an accompaniment to dance and movement. It is the use of time in music.

Children develop a sense of rhythm as they participate and move to strong beats and rhythmic patterns. As they gain control over their basic body movements, such as walking and clapping, they can put these movements to a beat. The toddler who begins to bounce when hearing music or the three-year-old who claps to the beat of a perky song, both demonstrate a beginning understanding and use of rhythm.

Activities appropriate for the development of rhythm in children include multiple opportunities to move to strong rhythms that vary in tempo. For young children, rhythm and movement go together. As children clap, stamp their feet, twist their shoulders, and walk in a parade, they develop their sense of rhythm.

Within the concept of rhythm is the underlying pulse that does not vary in a piece of music called its beat. A child's sense of beat takes longer to develop than the surface-level rhythms such as the syllables of the words in a song (Weikart & Carlton, 1995). For example, clapping the rhythm for "B-I-N-G-O" would be clapping once for each letter. Whereas, the underlying beat of the song would have four pulses (B-I-N/G-O, where N and G are combined for one beat). A metronome keeps the beat for musicians. It keeps the pulse of the music. A child's sense of beat is important for later musical competence, but is usually undeveloped in the preschool and primary years.

Harmony

If melody can be thought of as the horizontal movement of music, harmony can be thought of as the vertical element of music (Rozmajzl & Boyer-White, 1996). As the melody moves forward, notes of several pitches can be played simultaneously, creating **harmony**. For example, as the children sing a melody in unison, the piano or guitar can accompany them with chords that consist of more than one note played at once, creating a richer texture to support the melody. Children's earliest experiences creating harmony usually happens using their own voices in the form of rounds, such as in "Row, Row, Row Your Boat." When sung as a round, a harmonious, vertical texture is added to the song that is pleasing to the ear. In order to be able to sing rounds or create vocal harmony, children must be able to do two things at once. Holding one note while the teacher sings the melody, saying nursery rhymes as a round, or playing percussion instruments in a round help children develop these skills. They can also take on a simple part in a song, such as performing rhythmical speech patterns while others sing the melody. For example, some children can repeat "Tick, Tock, Tick Tock" while the others sing "Hickory Dickory Dock." This is called *ostinato patterns*. Young children rarely have the singing sophistication to sing harmonious parts to a melody (e.g., alto and soprano) simultaneously. This will come at a later time.

Music is another language for children to use to communicate. By responding to music and creating their own music, they communicate in ways that words cannot. Their worlds should be full of the harmony that only music can bring.

MOVEMENT AND DANCE

Learning through movement lies at the root of constructivist theory. Piaget contended that sensorimotor intelligence, beginning at the earliest stages of life, forms the foundation for all later learning. In this chapter we will look at another connection between movement and learning, learning *to* move. This area has been the focus of two branches of early childhood education. Teachers of the arts have concentrated on creative movement, including moving to music. Teachers of physical education have considered movement with more of a skills emphasis, such as the skills involved in throwing. This chapter combines the two approaches and describes the developmental and essential elements of both.

Learning to move takes more than maturation, it takes rich movement experiences and skillful guidance from adults. Developing the ability to move competently is age sensitive, but not totally age dependent (Gallahue, 1995). For example, when watching a group of seven- and eight-year-olds playing a game of kick-ball, we can expect to see a wide variety of developmental levels in the coordination, balance, strength, and locomotor abilities of the children. Children with physical disabilities and developmental delays may follow a different time frame. Yet there are general trends in children's movement development.

Newborn movements consist primarily of reflexes that allow them to eat, breathe, and function. Rudimentary movements, such as reaching, grasping, and crawling, predominate the child's life from about two months to around the age of two years. Between approximately two and seven years of age, children are developing what Gallahue (1995) and others call "fundamental movements." These include walking, running, skipping, hopping, throwing, kicking, climbing, swaying, and others, which will form the foundation for all future movement skills. This is also the time in which children are forming their sense of rhythm and beat. Emphasis during this time span is on learning a wide variety of skills. Teachers should build on the children's joy of movement during these years, without causing them to fear failure or embarrassment. At around the age of seven, some children are ready to begin to learn the specialized skills required for competitive sports or the performance level of dance. Other children may not be ready until they are closer to nine years old. At this age, specialized movement skills are just starting to form. Full competence is still years of experience and maturation away.

Elements of Movement

As children develop their abilities to move, there are specific elements that teachers need to plan for and observe along the way. Movement competency does not happen without carefully planned experiences that build on these elements. The foundation for all planning is providing each child with physical activities that use the following elements, which underlie expressive and athletic movements.

Rhythm

All movement has a rhythm. The rhythm may have a regular or irregular pattern. It may come from an internal or external source. Children under five years of age move more comfortably to an internal rhythm than an external rhythm (Weikart & Carlton, 1995). For example, when pretending to flap their wings like a bird to music, preschoolers will probably flap with as many rhythms as there are children. They are moving to their own internal rhythms, not the rhythm within the song. Some children may flap fast and wild, while others "soar" with arms outstretched and moving ever so slightly.

Children's sense of rhythm develops as they coordinate their movements to the music in pointing or wiggling their fingers to fingerplays or songs or as children develop control in movements such as running, kicking, and jumping. A child's sense of beat, or the steady pulse underlying a musical piece, develops later into the elementary years. Both rhythm and beat are important for movement competency, just as they are for musical competency.

Coordination

Coordination involves moving different body parts in synchrony with one another and moving in synchrony with others. Clapping one's hands, patting one's legs, and skipping require coordinating the movements of several body parts. Movements that require doing the same motion at the same time with different body parts, such as hand clapping, are easier than movements that require different parts to move at different times, such as skipping or pumping a swing. Learning to coordinate one's body parts to move in synchrony takes a combination of maturation and experience. Coordinating movements while sitting down is easier than when moving one's body through space. Coordinating one's own movements with those of others begins with rough approximations and leads to dancing types of coordinated movements in the later elementary years.

Time

Being able to start and stop one's own movements according to a signal, keeping one's body in motion for a designated amount of time, and speeding up and slowing down one's movements all relate to a time awareness (Weikart, 1989). Time awareness is necessary for dance forms, sports, and recreation. As children gain control over their movements, which takes maturation and a multitude of opportunities to practice, they can vary their movements according to time.

Space Awareness

When watching a group of preschoolers engaging in movement activities in close proximity to one another, one can quickly tell which children have yet to gain a sense of **space awareness**. The child who bumps into walls and chairs, falls onto another child, and otherwise invades the personal space of others needs more time to develop space awareness. The best way to develop this sense of space awareness is to use one's body to perform many movements, such as making shapes (e.g., a curled-up ball), extending the body vertically (e.g., stretch up to the sky) and horizontally (e.g., stretch out like a snake), and using the body to make other shapes. Children may need external cues to help them keep within their own personal space, such as "islands" to stay on that are outlined with masking tape on the floor.

Balance

Maintaining balance involves compensating for changes in the center of gravity as one moves. This can pose difficulties for young children since their centers of gravity change rapidly as they grow in size. Consider the origins of the word *toddler*. It descriptively captures the movements of a child new to walking. Dynamic balance involves maintaining the center of gravity while moving through space, such as when walking or riding a bicycle. Static balance involves maintaining the center of gravity without moving through space, such as standing on one foot or rocking in a chair. Both types of balance develop throughout the early childhood years, with many stumbles along the way.

Body Form

The way one moves and positions one's body comprises body form. Posture, flexibility, and body awareness also contribute to it. As children dance in front of a mirror, mimic others' movements, and move in a variety of ways, they develop the sense of body awareness—how their body works and moves. This is important for later interest in the aesthetics of movement as well as athletics.

Locomotion/Nonlocomotion

Moving one's body through space, such as when running, walking, hopping, or crawling, defines **locomotor movements**. Remaining static in space, such as when sitting or standing in one place, make up **nonlocomotor movements**. Nonlocomotor movements are easier for young children, generally up to the age of seven years old (Weikart & Carlton, 1995). Trying to coordinate moving through space and moving parts of one's body in different ways is usually beyond the young child's skill level. Thus, performing hand and arm motions with the upper body while sitting, learning to kick or catch a ball while standing in one place, and stamping one's feet instead of taking steps forward or backward are easier for young children to master.

Fine and Gross Motor Movements

Depending on which muscles in the body are used in movement actions, movements can be divided into two general categories: fine motor and gross motor. **Fine motor movements** use the smaller muscles of the fingers and hand. Writing and drawing are examples of fine motor movements. **Gross motor movements**, on the other hand, use larger muscle groups such as the whole arm or leg, upper torso, or lower torso. Children's development follows a trend from developing control of the gross motor movements before developing control of the fine motor movements. Yet opportunities to develop both types of movements are important throughout the early childhood years.

Strength

The muscles used to move one's body develop in strength with use and growth. Different movements involve distinct muscle groups, such as the upper or lower torso, arms, or legs. Muscle strength also involves cardiovascular ability. Young children's muscles and cardiovascular systems tire quickly but tend to recover more quickly than adults'. Muscle and cardiovascular strength both develop from persistent use. Active movement is necessary on a daily basis for young children, including running, climbing, swinging, stretching, and other activities that employ many muscle groups as well as the heart and lungs. Outdoor time is important throughout the year, even in the cold winter months, if children's muscles and cardiovascular systems are to develop strength.

Teachers can ensure that children have opportunities to build muscular and bodily strength by the equipment and play spaces they provide (e.g., balls, climbers, open areas, tricycles, swings, etc.), the encouragement and challenges they offer, and the models they set themselves.

Adults who play along with the children, toss the ball to them, lead them in simple exercises, and push them on swings communicate that active lifestyles are important to them, too.

As Gallahue (1995) so aptly states, "For young children, movement is at the very center of their lives" (p. 125). A constructivist program builds in the opportunities for movement development as it builds on the child's natural love of movement. Active learning involves more than active minds, it involves active bodies as well.

THE DRAMATIC ARTS

A young child's sense of story and drama are closely connected to their dramatic play. As Vivian Paley (1981) offers, when children share their own stories by acting them out, they "feel that they are playing together inside a story" (p. 167). Children are mesmerized by the stories they hear, see, or enact. Even the most active of children will usually focus their energies on a good story. Dramatic arts can include portraying a story through puppetry, mime, dramatic play, and acting.

A technique that Paley has developed to build on the children's sense of story and drama is called *story acting* (Paley, 1990). In this technique, children as young as three and four years old tell stories to an adult, who writes the stories down exactly as the child dictates. The story may be as simple as "A bunny runned in the woods." In the next phase, which is where the children's sense of drama enters, the children act out the story. The above story may have a bunny character and several children pretending to be the woods. The author may pick the part she wants to play. Additions and revisions to the story may be made by the author as she realizes that some parts are unclear or incomplete. Yet, only the author has the right to make changes in the story. The story acting technique has been used successfully across the preschool and primary ages. Older children start to write their own stories, some of which turn into continuing sagas taking the same characters into different situations, resulting in a novel or series of chapters. Groups of children can create jointly composed stories. The children's stories contain the elements of good literature—plot, characters, setting—which make the dramatizations more interesting and exciting.

Paley's story acting technique is not the only one that could be used in constructivist programs. Other techniques for introducing drama and literature to young children have been very successful (see Fox, 1987). But Paley's techniques fit into constructivist theory so well because they start with the child's stories and dramatizations. Each child has opportunities to be the author and the characters. Therefore, for the purposes of defining and illustrating children's sense of story and dramatization, Paley's technique provides the context and examples.

Elements of the Dramatic Arts

The following are some of the elements of story and drama that children understand and use.

Sense of Story

Stories have a beginning, middle, and end. They must start, take the audience members somewhere, then leave them with a sense of closure. Children oftentimes begin with "Once upon a time," just as do many of the fairy tales they have heard. They may tell us who is in the story (which they soon discover is vital for acting the story out) and what the characters are doing. A story without an ending, which is normal for the preschool storyteller, does not get by for long because curious classmates will want to know more. Children may ask, "What happens next?" and the author may compose the rest "on the spot," because his sense of story tells him—and his audience—that something is missing.

Fiction/Nonfiction

Most children are comfortable in the world of pretend. They mix pretense and reality into their dramatic play. They do the same in their story dramatizations. The characters may be real (e.g., Mommy, Daddy, Baby), but the situations may be pretend (e.g., the world of dinosaurs) or the characters may be fictitious (e.g., Ninja Turtles) but the situations real (e.g., going to school). Children blend myth with reality in their stories. Anything or anyone is possible. Trying to classify children's stories into fiction and nonfiction becomes difficult for the adult—and is usually unimportant to the children anyway.

Characters

Characters in the children's story dramatizations may be superheroes, animals, families, friends, classmates—everyone is there. Many children start with familiar characters (which is wise for any author) and experiment with the unfamiliar. Often their characters reenact a movie or familiar fairy-tale script. There might be an addition of new characters, such as a baby born to Cinderella after she married the prince and whose name happens to be the same as the author's! As the children become adept storytellers, they make their characters more interesting. They add descriptions and background information. The characters' personalities start to show through the dialogue and actions of the story. Characters may be "good" or "bad" guys. In fact, a common question asked by the actors playing the different characters is, "Is she good or bad?" That one piece of information helps the actor define how the character should act.

Setting

The **settings** for the stories are often given briefly or are simply inferred by the actors and audience. For example, consider a fairy-tale story that has castles and knights. Young children can transport themselves into that setting without worrying about how many years ago it happened or the name of the country, both of which would be quite meaningless to them anyway. They know what is important for their story—the people rode horses, used shields and swords, lived in families, and had all of the same basic needs that they have.

Plot

Something has to happen in the story, which defines the **plot**. For beginning storytellers, the plot may be a simple chronology of the character's day: "Laura got up. She ate breakfast. She went to school. She went to her friend's house. She went home for dinner." The author is using a familiar time frame (her daily schedule) to organize and sequence her plot. More experienced storytellers may begin with a dilemma, for example, somebody kidnapped the baby, and build the plot from there. The plot defines the possibilities for the actors; thus, the children have a natural motivation to make it interesting.

Conflict

Good stories have some sort of problem or **conflict** for the protagonist to resolve. The element of conflict is one of the later elements to appear in children's stories. Yet, conflicts abound in their spontaneous, unscripted dramatic play. For example, the dinner burns, wild animals attack, or the baby acts up. Some of the first conflicts to appear in the children's storytelling are reenactments of familiar scripts, for example, a television program they saw or a fairy tale. The conflict and the resolution of the conflict is predictable for the author—and the audience. Later, children will venture into unfamiliar and unpredictable problems and solutions.

Voice

Voice involves who is telling the story. Is there an "I" or is the storyteller an unidentified narrator? In addition to the answer to these questions, the story has an audience to whom the author speaks. With story acting, the audience is the author's classmates, who share similar experiences and ways of perceiving. If knowing one's audience is important, writing for an audience of same-age peers is an ideal place to start.

Story Acting with Seven- and Eight-Year-Olds

Ernie Walker, a teacher of a multiage second and third grade, attended a week-long seminar to learn to use story acting techniques in his classroom. He could not wait to get back to school and get started.

Before school began in the fall, he thought through how he would build in opportunities for story writing and story acting for the children. The classroom had several computers with easy-to-use word processing programs available. He decided to use these as the core of the story writing center. Next he recruited adult volunteers to transcribe the children's stories. He called several professors at a local teacher education program and asked them to help him find volunteers. He sent letters to the parents of the children in his class, and he contacted a senior citizen center. He was successful in getting enough volunteers to staff his writing center several times each day. He did a little workshop for the volunteers before school began to instruct them on taking transcription. He emphasized that the stories should be the children's. The words, the plot, the characters, everything should come from the children. Censorship would only occur if the plot went in violent directions. The volunteers practiced writing down dictated stories from each other. They were ready for their first storytellers.

The first week of school, Mr. Walker introduced the children to the storytelling/story acting cycle. He brought in some stories he had written (and several from his own children). The children acted out the stories, several times asking to do them more than once. Mr. Walker told them that there was a sign-up list for children who wanted to dictate their own stories. Children excitedly signed up.

The volunteers could hardly keep up with the demand. Children waited excitedly to dictate their stories. While they waited, they drew the illustrations, listened to their classmates' stories, and discussed their own stories. Mr. Walker built in a half an hour each day for story acting. This usually happened at the end of the day, just before dismissal. The children waited in anticipation for story acting each day.

After several weeks of dictating their stories, Mr. Walker was pleasantly surprised when several children came to him and asked if they could type their own stories when there weren't any volunteers at the writing center. "Sure." Mr. Walker smiled, thinking back to last year when the children all groaned when he required them to type at least one project on the computer.

Later in the month, several children came to him and asked if they could write a story as a group. Their goal was to put all of themselves into a series of adventures, so they wanted to work on it together. Once again, Mr. Walker marveled at the children's motivation and their desire to work cooperatively.

The school year progressed, with each child writing dozens of stories, which they kept on computer disks and on a giant bulletin board in the classroom. They even had a "story festival" when the children's families came into school and acted out the favorite stories with the children.

By the end of the year, the children's stories had all of the elements of experienced authors' stories. They had exciting plots with suspense, twists, and turns. The characters came alive, and the settings were diverse and detailed. Mr. Walker had never experienced such motivated and skillful story writing from second and third graders before. He was convinced that the acting out of the stories kept the children excited about their writing.

PROCESSES LEARNED THROUGH THE ARTS

Learning within the realm of the arts involves many processes. Children engage in these processes as they learn to use artistic representations. The processes defined below apply to all four areas of the arts discussed earlier in this chapter: visual arts, music, movement and dance, and drama. The materials used and the context of learning will differ, but the underlying processes occur in all areas of the arts.

Exploring and Discovering

As children first try a new art media, musical instrument, or dramatic theme, they will go through an exploration period. "How pliable is the clay?" "How loudly can the instrument play?" "What do the Ninja Turtles do in my story?" These are some of the questions they may subconsciously ask as they explore. Through exploration, they discover new combinations, reactions, and possibilities.

Investigating

Exploration and discovery are the beginning. To move beyond the exploration and discovery phases, children need teachers who will ask questions, pose dilemmas, and propel them to investigate the materials at higher levels. "What can you make out of clay?"; "What can you make your instrument sound like?"; "Do your Ninja Turtles have families?"; "How would dinosaurs move?" are the types of questions that help take children beyond exploration and discovery into new types of thinking. The teacher provokes further thinking with questions that ask the child to move into an area she had not thought of previously. In a Piagetian sense, the teacher's questions create the disequilibrium for the child to move to more sophisticated ways of thinking. The skill in knowing just how much disequilibrium will be effective comes from experience knowing the individual children and watching their reactions. Another way to guide children to the investigation process is by posing a problem, such as, "Would you like to make a panther to go with your story about panthers?" The child could investigate three-dimensional materials, such as papier-mâché or clay. Or she could investigate a variety of paints, pastels, markers, and crayons. The process of investigating the possibilities propels children's thinking to new levels.

Communicating

If children have many languages available through which to communicate, we can help them develop fluency in these languages. The arts allow children to communicate when words fall short. A picture, a piece of music, a dance, and a dramatization can communicate in non-literal ways.

In another vein, creating with art can be a social experience for children. They often talk to each other about their creations and ask about the creations of others, showing genuine interest in each other as artists. Some children may prefer to work alone, deeply engaged in their own thoughts about their creations. Some children respond readily to teachers' questions about their creations. Others would rather not put their thoughts into words. Teachers sensitive to the children's personal styles allow for a range of ways they can communicate. Just as artistic creations are personal, so are the ways that children engage in the creative process.

Creating and Imagining

The world of possible art creations is only limited by our imaginations. Creating and imagining are combined because creating is the external representation of the internal imagination. It is not in a linear relationship of imagination causing creation; instead, imagining and creating are part of the same process. With each new creation, the child's imagination can go in new directions. And with each new creation, the imagination expands.

Identifying, Differentiating, and Discriminating

Part of becoming a connoisseur of the arts is being able to differentiate among art forms for quality, type, and source. Children who have moved to an African percussion beat or examined an Ansel Adams photograph will start to recognize the genre and the artist's touch when they meet it again. Identifying art forms by differentiating qualities, such as color choices, brush strokes, or distinctive instruments, makes the art form familiar to the child. At first, the discriminating skills of the children will allow them to differentiate by obvious differences, such as the difference between oil and watercolor paintings. Later, they will develop the ability to focus on the more subtle differences, such as the use of light, instrumentation, or dance forms.

Problem Solving

Working—or playing—with art media offers natural opportunities for problem solving. "How can I make the legs look like they're running on my clay dog's body?" "How can I make myself move like a cat?" Trying new approaches in a risk-free environment with immediate feedback, such as the environment provided through the arts, is ideal for practicing the processes involved in problem solving.

Focusing

The concentration level of a four-year-old dictating a story, a five-year-old engaged in drawing, or a seven-year-old composing a song on a keyboard surpasses expectations. Even the most active of children can become absorbed in artistic expression. The arts draw us in to focus on the parts and the whole: the colors the child chooses to create a rainbow or the notes of a melody that we match our voices to. Children begin to focus on the parts of the whole that carry important meanings and on the whole itself, without which the meanings would be diminished.

Critiquing

Often considered a level of thinking beyond most preschool and primary children, the roots for **critiquing** and evaluating art forms can begin at a young age. More than a subjective, "I like it" or "I don't like it," critiquing involves explaining why an art form is pleasing or displeasing to a person. Children will have favorite songs, pictures, stories, and dances. Preferences are honored and valued by the teachers around them. Teachers need to be careful that children do not interpret critiquing as "putting down" each other's creations. It is best to use art forms that were not created by the children when practicing critiquing skills. The early childhood teacher's role is to set the stage for the more sophisticated critiquing skills that will come later.

Improvising

Many art forms are spontaneous and improvised. **Improvisation** is not random; it is guided by a dialogue with other artists and/or materials. Cues are taken, for example, from other musicians in an improvisational jazz performance or from the media when sculpting, painting, or drawing. A building made out of boxes will take different forms than one made out of clay. Drama provides a wealth of opportunities to improvise, since children may not know what lies ahead in the dialogue or actions of their fellow actors. Children learn flexibility, cooperation, and communication through their improvisations.

INSTRUCTIONAL PRINCIPLES

This chapter has outlined the basic elements within four areas of the arts (visual arts, music, movement, and drama) and the processes used in learning through these arts. Creating an atmosphere that moves children toward learning these elements and processes follows certain principles. The following principles are inclusive, applying across all four areas. Examples are given to illustrate how they might look in specific areas.

1. **Establish an atmosphere of trust**. Artistic expression flourishes when the artists feel free to express themselves. This is not to say that an "anything goes" atmosphere is ideal. Children who know that they must respect each others' rights as artists (e.g., treating others' creations with utmost respect) will trust that they will be treated likewise. Children whose artwork is greeted with encouraging, constructive criticism will learn to do the same. Acceptance also includes honoring a child's disappointment with a creation, even if the teacher thinks the work is fine. Trying to figure out why the child is disappointed can mean asking nonjudgmental, encouraging questions, such as "You think the colors look different when they dried?" or "Do you want to make another one?" This communicates respect much better than "Oh, it's fine just like it is."

2. **Value children's expressions.** Probably the best motivator teachers can give their students is to demonstrate that they value and respect the children's expressive attempts. Valuing does not mean using empty praise or token reinforcers, such as stickers. Valuing can be demonstrated by sincere interest, probing questions, and sharing the child's joy in successful creations. Valuing children's work can sometimes mean respecting the child's disappointment with a creation. If children's art has a wider audience that values the work, from the child's classmates to the parents and other children in the school, they start to appreciate the value of their own art.

3. **Appreciate individuality.** Artistic expression is inherently personal and individual. Asking children to make bunnies that all look the same or stories that follow a set formula discourages individuality and creativity. As children witness the many varieties of art created by their classmates, they too learn to appreciate their own and others' individuality.

4. **Resist comparing children's creations.** An extension of allowing individual expression is resisting comparisons between and among children. Assigning grades or points to artistic products, holding contests for the "best" products, and making comparative remarks can deflate the confidence of the beginning artist. At later stages, when the child is older, she can enter work in contests or audition for plays, if she chooses. During the preschool and primary years, the rewards can be in the intrinsic satisfaction the children get from communicating their ideas in new ways.

5. **Organize the space.** Artistic expression can get messy and noisy. The space arrangement can help to keep work areas clutter-free so that visual artistic creations, music, dance and movement activities, and story acting can happen. When arranging the painting and sculpting areas, water and smocks should be close by, along with the paper and paint supply. An area for exploring musical instruments can be positioned where the noise created will not bother other children. Providing headphones for the keyboard or taking the cymbals and xylophones outdoors are other solutions. When creating a temporary dance studio, the only things needed are an open space, a mirror, bar, place to hang the dance clothes, and a means of playing music. Any other furniture would get in the way of the dancers.

6. **Provide stimulating materials.** Since so much artistic expression results from a "dialogue" between the artist and the media, stimulating, interesting materials are a must. Yet a precaution is in order. Providing a "media of the day" or switching the art media too often prevents children from progressing past the exploration stage to a point where they can really create. This works against the children's

gaining a sense of autonomy and competence over the materials. Keeping a consistent selection of materials visible and within easy reach allows children to select materials to match their interests and ideas. New materials are introduced as the need arises due to children's interests or projects.

7. **Stimulate the senses.** The artist communicates what she perceives through her senses—visual, auditory, tactual, kinesthetic, and others. Becoming aware of the stimulations received through all of the senses, such as the buzzing of the bees, the smell of the rain, the feel of the wind, the texture of the sand, underlies the process of communicating sensations through art. As children take the time to "tune into" their senses and see, hear, and move in new ways, they open up the channels for further artistic expression.

8. **Encourage experimentation.** Most famous artists develop their ideas in a series of "studies" or drafts before they are satisfied with the results. They pose their ideas and hypotheses in an experimental sense, evaluate the results, and modify their plans. This experimental attitude prevails in an environment conducive to artistic development. The first attempt to compose a song, the first sketch of a subject, the first draft of a story are all subject to modification. The misconception that an artist creates a masterpiece each time he puts paint on paper may discourage many fledgling artists.

9. **Build in individual and group art experiences.** Too often, art experiences in the primary schools are confined to the time the music or art teachers have the whole class of children, usually once or twice a week for half an hour or so. Such scheduling works against many of the recommendations in this chapter. If artistic expression is to be a language available for young children to use in natural and meaningful ways, a group lesson in which everyone uses the same materials for a short amount of time cannot comprise the whole of a child's art and musical experiences. There is a place for weekly group experiences for direct instruction in art, movement, and music, but the budding artist needs more. Opportunities for children to individually select materials and activities to expand their artistic expressions lead to less rushed and more fluent uses. One possibility is introducing the materials to the whole group, then making them available for individual experimentation and expression from that point on.

10. **Provide the models.** Probably the most enlightening art lessons for children, next to creating art themselves, are the attempts by others around them to express themselves artistically. This includes teachers as well as other children. It's important that the children do not feel compelled to do as the teacher does, in other words, draw the same way, dance the same way—or compare their own creations to

the teacher's. Yet, sharing in the teacher's creative attempts, whether in a poem, painting, or dance, can provide a powerful model. The teacher who brings in a draft of the children's book he is writing or shows the photographs she took in her introductory photography class provides a model of an artist in the making.

Another way to model the artistic process is to invite an artist to come and work alongside the children as they create. A watercolor painter, an author, or a sculptor can set up a little studio in a visible place accessible to the children. The artist can go about the creative process, availing himself or herself to the children's queries. This indirect "artist-in-residence" approach allows children to witness a master at work.

Summary

A constructivist curriculum has at its center the meaningful construction of knowledge and the communication and representation of that knowledge. The arts provide the language, the media, and the means to aid children in that process. There is no doubt that the arts are basic in such a curriculum.

CHAPTER NINE

....

Putting It
All Together*

*This chapter was written with the assistance of Patricia E. Diebold.

9

The curriculum in a constructivist early childhood classroom is more than a compilation of different subjects taught in isolation. A constructivist curriculum connects subject to subject and child to subject in a way that makes sense to children. Teachers organize the learning environment so that children can actively construct the connections they need to make. Several ways of organizing the curriculum, the ways that some constructivist teachers "put it all together," will be the focus of this chapter.

INTEGRATING THE CURRICULUM

The preceding chapters in this book examined areas of the curriculum for the *Big Ideas*, processes, and principles in each. Breaking apart the curriculum is often necessary for analytic purposes. Yet, children do not naturally learn in separate, distinct subjects. Piagetian theory tells us that children constantly form schemata or interconnected cognitive webs to organize their knowledge. In the words of Caine and Caine (1991):

> Our minds organize pieces of related information into complex webs, called schemata. New information becomes meaningful when it is integrated into our existing schemata. In this way, knowledge builds on itself, and the schemata grow exponentially. (p. 6)

The challenge for teachers in a constructivist program is to organize children's learning experiences so that they will be stimulated to form these cognitive interconnections between and among subjects. In order to do this, teachers look to the processes and concepts—the *Big Ideas*—within each of the subject areas to guide their decisions about specific content to be taught. The *Big Ideas*, such as conservation in math, rhythm in music and movement, and scale in science and social studies, form the foundation of the curriculum upon which specific instructional decisions are based. The key to building such a curriculum is integration that transcends disciplinary boundaries. Such curricula are often called *integrated* or *interdisciplinary* approaches.

Trends toward integrated, **interdisciplinary curriculum** have been strong over the last decade. Yet oftentimes **integration** of the curriculum has been on a superficial level. For example, in a unit on zoo animals, the children may sort and count zoo animals in math, read about lions and tigers and monkeys in language arts, make zoo animal sculptures in art, sing about animals in music, create zoos in the blocks, and so on. This is an example of integration at the surface level. The connection among the disciplines of math, science, language arts, and the arts is only through the topic: zoo animals. The underlying processes within these disciplines are still unconnected.

Certainly, the *Big Ideas* of the various disciplines and their interrelated processes must be connected at deeper levels as well. For example, classification is an underlying process common to math and science. Classification of animals found in zoos can be based on where they live, how they bear offspring, or what type of feet they have. As children construct systems for classifying animals, they are using one of the *Big Ideas* of math and science. They use language in a meaningful context as they use the words for their classifications such as *mammals* or *webbed feet*. Social studies concepts such as the geographic location of different types of animals enters into the classification systems. For example, polar bears live where it is cold and alligators live where it is warm. Throughout their investigations of animals, integration is at a deeper level of understanding because the children construct the knowledge in real, concrete, and connected ways. They learn math, science, language, and social studies concepts at the same time as they classify zoo animals.

Approaches to integrating the curriculum often fall into two major types: those that use thematic units and those that use projects. Both approaches organize the curriculum with in-depth studies that blur the lines between and among disciplines of knowledge. Both build on the interests and prior knowledge of the children. The two approaches overlap one another in many ways, and constructivist teachers often use a combination of the two approaches. The thematic unit approach usually starts with predetermined units, which may come from a variety of sources, such as the school district curriculum guides. The project approach, on the other hand, allows ideas for projects to emerge from the interests and lives of the children. It is the more "bottom-up" approach.

Whether presented as thematic units or projects, an integrated curriculum provides a meaningful, nonfragmented, natural approach to learning. The curriculum more closely resembles the real world of complex problems and vast amounts of information. Ernest Boyer reminded educators that students need to "see relationships that add up to life" (1982, p. 582). Or, as John Dewey advocated, "Education is life; life is education." The constructivist educator's role is to help the children connect life and learning. How can we organize the curriculum so that it connects to real life?

The thematic approach and the project approach will be examined in more detail as examples of how the curriculum can be organized and presented in a constructivist program.

VIGNETTE 9.1

Integrated Curriculum with Kindergartners

Ms. Lisa Chase, a kindergarten teacher with over twenty years' experience, teaches in a school district that is moving toward an integrated curriculum at all levels. The middle schools are using an integrated team approach where teams of three or four teachers work with the same group of students to integrate the science, math, English, and social studies content. The high school offers courses that integrate two or more disciplines, such as history and literature. The school district curriculum guidelines outline skill and concept development benchmarks for students at the different grade levels in each of the disciplines. The guidelines also set forth broad thematic units for teachers at each grade level, but allows individual teachers the flexibility to select the content through which the concepts are taught.

The district mandates that kindergartners learn about cycles. Ms. Chase knows that the children in her kindergarten this year are fascinated with animals, so she decides to introduce the concept of cycles through a study of animals. She could have chosen to use plant cycles, the water cycle, or other cycles. However, being a constructivist educator, she wants to build on the children's interests and prior knowledge as much as possible. The unit on animal life cycles will include how different animals are born, fed, raised, form families, and die. Such study allows children to draw connections between what they already know about their own life cycles and the life cycles of other animals. An excursion to the zoo becomes an inquiry into the natural life cycles of various animals, from the baby elephant to the elderly orangutan. The children use their math skills to study the size relationships between the animals of different ages (the baby elephant is much smaller than the mother elephant) and types (the baby giraffe is much bigger than the baby monkey).

Several children ask Ms. Chase if they can build a miniature zoo in the classroom as a project. With Ms. Chase's guidance, they create the animals for their zoo out of modeling clay and habitats out of stones, twigs, and leaves. They even create a swimming hole for the polar bears. After several days, the whole class becomes involved in the project. As they create their zoo, the children research what the different animals look like, what they eat, and how they live. Each child or pairs of children select an animal that interests them to work on. Several of them even return to the zoo with their parents to take photos and gather more information about their animals. Ms. Chase realizes that the study on animal life cycles has taken off into directions she had not predicted.

At the end of the unit, the children invite their parents to school to see their completed projects. Ms. Chase stands back and listens as the children tell all about their animals. She knows that the children have learned much more than if she had required them to pursue projects of her choosing. She is convinced that the combination of thematic units and projects allows for the best of teacher-directed and student-directed learning.

Thematic Approach

Shoemaker (1989) identifies theme studies in the classroom as an approach that integrates both topics and concepts. She defines a **thematic approach** as "education that is organized in such a way that it cuts across subject matter lines, bringing together various aspects of the curriculum into meaningful association to focus upon broad areas of study" (1989, p. 9).

Thematic units organized around topics, such as the solar system or dinosaurs, provide a narrow area of study for a short period. On the other hand, thematic units organized around a broader concept, such as systems, cycles, or extinction, allow for a broader area of study that integrates many topics (Shoemaker, 1989).

Furthermore, thematic units must be interesting and meaningful for the children. After all, it is they who must integrate the knowledge in a meaningful way, through assimilation and accommodation, if they are to make sense of it. The strength of selecting a broad concept for study, such as cycles or systems, is that the children can pursue topics within the topic that interest them. The child who is fascinated by kittens can study the life cycle of cats—from the newborn litter at home to the elderly cat that lives next door. The child who has a baby brother at home can share fascinating facts about this newest family member. The theme must fit the children and their lives. Constructivist teachers create the environment for children to make connections between the concepts and the content.

Topics chosen depend on the developmental level of the children and their prior knowledge about the topics. In a unit on systems, a child who is fascinated with castles and knights could study the systems used within a medieval castle (from the water systems to the defensive systems). Even though the child may not use the vocabulary *cycles* or *systems,* the teacher organizes the learning environment so that the children experience these concepts directly. For example, the dramatic play area could be set up like a castle with a gravity-fed water system and a defense system consisting of a moat, tower, and sentries. The children will come to know the types of systems used in castles by connecting this knowledge with what they already know about the water system and defense system they use in their own homes every day. Even though they do not have water coming from a rooftop receptacle, they might have water towers close to their neighborhood. They do not have sentries armed with swords and shields at their doors, but they have locks, watchdogs, or burglar alarms. The teacher's role is to help the children make connections between the systems children already know and the new systems. In doing so, the children form **schemata** or cognitive webs to organize and use the information.

Organizing the curriculum around broad concepts provides a framework for exploring multiple topics. The *Big Ideas* and processes within each of the subject areas provides the learning objectives for the teacher to teach toward. For example, in the castle study, if the district mandates that children learn to use nonstandard measurements as part of the math curriculum, the teacher can set up a money system in the castle area using a balance scale and rocks painted gold and silver to represent a money system similar to those used in medieval times. The children can pretend to pay for their food and lodging using the gold and silver rocks. They are using a new kind of barter system, not so different from the money system we use today.

Setting up the environment takes research, creativity, and new knowledge on the part of teachers as they seek the connections between the instructional processes and the thematic units. Since teachers must meet the instructional goals and objectives of the schools or programs where they work, they can do so with the thematic units they and the students select. Constructivist teachers know that all processes, disciplines, skills, and objectives will not be integrated into each unit. However, once they start, teachers are surprised by how many processes, skills, and content areas they can integrate into a well-chosen thematic unit.

Project Approach

Another approach to integrating the curriculum is the **project approach**. This approach is commonly attributed to Katz and Chard (1989) and the Reggio Emilia schools of Italy. In the project approach, individual or groups of children, with the assistance of a teacher or teachers, determine a project they would like to do. It might be creating a butterfly garden in the school courtyard, making a dinosaur museum, or building a house out of surplus lumber. The important element is that the children are actively involved in every step of the project, from its inception to its completion. The children make decisions about the project that affect the direction it will take. Usually, the project becomes a joint effort of a group of children and adults. Parents and specialists in other fields may join in the effort. The teacher's role is to guide the project, integrate the learning processes, serve as a resource, and document the progress using work samples, observational records, photographs, and videotapes. Projects can last several days or an entire school year. Just as in the thematic units, a creative teacher can integrate all subject areas into a project. The children problem solve using math and science skills; they create maps and models (social studies); they read, write, speak, and listen (language arts); and they use the arts as they express their ideas with a variety of media. A project always starts with an idea, usually a child's, and the idea is carried through to a final product. The product is important, but not nearly as important as the processes that went into creating the final product. That is why documentation of the project-in-process and steps along the way is so important.

Using the Project Approach with Four- and Five-Year-Olds

Ms. Tricia Burger, a teacher of four- and five-year-olds, has been reading everything she can find about the project approach in early childhood programs. She decides to give it a try, targeting the sociodramatic play center as the focus of the first class project. She asks the children how they would like to set up the play center. It is currently set up like a house, with a kitchen, simple furniture, and dress-up clothes. The children generate many ideas, ranging from a drive-in restaurant to a library. One child excitedly offers, "A castle!"

"A castle?" replies Ms. Burger. "How could we do that?"

The child replies, "You know, we could make a moat and a tower and all of that."

The overwhelming consensus of the class is to make a castle in the dramatic play area for their project. Ms. Burger leads the children as they draw up their plans, brainstorm about the things they need, and start gathering "castle" items at home to bring into school. Ms. Burger becomes a resource herself as she answers children's questions; she becomes a co-investigator as she helps them find information; and she becomes a questioner when the children need a little push.

The next several days are full of activity as the children excitedly draw up their plans and bring items from home (everything from princess clothes to shields and armor). Ms. Burger visits the library and checks out as many books as she can find on castles. She reads the children fairy tales that have castles in them. They examine photographs of real castles. And their castle project keeps growing.

One day, a child runs into the room excitedly telling Ms. Burger that he has brought the tower. It is in his mom's car. Sure enough, a large refrigerator box is protruding from the back of his mom's station wagon. They drag the box into the room. At group time that day, Ms. Burger leads the children in a discussion of how they can make the box into a tower. The decision is to paint it to look like stone, cut a door and a window, and put a flag on top. The next several days, they do just that. The castle now has a tower.

Another idea of the children is to make horses for the castle. "How could we make horses?" Ms. Burger asks. "I know," exclaims one student. "I have one at home made out of a sock and a yard stick. I'll bring it in tomorrow." That leads to making sock horses in all colors, depending on the socks that are donated.

Ms. Burger wants the children to think about the social aspects of the castle. "How did they get water?" and "What did they eat?" are some of the guiding questions she asks the children. After studying the drawings of castles, they discover that the water came from a receptacle on top of the castle roof and the food was cooked over a fire. That leads to making a water system and a fireplace. Someone even brings in an iron pot to "cook" with.

The whole time that this project is going on, which was nearly a month, the children's journals and stories are full of castles, knights, and princesses. The dramatic play takes on familiar scripts (e.g., Cinderella) and scripts from the children's imaginations. One child brings in music that reminds him of castles so Ms. Burger sets up the tape player close to the castle so they can hear the music as they play.

When Ms. Burger notices the interest in the castle beginning to wane, she asks the children if they would like to try a different project and create a different dramatic play center. They decide that they need one more week with the castle, then they want to make a dinosaur cave. Ms. Burger is not sure how they are going to do that, but she knows that together they will figure out a way.

Katz and Chard (1989) suggest that the topics for projects come from the following sources: the children themselves, the local community, local events and current affairs, places, time, natural phenomena, concepts (e.g., opposites, patterns), general knowledge (e.g., inventions), and miscellaneous subjects (e.g., hats, puppets, etc.). The topics should be relevant, interesting, and meaningful for the children.

Using a Combined Approach

When setting up the constructivist curriculum, teachers may want to use a thematic unit approach, a project approach, or a combination of both. The two approaches overlap one another in many ways. They both organize the curriculum with inquiries into new or familiar areas. Thematic units and projects blur the lines between and among disciplines of knowledge. Both build on the interest and real lives of children. The major difference is the degree of emergence allowed in the two approaches. The thematic unit approach is often determined well in advance. In fact, the whole school may follow the same thematic unit cycle every year. The thematic unit approach organizes the curriculum in a more authoritative manner because the themes are usually selected by the teacher, the written curriculum of the school, or the textbooks. Constructivist teachers make the thematic units responsive to students by including them and their interests in the planning.

Projects, on the other hand, emerge from the students' interests. The project approach allows the curriculum to emerge from spontaneous, unpredicted events. For example, the teacher may observe the children's interest in the addition of a new wing to the school as the source of a project on building construction. Or, fascination with the puddles on the playground may turn into a project on puddles. The project approach is more responsive to the events and interests in the children's lives.

Both the project and thematic unit approaches allow teachers to integrate subject disciplines in ways that more closely resemble the real world. That is why both approaches are considered interdisciplinary, integrated approaches.

INCLUSION OF ALL CHILDREN

The current movement in all facets and all levels of education is toward including children with and without special needs in the same programs. The underlying rationale for inclusion is that all children belong together, not separated in segregated, exclusive programs (Salisbury, 1991). The charge for early childhood educators is to find ways to make the educational program "fit" the child, not the other way around. Allowing children with special needs to learn in the least restrictive environment possible not only benefits all children, it is mandated by law in the United States.

Implementing an early childhood program that includes all children demands a knowledgeable and skilled team of professionals. All children have unique and special needs; yet children with disabilities have needs that other children do not have (Wolery & Wilbers, 1994). Children's **special needs** include physical disabilities, mental disabilities, emotional disabilities, or a combination of several disabilities. Children with special needs require environments planned to "minimize the effects of their disabilities and to promote learning of a broad range of skills" (Wolery, Strain, & Bailey, 1992, p. 95). Planning such an environment becomes the joint effort of experts in many fields: early childhood education, special education, the medical fields, physical therapy, psychology, speech and language development, and so on. Planning the program also requires the direct involvement of the parents or guardians of the child.

Approaching the planning for each child with special needs as a team effort is not only good educational practice, it is required by federal law. The Individuals with Disabilities Education Act (IDEA), passed in 1990, requires an Individualized Education Program (IEP) for all children with identified special needs between the ages of three and twenty-one years. The program must be developed by a team of professionals and the child's family while the children are in preschool through secondary schools. The IEP must be reviewed and updated annually. The Individualized Education Program provides the goals and means of working toward these goals for each child. The early childhood teacher, as a member of the team, holds responsibilities in helping to implement the plan and work toward its goals. Part of the early childhood educator's responsibility is to learn as much as he can about the specific conditions affecting the children in his class. Bearing in mind that children with special needs are very different from one another (Wolery & Wilbers, 1994), consulting resources and experts on specific conditions becomes part of the research process each teacher of special needs children must pursue.

Constructivist approaches and inclusive programs are akin to one another. A constructivist teacher approaches the design and implementation of an enriched educational environment for all children from a research-based orientation. She strives to consider each child's learning needs and developmental level as the foundation for her curricular and instructional decisions. Planning for a child with special needs is more complex than planning for children without special needs and often requires the expertise of other professionals. Yet the constructivist approach of teaching for deep levels of understanding and building sound educational programs based on this understanding remains the same for all children.

In planning the educational program, the first responsibility of the early childhood educator is to strive to understand the children and to meet their specific needs. Setting realistic, obtainable goals for the child as part of the IEP is the second step. Brainstorming ways to obtain these goals with an interdisciplinary team comes next. As in all levels of curricular planning, a problem-solving atmosphere permeates the discussions and decisions made regarding the child's educational program. Strategies are formulated and tried by the teaching team. Adaptations and new strategies often result. The process of planning, evaluating, and further planning follows a cyclical path, with careful reflection and observation on the part of the team working with the child.

Including Children with Special Needs

Rose Hall, a kindergarten teacher with 15 years of experience, has always followed an approach to teaching that is now being called constructivist. She has resisted the pressures to push down the first-grade curriculum and over the years remained committed to a play-centered kindergarten curriculum. In May Ms. Hall's principal tells her that he would like to place six-year-old Rodney, a child with Down's syndrome, in her class next year. She has never had a child with Down's syndrome or mental retardation in her class before. She asks to attend the multidisciplinary team (MDT) meeting planned for June so that she can learn more about Rodney's needs.

In the meantime, Ms. Hall goes to the library and checks out several books on Down's syndrome. She reads them and takes copious notes on characteristics of the syndrome and recommendations for setting up educational programs for children with Down's syndrome. She learns that Down's syndrome children have a wide range of mental functioning, so each program must be based upon the individual child's abilities and needs.

In June, the MDT meeting includes Rodney's parents, a school psychologist, the principal, the special education teacher, the speech therapist, and herself. Ms. Hall learns that the child has been in a preschool program for the last two years. He has started to develop healthy social relationships and an understanding of school routines. The early childhood special educator and speech therapist have been working with him one-on-one several hours per week at the preschool. His speech is becoming more understandable. He is currently functioning on a three- to four-year-old level in most areas. The multidisciplinary team reviews Rodney's test scores and reports from his teachers and specialists. They schedule a second meeting to develop an Individualized Education Program (IEP) with goals and recommendations for the next year of Rodney's education.

Before the next team meeting, Ms. Hall makes arrangements with Rodney's parents to bring him by the school for a visit. They bring him in the next day. Rodney excitedly runs over to the blocks and starts building a tower. Ms. Hall knows that he will have no trouble feeling at home in her classroom.

The team meets to develop the IEP. Ms. Hall provides wording suggestions for the plan that fit with the goals of her current program. The IEP's goals for Rodney include developing positive social skills with his peers, developing beginning reading and writing skills, and forming beginning number skills such as counting objects to ten and sequencing three items according to length. The special education teacher and speech therapist will continue working with Rodney in a "push in" program, which means they will come into the classroom and work with him several times a week. They will also be available to consult with Ms. Hall about making adaptations in her curriculum to meet Rodney's needs.

Ms. Hall knows that challenges lie ahead for her and for Rodney because this is a new experience for both of them. Yet she is comfortable with the support staff that will be helping them both through the process. She also knows that Rodney's parents will provide support from home. With so many experts working together toward Rodney's success, she is excited about including him in her class.

Here are a few principles for early childhood educators to keep in mind when working with children with special needs:

1. **Plan to meet specific individual educational goals in a formal, yet natural way.** Goals for children with special needs must be formalized in the Individualized Education Program. These goals should be natural extensions of the program in which the child is included. The classroom teacher's participation in the multidisciplinary team meetings allows for congruence between the goals stated and the philosophy of the teacher.

2. **Strive for maximum participation and independence for the child.** The child should be expected to participate and be as independent as possible, depending on the type and degree of the disability. The teacher needs to know from parents and professionals how much she can expect from the child, so that unrealistic expectations do not frustrate both the teacher and child.

3. **Embed instruction into regularly occurring activities and routines** (Wolery, 1994). The current movement toward providing support for children with special needs within the regular classroom, oftentimes called "push in" services, makes it possible to provide instruction geared toward the child's special needs within programs taught by early childhood educators. Support provided for the child and teachers by the special educators is to assure maximum success within a regular program. The teacher and the other children are part of the educational program for the child with special needs. A little more patience may be required because of the extra time and energy a child with special needs requires, but the feeling of success for all involved make it time and energy well spent.

4. **Adjust the routines and activities to ensure success of all children.** If part of the day is unsuccessful for the child with special

needs, adjustments may need to be made. For example, if lunchtime results in one spill after another, serving the child's drink in no-spill cups may alleviate the problem. If group time extends beyond the child's attention span and she runs around the room after fifteen minutes, an alternate activity for the child after her attention span has waned may work. The key is practical solutions to make the environment work for the child's success and for all the children in the classroom.

5. **Implement logical, natural consequences for a child's behavior.** A child with special needs should not be permitted to break rules and conform to lower behavioral expectations than the other children. Assuming the child is capable of following a rule, breaking the rule should result in the same consequences. For example, if the consequence for eating the play dough is removing the child from the play dough table, the child with special needs must comply as well. Allowing a child with special needs to receive special privileges leads to resentment on the part of the other children and does not lead to the child's learning appropriate behavior. In fact, other children may want to act like the child with disabilities if they see inappropriate behavior reinforced or allowed by the teachers. Openly discussing the expectations for all children and the ways children and teachers can help each other meet these expectations can lead to understanding and empathy on the part of the children.

Inclusion of children with special needs is becoming a natural part of early childhood programs. Teams of professionals and parents committed to finding ways to make inclusive programs work are the key to their success.

Organizing the Day

The daily schedule for an early childhood program following a constructivist approach depends on many factors: the length of time the children attend the program (from a half day several days per week to over eight hours a day in a child-care program), age of the children, types of special classes offered (e.g., physical education, music classes, etc.), and other factors. With these factors in mind, the components of a solid early childhood program will be highlighted.

Planning the day in a constructivist program usually involves larger blocks of time within which children can make choices, work on projects, and change activities when their interest has diminished. For example, during a language arts block of time, several activities may be available: journal writing, reading silently, working on the computer, creating personal dictionaries, and illustrating and writing stories. All of these activities are within the language arts discipline, but children have some autonomy over which activities they choose. Some of the activities may be "requirements," especially for older primary children. Yet children may have a choice about the order in which they complete them. An effective strategy for older primary children is a contract system whereby the children and teacher sign a contract outlining what must be completed by a certain date. This serves as a record of the child's responsibilities that both the child and teacher can use as a reminder.

Another component of most early childhood programs is a time for play. This is in addition to an outdoor recess time. The play encouraged in constructivist programs stems from the types of play outlined in Chapter 4, as proposed by Piaget and Smilansky. Play centers include a dramatic play area, block area, sand and water table, art area, music and movement area, library area, small manipulatives area (e.g., puzzles, small building toys, etc.), writing area, and others. The areas are organized to allow children to engage in dramatic play, constructive play, and symbolic play, with or without peers. Children make choices about the type of activity, materials, and social arrangement they would like to engage in. Most programs allow from 45 minutes to one hour for this type of play. Programs that have children for a full day may even allow two blocks of time (morning and afternoon) devoted to play.

Another type of activity planned for children are large group times. These are times of the day when all of the children gather for time together. Usually they sing, listen to and discuss children's literature, story act, discuss the day's events, and share important happenings. The younger children need to have shorter meeting times than the older children. Many programs start and end their day with whole group meeting times.

Another scheduled part of the day is time for small group activities. These may include science experiments, math activities, language arts lessons, cooking, and other activities for groups of children guided by an adult. Several small groups may meet at once, or teachers may conduct the small group activities during the play time. If the latter is the case, teachers need to be sure that they do not require the children to miss all or most of their play period. Rebellion may result. Children protect their time to play.

As teachers plan the daily schedule, they want to keep to a routine that is predictable for the children. Children who know what will happen after lunch or before recess can pace themselves and come to depend on the repeated rhythms of the day. Also, a variety of teacher-directed and child-selected activities should comprise the daily schedule.

A sample daily schedule for a full-day program for five- to seven-year-olds may look like this:

Time	Activity
9:00–10:00	Language arts block (journal writing, story dictation, book projects)
10:00–10:30	Morning meeting (discuss schedule, sharing time, children's literature with social studies theme)
10:30–10:45	Snack
10:45–11:00	Outdoor recess
11:00–11:30	Large group story acting
11:30–12:00	Lunch
12:00–12:30	Sustained silent reading
12:30–1:00	Outdoor recess
1:00–1:45	Math/science block
1:45–2:45	Play center time
2:45–3:00	Closing meeting/dismissal

Of course, this is only one way of scheduling the day. There are an infinite number of possibilities. Teachers must work with the demands of the school, the needs of the children, their own preferences and teaching styles, and other factors when they build their schedule.

ORGANIZING THE ENVIRONMENT

Just as with the schedule, a teacher must use flexible, creative thinking to plan and organize the environment. The guiding principle is that the environment should work for the children. It must support the learning that takes place there; children's projects (finished and in-progress) should be all around the room. The work and play spaces must be accessible and usable for children. Too many prohibitions and restrictions will restrict and stifle the learning. Children must be allowed to "make a mess" within reason, because some of their choices and projects may be messy at times.

With those precautions in mind, there are a few requirements for a workable environment: spaces for large and small meetings of children and teachers; tabletop areas for drawing, writing, playing games, and so on; open spaces for movement and dance activities; a block center; a dramatic play center; a library/reading center; an art center; a small manipulatives center; a cooking area. Shelves and storage areas should be easy to reach and well marked so that it is easy to put things away. Walkways should be free of obstructions and stay clear of children's construction spaces so that accidental damage does not occur. "Soft"

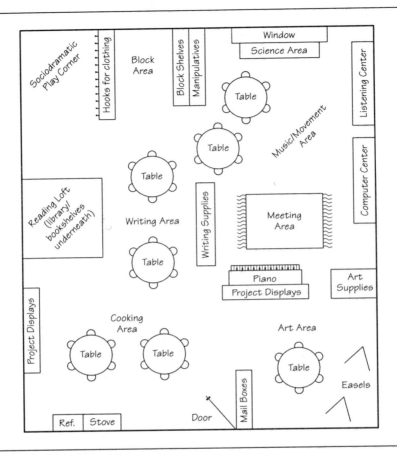

Figure 9.1 Diagram of Classroom

spaces with pillows and comfortable furniture should be available for curling up with a book.

A possible arrangement of an early childhood classroom may look like the diagram above.

The environment should communicate that this is a place for children to experiment, create, and construct. The teacher's job is to make sure that it invites children to engage in these processes.

ASSESSMENT

In a constructivist program, assessment is a natural part of the teaching/learning process. The teacher's purpose in assessing the children is to determine what they know and how they think about particular concepts. This is different from evaluation that places a judgment on the child at the end of a unit or grading period. Furthermore, the constructivist teacher is interested in how the children come to their current answers, that is, the processes and logical reasoning they use to make sense of the world. Erroneous answers are as enlightening as correct answers. In fact, as discussed in the preface, Piaget began his studies in young children's reasoning by analyzing their erroneous answers on intelligence tests.

Assessment of children's knowledge and ways of knowing should provide a profile of the child's level of understanding of a particular topic or concept. Furthermore, the information gained from assessing children is used for planning a curriculum that is appropriate for the children. This type of assessment takes on many forms, most of which look very different from the graded paper-and-pencil, single-answer tests that traditional programs use.

A constructivist teacher needs to have information about the children at the beginning of a unit of study. Then he or she can continue the assessment by listening and observing the children each day. The constructivist teacher's most valuable assessment tool is observation. It is critical that she arrange the environment and the schedule to allow her to observe, listen, and question the children as they go about their day. For example, when beginning a unit on animal habitats, the teacher needs to know what the children already know and think about habitats. She could do this by asking the children to draw and talk about pictures of animals in their homes, by reading a story about an animal family (e.g., "Goldilocks and the Three Bears") and then asking questions about the realism of the bear family's home, or by taking a walk and looking for animal homes. The teacher who listens and observes very closely will gather valuable information about what each child thinks about animals and their homes. Some children may think that most animals live in zoos; others may think that animals have kitchens and bathrooms in their homes; still others may think that all animals live underground. This information-gathering stage may last for several days.

The teacher may use the information about the children's understanding of animals upon which to base further instruction. She may plan a bird-watching expedition to the local park for the children to see birds making their homes in trees and telephone poles, not underground as some children thought. She may show a videotape of beavers making their lodges—without bathrooms and kitchens. Her purpose in planning further educational activities is to stimulate children to think at higher levels. She does this by providing new experiences that match and others that do not match the children's current ways of thinking.

Assessment and teaching are so interrelated in a constructivist program that the line between them is blurred. It is difficult to differentiate the assessment activities from the instructional activities in a constructivist classroom because instruction and assessment occur simultaneously. Each time the teacher poses a question based upon a child's earlier comment, he is assessing *and* teaching. Each time he collects a sample of the child's work, he is "capturing" the child's thinking at that point so that he can track the child's development over time and with further instruction.

Another means for constructivist teachers to determine the children's level of understanding is by interviewing. The interview may revolve around a task, such as ordering a set of rods from shortest to longest, a discussion about a story or event, such as about another child's infraction of the rules, or just about any activity that taps into the child's reasoning and thinking. The interview becomes the means for the teacher to gain insight into the child's knowledge of a particular topic. As the child places the rods into a logical order, the teacher observes the means by which she does so. Does she match two rods at a time and place them in ordered pairs? Does she use the words *shortest* and *longest* as she places them in order? All of this information gives the teacher insight into the logical reasoning the child is using and the vocabulary she has developed to express the relationships between objects that vary in length.

Just as teachers use various methods of assessing children's understanding, school districts and early childhood programs use assessment tools to track children's progress. Most schools have checklists of expected skills and concepts for designated grade levels that teachers use to record a child's progress. Many schools and programs are moving toward developing assessment methods that are curriculum-based. Teams of teachers and administrators often volunteer to develop the assessment tools for their programs or schools. The degree of flexibility in assessment methods depends on the school or program and the type of tools used. Constructivist teachers can work within many types of systems, collecting information on the children's development as an extension of the teaching/learning process.

• •

VIGNETTE 9.4

Assessment of Six-
and Seven-Year-Olds

Mr. Robert Levito, a teacher with several years' experience teaching first and second grades, has a multiage group of first- and second-grade children this year. He realizes that he will have to adjust his methods of assessing and grading the children, something he is now ready to try after having several years of experience teaching these levels. The school board has given him and several other teachers permission to develop alternative means of assessment for the multiage classes as long as they can document the children's progress for purposes of accountability. The team of teachers has one year to develop alternative methods of assessment and a second year to field test these methods. At that point, the school board will decide to approve or not to approve the proposed methods. Parents have the option of enrolling their children in the multiage classes, with the understanding that the children will be part of an experimental program. Mr. Levito has such a positive reputation among the parents that he has more children on the waiting list for his class than he can take.

The team of multiage teachers meet weekly to develop their assessment tools and share their experiences. Mr. Levito enthusiastically participates in each of these sessions, as do the other teachers who are bringing their years of experience and a newfound excitement to their new roles. A university faculty member who is an expert in assessment techniques agrees to meet with the team once a month on a consultant basis.

The team decides to develop several assessment tools to help them collect and standardize their data. They decide to develop profiles for each of the major subjects—reading, writing, math, social studies, and science—which consist of specific outcomes arranged developmentally, with the easier levels preceding the more difficult outcomes. They also decide to agree to a work-sampling system whereby each teacher will collect samples of the children's work, including writing samples, math and science tasks, and art samples, to be reviewed by outside evaluators according to criteria developed by the team. The criteria are developed by researching the assessment tools used within the different disciplines and "borrowing" and adapting the ones that make sense to the team. A third assessment tool that the team decides to use is a series of performance tasks, one per grade level per subject, that will be used to gather information about the children's level of understanding on specific assignments. The last assessment tool is a narrative to be written for each child four times a year. These narratives, which summarize the findings from the other three assessment tools, will replace the traditional report cards sent home to parents. As traditionally done, parents will be invited for parent-teacher conferences to review the data and narratives twice a year—once in the fall and once in the spring.

Mr. Levito volunteers to work on the subcommittee developing the math profiles and performance tasks. This committee will also decide on the type of work to be collected for the work-sampling system in math. They go about their task by researching the latest research literature, standards developed by national organizations within the profession, curriculum guidelines for the state and their school district, and systems used by other schools. Every other week, the committee members report back to the team on their findings and progress. This is the time for them to refine their efforts and change directions if necessary. Surprisingly, by the end of the fall, each subcommittee has already developed a rough draft to present to the team.

During the spring, the team members field test the profiles, work-sampling systems, and performance tasks. Teachers prepare narratives for each of the children in their classes. At the end of the year, they make a presentation to the school board reporting on their progress to date. Several parents volunteer to testify about the thoroughness of the data collected on their children.

Over the summer, the team continues to meet to refine and prepare their assessment tools for widespread application the second year. They print all of their assessment tools and supporting materials in book form. The hundred-page volume looks impressive. It reflects the hard work of the team of teachers. Each teacher sets out to use the instruments, excited about the progress made. But they are even more excited about the way they have been trusted as professionals to apply their knowledge of the curriculum, of children, and of the latest research on teaching and learning to develop a program that works for them.

INSTRUCTIONAL PRINCIPLES

Throughout this book, a series of principles summarized the *Big Ideas* for each of the content areas. These principles encapsulated the main ideas for teachers to remember when applying constructivist theory to teaching young children important concepts in math, language arts, science, social studies, and the arts. Principles for using a play-centered curriculum and guidance system based on moral development were also included. The following principles are general guidelines to use throughout the curriculum because they address the "big picture" of how a constructivist classroom can look and function.

1. **Be organized but flexible when developing the environment, schedule, curriculum, and assessment tools.** Oftentimes people mistakenly refer to a constructivist program as being unstructured and somewhat disorganized. The structure and organization of a constructivist classroom is less obvious to the casual observer because it is so flexible and responsive to the children. The goal for constructivist programs is for students to form their own cognitive structures and connections within their thinking. Therefore, the environment must allow for children's creative thinking and problem solving. A classroom that rigidly structures the learning environment to the point of communicating, "Do as I do, and think as I tell you to think," results in the mindless memorization of information and a stifling of children's autonomous reasoning.

The organization of a constructivist classroom allows the teacher and environment to be responsive to the students, their developmental levels, and individual needs and interests. The classroom is usually less formal and rigid than traditional classrooms. A visitor to a constructivist classroom may find children and adults sitting on the floor, conversing, using many materials, and making choices. This leads to a more informal environment, but it is one that must be organized for all of this activity to take place.

2. **Treat learning and development as inseparable and interdependent processes.** Fosnot (1995) put this same principle in even stronger language when she said that "learning *is* development" (p. 29). Piagetian theory tells us that development is the result of physical maturation and the use of increasingly more sophisticated cognitive constructs. In this sense, development and learning are interchangeable. Neither maturation nor cognition alone can account for the changes that we call learning. Thinking in new ways or learning new concepts sometimes must wait for physical maturation to occur. For example, a child who lacks conservation in his thinking will be confused by concepts of equivalence in mathematical equations. A degree of maturation and a multitude of experiences must occur before the child begins to use conservation and is therefore able to understand concepts based on equivalence. Then, once the child understands conservation, he will not regress to his earlier misunderstandings. Learning and development occur when children change and adapt their thinking to accommodate new knowledge and new experiences.

3. **Build in opportunities for children to learn from each other.** Building understanding does not happen in isolation; it happens as a result of learning together. Children learn from each other as they question, watch, and speak to each other. They learn from the teachers and adults around them. Furthermore, the adults learn from the children. A true community of learners exists when all members assume that no one has all of the answers and that no one comes to the learning situation with little or no knowledge— including the children. Each learner contributes to the learning process. Children are preparing to work and live in a world of global interdependence and information that grows exponentially. They will not be able to be experts in all areas; they will have to rely on others to work with them to solve problems that we cannot even fathom today. Learning from each other can start in the early childhood years.

4. **Build on children's knowledge and interests.** Students of all ages learn best when they are interested. This is not to say that they

should limit their studies to only those topics that they already have an interest in. Sometimes interest has to be piqued by teachers who can show the connections between new knowledge and their own lives. For example, a child may not be interested in the life cycle of a butterfly until she has watched it unfold in front of her. After seeing the caterpillar change into a chrysalis and then one day open up into a beautiful butterfly, she may want to learn more about how this happens. Young children usually approach each new experience in a spirit of wonder and curiosity. The role of constructivist educators is to channel that curiosity into new learning experiences.

5. **Allow for choices that lead to autonomy.** Constructivist programs build in opportunities for decision making and self-directed learning. This can be done in small ways, such as the choice of media to use in an art project, or large ways, such as providing input into the class project selection. Learners who make choices and take responsibility for those choices become autonomous learners. Autonomous learners have confidence in themselves as learners, are willing to take risks, and learn from their mistakes.

6. **Have realistic expectations.** One of the unfortunate characteristics of today's push toward higher expectations and academic rigor is the tendency to "push down" learning experiences used in the older grades onto children in the younger grades. Kindergartners who sit at desks and do paper-and-pencil work for much of their day is one example. Constructivist theory dictates that learning should be **developmentally appropriate,** which means that teachers must formulate experiences that are meaningful for the children's level of understanding. Preschool and kindergarten children learn from concrete experiences with real objects, not symbols presented on work sheets. Memorizing lists of words or mathematical facts does not lead to academic rigor. It leads to frustration and wasted time on the parts of the children and the teacher. Time spent doing meaningless activities would be better used in meaningful experiences such as experimenting, creating, dramatizing, and playing.

7. **Approach the curriculum and instruction in a problem-solving, inquiry mode.** Uncovering, rather than covering, the curriculum is a metaphor constructivist educators like to use. Students and teachers approach new topics with a hunger to learn more, to test their current thinking, and to uncover as much as they can about the topic. They are propelled by their disposition to learn. Receiving a grade is no longer needed as the motivator for learning. Learning is perceived in the Piagetian sense of developing and striving for equilibrium. Students start with questions that are real

and pressing for them—the source of disequilibrium—and approach learning with a need to know. The teacher's role is to create the right amount of disequilibrium, pique the students' curiosity, and work with them to find the answers to their questions in their quest toward equilibrium.

8. **Strive for connections within and across the curriculum.** If the thematic units are selected carefully and the projects include many areas of study, children will begin to understand the interconnections between math, science, social studies, language arts, and the arts. Once teachers begin to think in interconnections, they will discover connections everywhere. In a study of families, savvy teachers will find all kinds of families—families at home, number families, animal families, families of historical figures, and extended families that include grandparents, aunts, and uncles. Even musical instruments come in families!

9. **Assess continuously and naturally.** Assessment in a constructivist program is the glue that connects teaching and learning. The teacher needs to know where the students are before making decisions about what to teach next. Constructivist teachers become master observers of children because they are constantly listening, questioning, and watching. They take notes and record the children's answers and spend time analyzing the data they collect for clues about the children's thinking. Teachers constantly form hypotheses about the children's understanding, test these hypotheses, and adapt instruction based upon their findings. Teaching becomes a constantly evolving research study. The questions never cease and neither does the teachers' curiosity and discoveries about the students.

10. **Allow for errors.** Young children's "errors" provide valuable data for teachers to analyze. Each error provides clues into the child's reasoning. Consider the child who insists that items in the estimating jar be recounted by ones after they are counted by twos because she is sure that her estimate of "19" was skipped. Instead of being considered an error, the teacher agrees to recount the items. The child, although still unconvinced, is using a logic natural for pre-operational thinkers. The teacher has learned important information about the child because of her "error."

These principles are guidelines for teachers new to constructivist practices to consider. They can also serve as a checklist to remind teachers what to look for and strive for in their programs. In the spirit of the approach presented in this book, readers must make their own connections and form their own understandings about what will work for them.

Epilogue

The intent of this book has been to provide the disequilibrium for readers to question, ponder, and reconsider their own theories about how children learn and develop their own ideas about how we can best teach young children. There are many "right" ways to teach within a constructivist approach. The examples and ideas presented in this book give the reader a peek into sample constructivist programs and into the minds of some constructivist teachers. The *Big Ideas* processes and principles for a constructivist curriculum presented here can provide a framework for curricular decision making within and across the disciplines. Yet learning to use a constructivist approach cannot come from a book. The learning occurs when the reader brings real-life experiences and prior knowledge to the new ideas presented and decides if there is a fit. Changes in thinking occur when there is a conflict between one's prior way of thinking and the new knowledge. This meeting of the minds between author and reader is what this constructivist author hopes to accomplish with the ideas proposed in this book.

REFERENCES

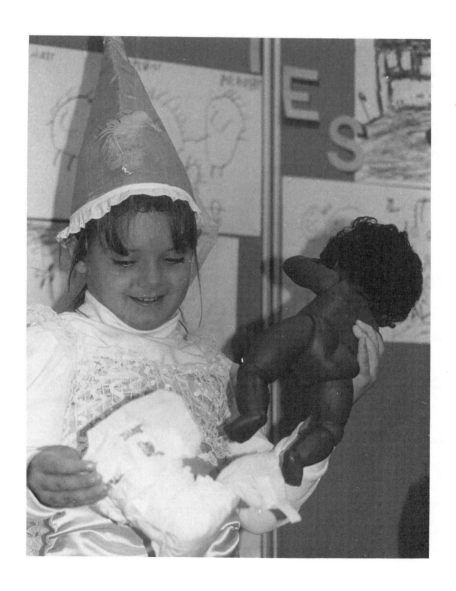

References

Athey, I. (1988). The relationship of play to cognitive, language, and moral development. In D. Bergen (Ed.), *Play as a medium for learning and development: A handbook of theory and practice.* Portsmouth, NH: Heinemann.

American Association for the Advancement of Science. (1990). *Science for all Americans.* New York: Oxford University Press.

American Association for the Advancement of Science. (1993). *Benchmarks for science literacy.* New York: Oxford University Press.

Baratta-Lorton, M. (1976). *Mathematics their way.* Menlo Park, CA: Addison Wesley.

Berk, L. E. & Winsler, A. (1995). *Scaffolding children's learning: Vygotsky and early childhood education.* Washington, DC: National Association for the Education of Young Children.

Boyer, E. L. (1982). Seeing the connectedness of things. *Educational Leadership, 39,* 582–583.

Brittain, W. L. (1979). *Creativity, art, and the young child.* New York: Macmillan.

Bredekamp, S. (Ed.). (1987). *Developmentally appropriate practice in early childhood programs serving birth through age 8.* Washington, DC: National Association for the Education of Young Children.

Brooks, J. G., & Brooks, M. G. (1993). *In search of understanding: The case for constructivist classrooms.* Alexandria, VA: Association for Supervision and Curriculum Development.

Burns, M. (1992). *About teaching mathematics: A K–8 resource.* Sausalito, CA: Math Solutions.

Caine, R. N., & Caine, G. (1991). *Teaching and the human brain.* Alexandria, VA: Association for Supervision and Curriculum Development.

Copeland, R. W. (1984). *How children learn mathematics: Teaching implications of Piaget's research* (4th ed.). New York: Macmillan.

Corsaro, W. A. (1985). *Friendship and peer culture in the early years.* Norwood, NJ: Ablex.

DeVries, R. & Kohlberg, L. (1987). *Constructivist early education: Overview and comparison with other programs.* Washington, DC: National Association for the Education of Young Children.

DeVries, R., & Zan, B. (1994). *Moral classrooms, moral children: Creating a constructivist atmosphere in early education.* New York: Teachers College Press.

Edwards, C., Gandini, L., & Forman, G. (1993). Introduction. In C. Edwards, L. Gandini, & G. Forman (Eds.), *The hundred languages of children: The Reggio Emilia approach to early childhood education.* Norwood, NJ: Ablex.

Engel, B. S. (1991). An approach to assessment in early literacy. In C. Kamii, M. Manning, & G. Manning (Eds.), *Early literacy: A constructivist foundation for whole language.* Washington, DC: National Education Association of the United States.

Ferreiro, E. (1991). Literacy acquisition and the representation of language. In C. Kamii, M. Manning, & G. Manning (Eds.), *Early literacy: A constructivist foundation for whole language.* Washington, D.C.: National Education Association of the United States.

Ferreiro, E. & Teberosky, A. (1982). *Literacy before schooling.* Portsmouth, NH: Heinemann.

Fisher, A. (1992, September). Why Johnny can't do science and math. *Popular Science, 98,* 50–55.

Fosnot, C. T. (1996). Constructivism: A psychological theory of learning. In C. T. Fosnot (Ed.), *Constructivism: Theory, perspectives, and practice.* New York: Teachers College Press.

Fox, M. (1987). *Teaching drama to young children.* Portsmouth, NH: Heinemann.

Freire, P. (1990). *Pedagogy of the oppressed.* New York: Continuum.

Fromberg, D. P. (1995). *The full-day kindergarten: Planning and practicing a dynamic themes curriculum* (2nd ed.). New York: Teachers College Press.

Gallahue, D. L. (1995). Transforming physical education curriculum. In S. Bredekamp & T. Rosegrant (Eds.), *Reaching potentials: Transforming early childhood curriculum and assessment: Vol. 2.* Washington, DC: National Association for the Education of Young Children.

Gardner, H. (1980). *Artful scribbles: The significance of children's drawings.* New York: Basic Books.

Golomb, G. (1973). Children's representation of the human figure: The effects of models, media, and instruction. *Genetic Psychology Monographs, 87,* 197–251.

Goodman, K. (1986). *What's whole in whole language?* Portsmouth, NH: Heinemann.

Haines, B. J. E., & Gerber, L. L. (1996). *Leading young children to music* (5th ed.). Englewood Cliffs, NJ: Prentice-Hall.

Harste, J. C., Woodward, V. A., & Burke, C. L. (1984). *Language stories and literacy lessons*. Portsmouth, NH: Heinemann.

Haskell, L. L. (1979). *Art in the early childhood years*. Columbus, OH: Charles E. Merrill.

Kamii, C. (1982a). Encouraging thinking in mathematics. *Phi Delta Kappan, 64* (4), 247–251.

Kamii, C. (1982b). *Number in preschool and kindergarten: Educational implications of Piaget's theory*. Washington, DC: National Association for the Education of Young Children.

Kamii, C. (1984). Autonomy: The aim of education envisioned by Piaget. *Phi Delta Kappan, 65* (5), 410–415.

Kamii, C. (1985a). Leading primary education toward excellence: Beyond worksheets and drill. *Young Children, 40* (6), 3–9.

Kamii, C. (1985b). *Young children reinvent arithmetic: Implications of Piaget's theory*. New York: Teachers College Press.

Kamii, C. (1989). *Young children continue to reinvent arithmetic*. New York: Teachers College Press.

Kamii, C. & DeVries, R. (1993). *Physical knowledge in preschool education: Implications of Piaget's theory*. New York: Teachers College Press.

Kamii, C., & Kamii, M. (1990). Negative effects of achievement testing in mathematics. In C. Kamii (Ed.), *Achievement testing in the early grades: The games grown-ups play* (pp. 135–145). Washington, DC: National Association for the Education of Young Children.

Katz, L. G. (1988, April). What should young children be doing? *New York State School Board Association Journal*, 23–27.

Katz, L. G., & Chard, S. C. (1989). *Engaging children's minds: The project approach*. Norwood, NJ: Ablex.

Kellogg, R. (1969). *Analyzing children's art*. Palo Alto, CA: National Press.

Kingsolver, B. (1995). *High tide in Tucson: Essays from now and never*. New York: Harper Collins.

Labinowicz, E. (1980). *The Piaget primer: Thinking, learning, teaching*. Menlo Park, CA: Addison-Wesley.

Labinowicz, E. (1985). *Learning from children: New beginnings for teaching numerical thinking*. Menlo Park, CA: Addison-Wesley.

Leeb-Lundberg, K. (1988, February). Math is more than counting. *Scholastic Pre-K Today, 2* (5), 21–24.

Lowenfeld, V. (1947). *Creative and mental growth*. New York: Macmillan.

Manning, M., & Manning, G. (1991). Modeled writing: Reflections on the constructive process. In C. Kamii, M. Manning, & G. Manning (Eds.), *Early literacy: A constructivist foundation for whole language.* Washington, DC: National Education Association of the United States.

Marion, M. (1981). *Guidance of young children.* St. Louis: C.V. Mosby Co.

Much, N. C., & Sweder, R. A. (1978). Speaking of rules: The analysis of culture in breach. *New Directions for Child Development, 2,* 41–59.

National Council for the Social Studies (1994). *The curriculum standards for social studies: Expectations of excellence.* Washington, DC: NCSS.

National Council of Teachers of Mathematics (1989). *Curriculum and evaluation standards for school mathematics.* Reston, VA: NCTM.

Nucci, L. P., & Turiel, E. (1978). Social interactions and the development of social concepts in preschool children. *Child Development, 49,* 400–407.

Paley, V. G. (1981). *Wally's stories: Conversations in the kindergarten.* Cambridge, MA: Harvard University Press.

Paley, V. G. (1990). *The boy who would be a helicopter: The uses of storytelling in the classroom.* Cambridge, MA: Harvard University Press.

Parten, M. B. (1932). Social participation among preschool children. *Journal of Abnormal Psychology, 27,* 243–269.

Piaget, J. & Szeminsk, A. (1952). *The child's conception of number.* New York: Humanities Press.

Piaget, J. (1962). *Play, dreams, and imitation in childhood.* New York: Norton.

Piaget, J. (1965). *The moral judgment of the child.* New York: Free Press.

Piaget, J. (1967). *Six psychological studies.* New York: Random House.

Piaget, J. (1969). *Science of education and the psychology of the child.* New York: Viking.

Piaget, J. (1973). *To understand is to invent: The future of education.* New York: Grossman.

Piaget, J. & Inhelder, B. (1969). *The psychology of the child.* New York: Basic Books.

Reys, R. E., Suydam, M. N., & Lindquist, M. M. (1992). *Helping children learn mathematics* (3rd ed.). Boston, MA: Allyn and Bacon.

Rogers, C. S., & Sawyers, J. K. (1988). *Play in the lives of children.* Washington, DC: National Association for the Education of Young Children.

Rowan, T., & Bourne, B. (1994). *Thinking like mathematicians.* Portsmouth, NH: Heinemann.

Rozmajzl, M., & Boyer-White, R. (1996). *Music fundamentals, methods, and materials for the elementary classroom teacher.* White Plains, NY: Longman.

Rubin, K. N., Fein, G. G., & Vandenberg, B. (1983). Play. In E. M. Hetherington (Ed.) & P. H. Mussen (Series Ed.), *Handbook of child psychology: Vol. 4. Socialization, personality, and social development* (pp. 698–774). New York: Wiley.

Salisbury, C.L. (1991). Mainstreaming during the early childhood years. *Exceptional Children, 56,* 540–549.

Scarselletta, D. (1988). Observing children's social play: The basis for a system of coding. Unpublished master's thesis, State University of New York at Plattsburgh.

Schifter, D., & Fosnot, C.T. (1993). *Reconstructing mathematics education: Stories of teachers meeting the challenge of reform.* New York: Teachers College Press.

Scieszka J. (1989). *The true story of the three little pigs.* New York: Scholastic.

Seefeldt, C. (1987). The visual arts. In C. Seefeldt (Ed.), *The early childhood curriculum: A review of current research.* New York: Teachers College Press.

Selman, R. (1980). *The growth of interpersonal understanding.* New York: Academic Press.

Shoemaker, B. J. (1989). Integrative education: A curriculum for the twenty-first century. *Oregon School Study Council Bulletin, 33* (2).

Siegrist, F., & Sinclair, H. (1991). Principles of spelling found in the first two grades. In C. Kamii, M. Manning, & G. Manning (Eds.), *Early literacy: A constructivist foundation for whole language.* Washington, DC: National Education Association of the United States.

Smetana, J. G. (1984). Toddlers' social interactions regarding moral and conventional transgressions. *Child Development, 55,* 1767–1776.

Smilansky, S. (1968). *The effects of socio-dramatic play on disadvantaged preschool children.* New York: Wiley and Sons.

Smilansky, S., & Shefatya, L. (1990). *Facilitating play: A medium for promoting cognitive, socio-emotional and academic development in young children.* Gaithersburg, MD: Psychosocial & Educational Publications.

Taylor, D. (1989). Toward a unified theory of literacy learning and instructional practices. *Phi Delta Kappan, 71* (3), 184–193.

Thompson, C. M. (1995). Transforming curriculum in the visual arts. In S. Bredekamp & T. Rosegrant (Eds.), *Reaching potentials: Transforming early childhood curriculum and assessment: Vol. 2.* Washington, DC: National Association for the Education of Young Children.

Van de Walle, J. A. (1994). *Elementary school mathematics: Teaching developmentally* (2nd ed.). New York: Longman.

Van Hoorn, J. Nourot, P., Scales, B., & Alward, K. (1993). *Play at the center of the curriculum.* New York: Merrill.

Vygotsky, L. (1962). *Thought and language.* Cambridge, MA: M.I.T. Press.

Vygotsky, L. S. (1978). *Mind in society: The development of higher mental processes.* (Edited and translated by M. Cole, V. John-Steiner, S. Scribner, & E. Souberman.) Cambridge, MA: Harvard University Press.

Wadsworth, B. J. (1978). *Piaget for the classroom teacher.* New York: Longman, Inc.

Waite-Stupiansky, S. (1987). *A naturalistic study of ownership interactions among nursery school children.* Unpublished doctoral dissertation, Indiana University, Bloomington.

Weikart, P. S. (1989). *Teaching movement and dance: A sequential approach to rhythmic movement* (3rd ed.). Ypsilanti, MI: High/Scope Press.

Weikart, P. S., & Carlton, E. B. (1995). *Foundations in elementary education: Movement.* Ypsilanti, MI: High/Scope Press.

Winner, E. (1986, September). Where pelicans kiss seals. *Psychology Today,* 25–26, 30, 32–35.

Wolery, M. (1994). Implementing instruction for young children with special needs in early childhood classrooms. In M. Wolery & J. S. Wilbers (Eds.), *Including children with special needs in early childhood programs* (pp. 151–166). Washington, DC: National Association for the Education of Young Children.

Wolery, M., Strain, P. S., & Bailey, D. B. (1992). Reaching potentials of children with special needs. In S. Bredekamp & T. Rosengrant (Eds.), *Reaching potentials: Appropriate curriculum and assessment for young children: Vol.1* (pp. 92–111). Washington, D.C.: National Association for the Education of Young Children.

Wolery, M., & Wilbers, J. S. (1994). Introduction to the inclusion of young children with special needs in early childhood programs. In M. Wolery & J. S. Wilbers (Eds.), *Including children with special needs in early childhood programs* (pp. 1–22). Washington, DC: National Association for the Education of Young Children.

Zellich, K. (1994). Exploring art and construction in early childhood education. *The Constructivist Educator,* 3 (1), 1–3.

Index